Final Notes
from a Great Island

A Farewell Tour of Singapore

Neil Humphreys

Marshall Cavendish
Editions

Published by Marshall Cavendish Editions
An imprint of Marshall Cavendish International
1 New Industrial Road, Singapore 536196
© 2006 Marshall Cavendish International (Asia) Private Limited

Reprinted 2006 (twice).

Other Marshall Cavendish Offices

Marshall Cavendish Ltd. 119 Wardour Street, London W1F 0UW, UK • Marshall
Cavendish Corporation. 99 White Plains Road, Tarrytown NY 10591-9001,
USA • Marshall Cavendish International (Thailand) Co Ltd. 253 Asoke, 12th
Flr, Sukhumvit 21 Road, Klongtoey Nua, Wattana, Bangkok 10110, Thailand •
Marshall Cavendish (Malaysia) Sdn Bhd, Times Subang, Lot 46, Subang Hi-Tech
Industrial Park, Batu Tiga, 40000 Shah Alam, Selangor Darul Ehsan, Malaysia

Marshall Cavendish is a trademark of Times Publishing Limited

National Library Board Singapore Cataloguing in Publication Data
Humphreys, Neil.
Final notes from a great island : a farewell tour of Singapore / Neil Humphreys.
– Singapore : Marshall Cavendish Editions, c2006.
p. cm.
ISBN-13 : 978-981-261-318-9
ISBN-10 : 981-261-318-8
1. Singapore – Anecdotes. 2. Singapore – Humor. I. Title.
DS609
959.57 -- dc22   SLS2006026175

Printed in Singapore by Fabulous Printers

ACKNOWLEDGEMENTS

I must thank all at Marshall Cavendish for enquiring about the possibility of a third book every seven minutes. Joo Sin and Leslie championed that cause for a couple of years before I finally caved in. My indefatigable editor Katharine was then on hand to point out my various shortcomings. Usually every seven minutes.

This kind of book could not have been written without the dedicated support of staff at the National Heritage Board, the National Archives of Singapore, the National Museum of Singapore, the People's Association, the National Library Board, the Raffles Museum of Biodiversity Research and the magnificent National Parks Board. The great team at Sungei Buloh Wetland Reserve tracked down "Mr Bob" for me and NParks' Benjamin Lee went to commendable lengths to ensure that I did not die in the jungle.

Everyone at *TODAY* deserves praise for not laughing when I announced my grand plan to drop everything and embark upon a tour of Singapore. Mano, Margie, Clement and Zul offered content suggestions, many of which I dutifully pinched, and Puay Koon even agreed to illustrate my tour with a superb map. I should also apologise to my fellow columnist Siva Choy for stealing his story on the Dagenham Girl Pipers.

A decade ago, my mother ordered me to "see a bit of the world". Scott accompanied me and David guided us to Toa Payoh for a short holiday. The incomparable people of Singapore did the rest and I am indebted to all of you.

But I dedicate this book to the wonderful woman who shared my Singapore story. Thanks, Tracy, for making it such an entertaining journey.

PROLOGUE

On 1 January 2006, my wife and I thought we were going to be arrested for loitering. We certainly looked like burglars. We were standing beside the rubbish chute on the 40th floor of the biggest Housing and Development Board (HDB) apartment block in Singapore when the shocked owner of the nearby flat appeared.

"Er, good evening and Happy New Year," I mumbled to the middle-aged Chinese woman. "We're hoping to see the fireworks."

The startled woman digested this information slowly, clearly unsure whether to call the police or hit me with her full bag of soiled nappies.

"Oh, I see. The fireworks have already finished," she replied warily. "About five minutes ago."

"That's a shame. We really wanted to see them. Okay then, we'll go back home."

"Yah. The view was great from up here. Could see everything. The fireworks were so bright and colourful. Went on for a long time, you know."

Now she was just rubbing our noses in it. We stepped aside so she could throw the bag down the chute and then headed sheepishly towards the lift.

"Happy New Year," the woman shouted after us, now reassured that we were not casing her property. "Have a good 2006."

Her sincere words were most appreciated and timely. We needed all the good fortune we could get. We had welcomed in the New Year from the woman's apartment block knowing that it would be our last in Singapore. The travel bug that brought us to Southeast Asia had gripped us again and we were now ready to head down under because we were convinced that we really needed to spend some time in a country that offered "roo poo", several of the world's most venomous snakes and Steve Irwin. The year 2006 marked our tenth here and it seemed appropriate to move on after enjoying an unforgettable decade in Singapore. That in itself was a remarkable achievement considering I only came to this sunny island for a Christmas holiday.

On 20 November 1996, I set foot on Singaporean soil for the first time. My reasons for visiting were extremely honourable: I wanted to see an exotic world beyond the red-bricked, monotonous council houses of Dagenham, England, and, more pertinently, my dear Singaporean friend David had offered free accommodation. I arrived with my old mate Scott, an architecture graduate from Yorkshire, ready to conquer the country. He planned to contribute to the soaring skyline around Raffles Place and I would ... Well, I would think of something.

Unfortunately, I did not. Scott received two tentative job offers within a fortnight. I, on the other hand, received lots of curt advice.

"I see you've got a good degree," one stockbroker said during a very brief interview at her swanky Robinson Road office. "But what can you offer *us*? What can you actually *do* in Singapore?"

And the truth was, not a lot. A six-month stint at a London stockbroking firm got me that interview, but my degree was in history. That proved to be about as useful as a Singaporean concert pianist living in London. My chances of succeeding in this country were only marginally better than the political opposition. As we sat in the flat that belonged to David's family in Lorong 8 Toa Payoh, Scott tried to be upbeat.

"You'll get a job here, Neil. The economy's booming," he said encouragingly, while trying to batter a feisty gecko with a packet of curry noodles.

"Yeah, in bloody electronics, engineering and construction. What do they need me for? My degree is in modern history. The job market isn't looking for someone to tell them who won the Crimean War."

I found the irony deeply depressing. The Singaporean economy reached its ceiling in late 1996 as Toa Payoh residents waited greedily for their five-roomed flats to hit the half a million mark. Teenagers had never experienced a recession, no one had heard of SARS and the phrase "Asian Currency Crisis" sounded like a bizarre oxymoron. Newspapers even reported the phenomenon of negative unemployment. In some sectors of the economy, there were more jobs than people.

Imagine that.

And I still could not get a bloody job.

Imagine that.

But Singapore was a different country then, in every sense. The pound cost only S$2.20, which meant a 50p bag of chips in England set me back just over a dollar. Today, every pound is almost 80 cents more expensive. And that bag of chips now costs Londoners £1. When I used to say I was from London, Singaporeans occasionally replied, "Ah, Nick Leeson." Now, they say, "Wah, so expensive."

In 1996, Singaporeans bought pirated VHS tapes from the Malaysian town of Johor Bahru on the other side of the Causeway for $10 and hid them in their golf bags and glove compartments on the drive back. Today, Singaporeans buy DVDs for $5 each and have them delivered to their homes. Failing that, a Chinese auntie turns up once a month to sell them from a rucksack, in an office broom cupboard. On the big screen in 1996, cinemas were showing some awful, low-budget film called *Army Daze,* which had grown men wetting themselves with laughter in auditoriums across the country. Not familiar with Singlish or local culture, I thought it was a terrible film. Now familiar with Singlish and local culture, I still think it is a terrible film.

On our first weekend here, Scott and I tried to find out the latest English Premiership scores, but there were no live matches. Indeed, English-language television appeared to be preoccupied with showing reruns of *Mr Bean*. Thank God that does not happen anymore. In the end, we found the BBC World Service on a crackling old radio in the apartment and sat on the floor in our sweaty boxer shorts waiting for intermittent sports updates. Today, you cannot flick through Singapore's cable channels without finding a washed-up English footballer spouting meaningless clichés to bored Asian audiences.

On the other hand, locally produced English programmes were at the peak of their popularity then, with *Under One Roof* and *Growing Up* regarded as must-see TV, even for foreigners like myself. The first was a comedy about a local family who spent most of their time arguing in a living room. The latter was a period drama about a local family who spent most of their time arguing in a living room. Both programmes are no longer on the air and Singaporeans now gather to watch a comedy about a building contractor named Phua Chu Kang, who wears yellow wellington boots, shouts at everybody in Singlish and picks his nose with a long fingernail. Oh, he is such a hoot.

Singlish was a bit of a mystery then, too. My initial inability to understand the nuances of the local dialect painted a terrifying picture of how children were disciplined here. In England, naughty children were "told off" by their parents. In Singapore, they were "scalded" by their parents. The Asian emphasis upon the hierarchical extended family is well-known, but chasing little Harry around the living room with a hot iron because he admonished the maid seemed a tad excessive. I soon discovered, of course, that Singaporeans were not saying "scalded", but "scolded", a quaint verb, last uttered in Britain by Queen Victoria in 1847 when she "scolded" Prince Albert for admonishing the maid.

The intricacies of Singlish were as confusing as they were entertaining. I was alarmed by how comfortable local men were discussing their reproductive organ. I can vividly recall David saying, "That guy likes to talk cock." Does he now? The dirty old bastard. And I thought Singapore was a conservative society. Growing up in England, friends would discuss their erratic bowel movements before they would ever tackle the subject of their tackle.

But everyone "talks cock" in Singapore now. There is a website devoted to that very pastime. There was even a movie, unoriginally called *Talking Cock, The Movie,* which I shamelessly mention only because I played Singapore's founder Sir Stamford Raffles in the opening scene.

Other than its residents' desire to still talk cock, little else remains from the Toa Payoh of 1996. My adopted hometown, one of Singapore's oldest and proudest estates, was transformed in the ensuing decade. The hawker centre where I had ginger beef in oyster sauce on my first night was knocked down, along with the old bus interchange. Apartment blocks were upgraded and painted several times, new parks and gardens were landscaped and new public facilities were opened. The shops where I bought my first mobile phone, CD, VCD, DVD, badminton racquet, tennis racquet, polo shirt and some ill-fitting underpants all came and went. In Dagenham, my former hometown in England, a new shop could stop the traffic.

Even the swanky, 40-storey apartment block where my wife and I missed the firework display did not exist in 1996. Toa Payoh, like Singapore, is a different world now.

And I planned to explore that world one more time before I left. I did not want to say goodbye to a country standing beside a rubbish chute filled with dirty Pampers, staring up at an empty sky. Where is the fun in that? No, Australia could wait. I wanted to see Singapore as I had first seen the country 10 years ago: on foot and unaware. I would venture to places I knew well, places I was vaguely familiar with and places I had never heard of. I would embark upon a farewell tour of an island I fell in love with a decade ago when I called my mother and said, "Singapore's all right, I suppose. But I'll probably be back in England within three months."

Neil's Farewell Tour

CHAPTER 1

Singapore was laid out on the map before me. The north offered Woodlands, the gateway to Malaysia and beyond, and Kranji, home to the only wild crocodiles left on the island. The west promised the Chinese Garden, where I make an annual pilgrimage on my birthday. The south boasted a vomiting lion-fish and the east had Fairy Point. Fairy Point? That caused a double take. I had never heard of the place and certainly did not know that there was a designated area for fairies tucked away in the northeastern corner of Changi. That was definitely on the must-see list.

So I closed the door behind me, took a deep breath and spent a few days walking around Toa Payoh. You do not want to overexert yourself on these things. My trip needed the royal stamp of approval as I intended to follow in the footsteps of my queen. In 1972, Queen Elizabeth II, her hubby Big Phil and daughter Anne visited Toa Payoh and toured the blocks of 53 and 54 in Lorong 5 and I thought that exact location would make an appropriate starting point. Not because I am a royalist, but because it is only a 10-minute walk from my apartment.

On the way, however, I was sidetracked by the biggest pair of pink knickers I had seen since my grandmother used to perform the cancan in her living room. I ambled past Block 99A and there they were in all their hypnotic glory. They caught my eye because they were one of three equally roomy, and equally pink, pairs, and they were not pegged to a bamboo pole, the traditional platform for breezy knickers, but hanging beneath a window. It was a cunning method because that side of the apartment block enjoyed direct sunlight. Every time the clouds parted, the pink frillies glowed, like a scene from the old TV programme *Highway to Heaven*. God obviously likes pink knickers.

Those glowing knickers brought my attention back to Queen Elizabeth II and her visit to the Big Swamp. In Chinese, *Toa* means "big" and *Payoh* is the Malay word for "swamp". So the royal family popped by the Big Swamp. Marvellous. Apparently, there had been a number of letters to *The Straits Times* in the 1960s and 1970s demanding that such an uncouth name be changed to something more tasteful (and snobbish) like Orchid Avenue. Fortunately, common sense prevailed.

Toa Payoh was built on swampy ground and it was the largest housing estate in Singapore (rather like my native hometown of Dagenham curiously enough, which was once the biggest municipal housing estate on the planet and was built on Essex marshland beside the River Thames to the east of London), hence the name. The Big Swamp is both relevant and unique. Orchid Avenue belongs on a Monopoly board.

As I stood in front of Block 53, it was obvious why those wily government chaps of the People's Action Party (PAP) had picked this particular block for the queen's inspection. It provided a microcosm not only of Toa Payoh, but of Singapore's public housing in general, encapsulating the success of the Housing and Development Board (HDB) in sweeping away the decaying kampongs and creating a modern, urban metropolis in their place. Attempts to re-ignite the kampong spirit of community were evident at every turn. The block boasted an amphitheatre for grassroots events, a street soccer pitch, a basketball court, a decent playground, three barbecue pits (all numbered, naturally) and a fitness corner with pull-up bars, parallel bars and monkey bars.

The fitness corners are reasonably popular with the elderly across the country, but I have always viewed them as a touch Orwellian: a healthy nation is a fit nation is a happy nation and all that nonsense. But my cynicism probably was not helped by my attempt to try one pull-up. The blood rushed to my head, I felt faint and someone in a flat above giggled.

Block 53 had also been painted since I had last seen it. More aesthetically pleasing shades of peach, orange and white replaced the dark greens, blues and purples I recall of Toa Payoh when I first arrived. Indeed, gentler, more soothing pastel colours appear to have covered the harsh primary-coloured blocks that were once eyesores around the country and HDB deserves credit for that. There are also fewer blocks with their number painted down the side. I apologise if you happen to live in one of those apartment blocks, but they remind me of kindergarten drawings when a child paints "No. 15, Mummy and Daddy's House, Singapore, Asia, the Earth, the Universe" in the middle of it.

What were the town planners thinking? I think they were pissed. Sitting around the plans after a hearty lunch and a few Tigers in the midday sun, someone probably slurred, "We should paint the block numbers 50 feet high, in bright red paint, down the side of each block."

"Er, why?"

"Because red's a lucky colour."

"Yeah, but won't it be a bit dazzling for residents and passersby, like the pilots of a commercial flight for instance?"

"Nah, it's perfect. Think about when you're pissed and you can't remember exactly where you live. You'll be able to tell the taxi driver to look out for a 50-foot-high block number ... Don't spill your beer on the plans."

Block 53 had a viewing gallery at the top when it was first opened to enable residents and visitors to watch Toa Payoh (and the other HDB estates in nearby Ang Mo Kio and Bishan) slowly rise up around them. There was no cable television in those days.

I was heading for the lift of Block 53 when a voice beckoned.

"Hey, you okay? You look lost?" A middle-aged Chinese chap, holding a bag of shopping, stood beside me, eyeing my notepad with a benign mixture of curiosity and concern.

"No, no. I'm an author. I mean, a writer. You know, a journalist."

My hang-ups have always made it ridiculously difficult for me to explain what I pretend to do for a living. An author is something well-spoken children from English counties like Berkshire or Hampshire say they want to be when they grow up and no one in their family laughs. A writer is what teenagers assume they are when they have written four angst-ridden poems as a woefully inadequate substitute for sex. And a journalist is someone who stands bravely in front of a toppling statue of a murderous tyrant in Baghdad, explaining how much the locals appreciate a good, strong Bush. I, on the other hand, stood in Toa Payoh with a lovely man who was holding a bag full of Maggi noodles.

"So what are you doing here?" he asked warily.

"Well, I heard that the British queen once visited here back in 1972."

"Yah, yah, the queen come here. She come to my block," he said excitedly.

"And did you get to meet her?"

"No, I was out."

I thought that was marvellous. Britain's monarch, the queen of the Commonwealth and the former figurehead of the old empire, popped by for a glass of 7-Up and Mr Maggi Mee was out.

"No, no. I mean, I was out of Toa Payoh," he corrected me. "I moved here later but my friends still remember her coming here."

Like many of the town's residents, Mr Maggi Mee was proud to live in Toa Payoh. He had lived in the block for many years, worked hard, put his son through a decent education and spoke with tremendous pride when detailing the academic record of his son, who taught at one of the country's finest schools. It is a familiar story in Toa Payoh. The once working-class town (many of the residents now fall into the lower middle-class bracket) bears many similarities with Dagenham, with one major difference. A child's education takes precedence over everything else, as Mr Maggi Mee pointed out: "You got children? ... No? ... When you do, make them study hard. When your son makes you proud, it's the best. When your son is an idiot, it's the worst. Don't have a 'half-past-six' son."

I adore that expression. A popular, and unique, Singlish turn of phrase, it loosely means "incompetent" or "screwed up", but "half-past-six" is much more creative. Its origin is supposedly sexual and refers to the angle of the penis. Naturally, half-past-six is droopy, while midnight is impressive. Quarter-past-three needs urgent medical attention.

"No, lah," Mr Maggi Mee continued. "Half-past-six son no good. Don't want one who smokes, drinks or takes the ganja and that white powder. What's it called?"

"Cocaine?"

"No, not that one. The other white powder. Heroin! That's it. Don't take that white powder heroin."

He sounded like a government health campaign. I only asked if he had met the queen. But I shook his hand and said goodbye, promising not to have a half-past-six son, before heading up to the 19th and top floor. Those Singaporean urban planners of the 1960s were rather clever chaps, weren't they? Toa Payoh lies pretty much in the middle of the diamond-shaped country, the municipal jewel in the centre. And Block 53 finds itself at the heart of the Big Swamp and provided both the perfect location for a royal visit and a viewing gallery.

The queen is still going strong, but the same cannot be said about the viewing gallery. I sneakily climbed a stairwell that was clearly off-limits on the 19th floor, only to find a door locked with the biggest padlock this side of Changi Prison. This happens a lot here. The government builds something, then does not fully trust its populace to use it properly.

Even from the 19th floor, however, the view was spectacular. Providing almost complete and unblocked 360-degree panoramic views of the entire country, this was not an arresting vista. It was an IMAX experience. Seu Teck Sean Tong, the bright, exotic Buddhist temple of Toa Payoh, was below me, a building that has long provided an imperious entrance to Toa Payoh for those travelling in from the north, via Braddell Road. And spotting the housing estates of Ang Mo Kio and Bishan a little further north was easy enough.

Walking around the corridor, I picked out the skyline of Raffles Place in the south, two of the floodlights of the National Stadium in the east and the green summit of Bukit Timah in the west before returning to my original vantage point, which was wedged between two plant pots that belonged to a resident whom I hoped would not pick that particular moment to water her miniature botanic garden. The clouds cleared a little and I spotted what could only be the Malaysian coastline of Johor. Hazy, a little blurred but clearly too distant, and too green, to be Singapore, Malaysian land was clearly ahoy beyond Selat Johor (the Johor Straits).

Pleased with my powers of observation, I left a happy man, albeit a slightly hurried one because one or two heads had begun to pop through the grilles of their front doors. Nevertheless, it was well worth the uneasy stares. While the coach parties and the backpackers hand over a small fortune for their minimum-charge drinks at plush rooftop bars and restaurants around Orchard Road and City Hall, similar views are free in Toa Payoh. But then, more tourists should come here anyway.

Although Queenstown came first, Toa Payoh was the first complete estate in Singapore. It is the HDB's crowning glory with polished gems on every corner. With the kampongs being bulldozed by the day, town planners built Singapore's "Dagenham" on the Big Swamp, throwing up homes for 200,000 people, one tenth of the entire country's population at that time. Missing the communal collectivism of the kampongs, not everyone was pleased to be moving to a concrete block, so developers moved quickly. Toa Payoh soon had everything: shopping centres, schools, clinics, a fine public swimming pool, sports halls and community centres, a cinema, gardens, playgrounds, a town park, hawker centres and a sports stadium. All of which were valiant attempts to foster a sense of community and belonging in a new, alien environment.

Over 90 years after the London County Council first conceived the housing estate where I would eventually be raised, Dagenham is still suffering from the short-sightedness of its architects. Social amenities and facilities never kept apace with the bricklayers throwing up the houses and my old estate increasingly resembles a ghost town, with boarded-up shops covered in graffiti and "to let" signs dotted around an estate that is in desperate need of some regeneration.

Toa Payoh has not made that mistake. As a social experiment, it was nigh on flawless. Singapore's public housing policy is undoubtedly one of its greatest success stories, epitomised by my adopted home. The oldest satellite town now looks like one of the newest, having had an extreme makeover in recent years. Boasting a new shopping hub and the country's only entirely air-conditioned bus interchange, Toa Payoh has upgraded just about everything since I first arrived, namely the apartment blocks, the swimming pool, the cinema, the central community centre, the schools, the public library, the food courts and the town garden. Everything. Like many other housing estates across Singapore, nothing is permitted to stand still in Toa Payoh. There are even two private condominiums in the area now, which means other *ang mohs* are encroaching upon my Toa Payoh turf. Apparently, they kept coming across books and newspaper columns that told them what a great place it was.

Even the queen thinks so. In 2006, she returned to Toa Payoh to revisit the same family she enjoyed a 7-Up with all those years ago. The family still lived in Toa Payoh but had moved to a newer block. I hear that the queen still lives in the same house and that it is getting on a bit. But Her Majesty cannot seem to get enough of this place and who can blame her?

As I wandered along Toa Payoh's Lorong 5, I was reminded, yet again, how grateful I am that my dear friend David was not only Singaporean, but also lived in Toa Payoh. I recalled his kind invitation to visit his homeland as we sat in our room in Grosvenor Place, one of the better halls of residence for Manchester University students, while it inevitably pissed down outside. Scott and I were initially apprehensive. Scott was not sure if he would get work as an architect in such a competitive industry. I was undecided if I wanted to live in China.

If our Singapore story had begun in Yishun or Bedok it might have been equally exotic, but Toa Payoh became our first home. And the Big Swamp proved to be my only home for a decade. If it was good enough for the queen—twice—it was good enough for me. Extremely pleased with that thought, I headed over to the Lorong 8 hawker centre. I was hungry and it was getting late. It was almost half past six.

CHAPTER 2

It is not often that you are greeted by the sight of six arseholes. But there they were. Six photographs each depicting a pair of buttocks being pulled apart by a pair of hands.

Of course, these bottoms were no ordinary bottoms. Oh no. These bottoms suffered from acute piles. I am not a doctor, or any kind of anal specialist for that matter, but when the hands are pulling the cheeks so far apart that an MRT train could pass through, it is fairly obvious what is wrong. The photographs were mounted proudly on a sizeable piece of bright yellow card, which rested on an easel. On the off chance that the passer-by somehow missed the sore sphincters on display, a couple of colourful arrows had been drawn on the card with a disturbingly energetic marker pen to capture your attention. It was surreal. I had not seen so many arseholes in one place since a gang of drug addicts mugged me in a Dagenham park in 1996.

But this home-made board of bums was not pinned up on a wall of a doctor's surgery, but at a *pasar malam*, a night market, where I usually enjoyed a cup of sweetcorn. I threw the sweetcorn straight into the dustbin and cut out the middleman. The stall full of bottoms sold some ridiculous cream that promised to cure all of the terrifying ailments depicted in the gory photographs. Surprisingly, the remedy for piles sat proudly beside a stall selling pineapple tarts, the sausage-shaped ones, which looked remarkably similar to some of the symptoms displayed in the photographs. Not surprisingly, sales appeared slower than usual at the pineapple tart stall.

I had two queries regarding the piles cream. First, how brave do you have to be to approach the stall owner? Surely, pointing to one of the bottoms on the menu and saying "I've got that one there. How?" was not an option. Second, and more important, who were the lunatics who agreed to pose as the models? That is surely not a photo shoot to put on your résumé.

Obese people are often willing to pose for "before" and "after" shots for slimming campaigns, but would you get your arse out for a "before" and "after" piles campaign? The photographer must have barked out some bizarre requests at the shoot. "A little more to the left, that's it ... More cheek darling, more cheek ... Push them together, now pull them apart ... Beautiful, baby, beautiful. That's a wrap ... Fancy a cup of sweetcorn?" I can only hope the hands that pulled the cheeks apart in each photograph belonged to the owner of the bottom.

Pasar malams are fabulous though, aren't they? The night markets are one of the highlights of living in Singapore and I cannot comprehend why the Singapore Tourism Board does not do more to woo tourists away from Chinatown and Little India and send them into the unique world of *pasar malams* around the HDB estates. Whenever I am preparing for a trip back to England, the following text message goes out to everyone I know: "Is a *pasar malam* in your town? Need fake branded purses and bags for mum and sister." At *pasar malams,* I have seen handbags manufactured by "Pradha", "Pada" and occasionally even "Prada", which only adds to the fun.

Street markets have fascinated me ever since my mother dragged me around the Dagenham Sunday Market every, well, Sunday. I only went along because she always promised to buy me a "Dagenham Dog", which was an enormous hotdog with greasy onions. When I got older, a "Dagenham Dog" ended up meaning something else entirely. But they were still just as greasy. On this occasion, the *pasar malam* was one of the larger ones that visit Toa Payoh Central just before Chinese New Year and occupied the space around the amphitheatre.

Selling everything from mobile phone covers and screwdrivers to pyjamas and cream for piles, *pasar malams* exude a warmth and cosiness rarely surpassed anywhere else on the island. My wife has followed the travelling markets all over the country, always checking with the stall owners where their next port of call will be. The byword of any *pasar malam* is cheap and their appeal is universal. Children look at the toys (including the first fake Monopoly board game I had ever seen), teenagers buy the latest CDs and jeans (both inexpensive and of dubious origin), women go for the purses and handbags (Gucci and his brothers "Guci" and "Gucii"), men hover around the DIY stalls and I buy Malaysia's finest Ramly burgers.

The *pasar malam* was beside the Toa Payoh Community Library, which I popped into because it has the coolest air-conditioning and I needed to use the toilet after the Ramly burger. During my first year in Singapore, the library (which opened in 1974, the same year I was born) became something of a second home. Just before Christmas in 1996, my future wife joined me in Singapore and we rented a room from a tyrannical Indian landlady, who had a penchant for removing her clothes and baring her boobs to the world on laundry day. Her massive breasts could plug a sink. And as she leant over to do her washing, they almost did. So we were desperate to get out of the flat of the world's oldest glamour model as often as possible.

My wife has always loved public libraries while a lovely lady called Juliet McCully had decided to give me a job at her speech and drama school on the proviso that I hit the textbooks and attained the relevant teaching diploma. So we spent many happy evenings together in the Toa Payoh Community Library.

Singapore really does boast one of the greatest public library systems in the world and, more impressively, the library is still considered a viable place to hang out by children and teenagers here. In contrast, libraries in Dagenham are frequented by senior citizens who borrow books about steam engines and Tupperware. At the age of four, I was thrown into the nearest library by my mother and ordered to read more. I subsequently spent many happy years at that library, looking up rude words in all the dictionaries and finding illicit passages detailing hot steamy sex in the romance novels. When I returned to Dagenham a couple of years ago, my old library resembled a prison. It was surrounded by high perimeter fencing topped off with ferocious-looking spikes to prevent climbing. The library itself had shrunk; there were fewer books available to take out thanks to a reduction in local government funding. Working-class children need well-stocked municipal libraries and parents must force them, at gunpoint if necessary, to use them regularly. The public library is more than a source of entertainment; it is an escape route. Singaporeans should never take their magnificent library service for granted.

After rearranging my books in the Singapore section, I left the library and walked back through the first L-shaped shopping centre built here in the 1960s. With Chinese New Year approaching, the festive lights were coming on and the streets of Toa Payoh were packed with families. The relaxed mood is always convivial for shopping in the evenings. At dusk, the humidity relents a little and I often sit on one of the many benches the town council kindly provides as my wife dashes from one shoe shop to another. She is no Imelda Marcos; she just gets rather excited when she spots shoes going for less than $5, something that seems to happen quite a lot in Toa Payoh. Why are tourists not flocking to this place?

The atmosphere is quite wonderful. Apart from an overriding sense of safety and security, there is always a communal feel to shopping in Toa Payoh. Customers and shop owners know each other and chat. Uncles sell ice cream or hot chestnuts from their bicycles. Aunties read palms for a few bucks and tell strangers their fortunes. Mothers stop in the packed street to gossip while their children play or browse around the toy shops. The mothers never have to worry where their children are. It is Pleasantville, Singapore-style, and it still exists in the 21st century. I see it every night in Toa Payoh.

This scene was repeated at Heathway, the nearest shopping parade to my Dagenham home, when I was young. I knew the butcher, the baker, the greengrocer and the fish and chip shop owner because my mother sent me on regular errands to all four. Alas, there was not a candlestick maker. Today, however, Dagenham children are thrown into the car, buckled to the backseat and driven to a nondescript, all-under-one-roof shopping monstrosity on the outskirts of town. It is a dull, retail behemoth where greasy teenagers earn £5 an hour to tell you that the product you want does not fall within their area of expertise so could you kindly get lost because a senior citizen has fallen into the cornflakes' display. Britain's concrete car parks and shopping blocks are uniform, impersonal and repetitive, but they are cheaper than neighbourhood shops and an inevitable consequence of globalisation, apparently.

If you want to sample that future of shopping in Toa Payoh, step away from the family-run businesses around the older parade and head for the ultra-modern HDB Hub. Opened in June 2002 at the costing of over $380 million, the Hub has a shopping centre and a 33-storey office tower that now overshadows, literally and metaphorically, the neighbouring older mall.

It did bring about 5,000 office workers to the town centre, but they work mostly at the bland HDB headquarters, a skyscraping eyesore that towers above Toa Payoh. And yet its image is wiped from your memory as soon as you have passed it. It may have cost over $380 million but it is instantly forgettable. Whichever way you look at it, that is quite an achievement. Of course, you will find everything you could possibly need for a healthy, balanced lifestyle there: a McDonald's, a Burger King, a Coffee Bean, a Mos Burger and a Kodak photo-developing shop. The trouble is, they are everywhere else too. Eventually, a shopping trip in Toa Payoh will be about as gripping as a shopping trip in Dagenham because the shops will be exactly the same.

Before it got too dark, I bought some *ikan bilis* (dried anchovies) and gladly left the Hub hordes to have a quick peek around Toa Payoh Town Park. Although small and across the road from the choking fumes of the bus interchange, this green spot has always been a pleasant diversion with its stone bridges that surround its centrepiece—a 0.8-hectare carp pond that is also filled with turtles. When Scott and I first arrived, we often spent weekends at the park feeding the turtles after a Chinese uncle showed us how it was done. Okay, it was hardly a trip to Disneyland but we had not been in the country long and needed an afternoon attraction that cost less than $2.

It started to drizzle as I peered into the pond but several plump turtles popped their heads out of the murky water and, in my eagerness to feed them, I inadvertently almost knocked their heads back into their shells with a handful of dead anchovies. At that moment, two urchins appeared from nowhere, looking like they had stepped out of a Charles Dickens novel and into Toa Payoh. The older Malay boy, about 11 years old and clearly the brains of the operation, pushed a bicycle along the edge of the pond while his younger brother, a tubby lad of about 7, leant over the water's edge and dropped in a toy boat. Then he began slapping the boat on the surface of the pond. All that frenzied thrashing caused the turtles to disappear.

"What are you doing, boys?" I asked, a tad annoyed.

"Fishing, lah," said the tubby one, flashing a cheeky grin.

"Why are you banging that boat against the water?"

"So the fish will come over and see what I'm doing." The logic was flawed but he was serious about the job at hand.

"If the fish do come, how will you catch them?" I enquired.

"With my hands, loh." His contemptuous look suggested I had just asked the stupidest question he had ever heard.

"Do you think you'll need a fishing rod?"

"No need, lah. Aiyoh, just grab them."

And he continued to thrash the boat around in the water like a deranged munchkin while his older brother shouted words of encouragement. Bidding a fond farewell to my fisherboy friends, I had a quick look at one of the strangest buildings in Singapore. Okay, one of the ugliest.

The Toa Payoh Viewing Tower stands at the end of the town garden and looks down upon the town centre. Built in the 1970s to complement the garden, the vertical tower stands at a height of 27 metres. It has a light green exterior with a dark green spiral staircase running through the middle. The top of the cylindrical building juts out on one side, something architects usually call a feature. This means, of course, that the "iconic" tower resembles a giant penis, complete with bulbous foreskin at its summit. Being green merely underscores its aesthetic shortcomings, suggesting that the penis has recently caught a venereal disease of some unsavoury description.

As part of the town park's recent upgrading, the tower was repainted and given a little moat with cute fountains spouting muddy water. There was even a small path leading up to the entrance of the tower, which was blocked by a green grille. Naturally. When are the authorities going to learn to trust their own people? For whatever reason, the viewing gallery over at Block 53 was locked, the empty shell of what used to be a restaurant overlooking the carp pond was locked (even though the second storey provides pleasant views of the park) and the Toa Payoh Tower was locked. The message was clear: Look but do not touch because you cannot be trusted. That is how you speak to highly-strung grandchildren.

When I came to Singapore, the tower was still open and I climbed to the top to get a bird's eye view of Toa Payoh. There were used condoms all over the floor. Many couples once took their wedding photographs in Toa Payoh Town Garden. Even more couples used to have sex at the top of its tower. Combining two significant erections at least gave the tower a purpose. It is no coincidence that the government's preoccupation with falling birth rates has intensified since the town council closed the Toa Payoh Viewing Tower. To the people in power, might I make a humble suggestion: Reopen the green penis and the townsfolk will gladly shag for Singapore once again.

CHAPTER 3

I decided to return to my first home in Singapore, only to find it was a mess. I moved into the HDB flat of David's late grandparents in Block 230, Lorong 8, Toa Payoh, in November 1996. We lived on the 13th floor. That was not unlucky, but sharing a bedroom with my then girlfriend (now wife) and my best friend Scott was a touch horrific. Allowing us to stay at the apartment, rent-free, for a couple of months was an extremely touching gesture on the part of David's family but our living conditions were becoming a Freudian nightmare. So Scott rented a room from a lovely Indian family while my girlfriend and I rented a room from a mad Indian woman who made *roti prata* with her enormous boobs exposed. We all remained in Lorong 8, though. Returning there now, the place was in a terrible state.

The government's Main Upgrading Programme (MUP) was in full swing, which meant new car parks, gardens, a basketball court and renovated apartment blocks were on the way. I visited in the interim period and found myself surrounded by scaffolding, tins of paint, bags of cement, water-filled ditches and yellow boots. The incessant drilling was intolerable. But I was here now and decided to have one last peek at our first home on the 13th floor. As the lift doors opened, I heard a voice mutter "*chee bye*". The block was haunted by a foul-mouthed ghost. I immediately wanted to move back in.

Disappointingly, the Hokkien vulgarity came from a plasterer beneath my feet, who was busy laying new tiles outside the lift.

I had unknowingly stepped on his work, knocking a couple of tiles out of place. He had a right to be cross.

But isn't *chee bye* a wonderful vulgarity? It is truly delightful and easily my favourite Singaporean expletive, precisely because it does not sound like one. It is Hokkien for "vagina", but it is so much jauntier than its British four-letter equivalent, which sounds so guttural, particularly when it is said sneeringly through the side of a Londoner's mouth. Like my mother's. That always got my attention when she called me in from the street.

Chee bye, on the other hand, comes across as a formal farewell to the unfamiliar ear. You can almost imagine Jeeves and Wooster crying "Cheerio! Bye!" Such a breezy exclamation, it appears to crop up at the most inappropriate junctures. Two drunks argue in a Toa Payoh coffee shop and, no matter how personal and objectionable the bickering gets, they conclude by shouting "Cheerio! Bye!" Well, that is jolly decent of them, isn't it?

Having apologised profusely to the plasterer, I found myself in a scene from a science fiction movie. The door to each unit was covered in plastic sheets. It was like *E. T.* At any moment, I expected a scientist to step out from one of the units in a radiation suit and take away my BMX. I got nowhere near my old flat. Even the lift was boarded up, which at least provided some priceless examples of Singaporean graffiti.

In a society where respect for law and order is a given, examples of anarchic behaviour often seem so pitiful, they are almost endearing. Rather like those American teenagers who occasionally loiter around Orchard Road with their skateboards, baggy pants and baseball caps, imitating white trash from a Detroit trailer park. In reality, of course, they invariably attend an international school here, their fathers are high-salaried executives and their real home is a leafy suburb in Middle America.

Singaporean graffiti is equally as lame. On one side of the lift, someone had scribbled "Your backside!". Perhaps he manufactured cream for piles. Underneath that hard-hitting attack, someone had retorted with "NO NEED TO SHOUT! Don't grumble like old lady!". On the other side of the lift, a vandal had changed tack by writing "Merry Xmas, may peace with you". The scribbler was so sincere, he obviously felt correct grammar was not required. Indeed, when Singaporean graffiti does bear similarity to the more explicit stuff often spotted inside London's telephone boxes, the grammatical deficiencies weaken its impact. In a public toilet in the Specialists' Shopping Centre, I once read "Miss X will hard suck you". Now, that would make your eyes water. And it would make you grumble like an old lady, too.

Speaking of grumbling old ladies, I felt compelled to return to the home of one of the most famous in Singapore. I wanted to revisit my second home in Lorong 8 to see if my infamous bare-breasted landlady still ruled the apartment block with an iron fist and her enormous boobs. So I left the dusty, discordant upgrading work of the government and headed over to the ageing, largely neglected world of the political opposition.

Toa Payoh is truly a fascinating place to begin a valedictory tour of Singapore, and not just because it happens to be my home. The town encapsulates the general landscape of the country and Lorong 8 illustrates its political make-up. It is a street where two distinct political worlds collide. My first block, 230, falls under the jurisdiction of the Bishan-Toa Payoh Town Council, a Group Representation Constituency (GRC), which was formed in January 1997 and covers three main estates: Toa Payoh, Bishan and Thomson. It is controlled by the PAP, the party of government led by Prime Minister Lee Hsien Loong.

A five-minute walk led me to my second home in Singapore, Block 220, which is also in Lorong 8. But this small corner of Toa Payoh falls under the Potong Pasir Town Council, a single member constituency currently under the control of the Singapore People's Party's secretary-general, Chiam See Tong, who has gamely been the constituency's MP since 1984. I say gamely because he is up against an incumbent party that has been returned to power with massive electoral majorities since Lee Kuan Yew took control in 1959. Chiam and the residents of Potong Pasir are well-respected by politicians on all sides of the spectrum, and they damn well should be.

The contrast between the two sides of the same street was obvious. The area around Block 230 was being transformed with an amphitheatre, new sports facilities, car parks, gardens and upgraded homes. But the area around Block 220 desperately lacked such swanky social amenities. There was no multi-storey car park, the units had no additional rooms, the children's playground was basic, there were no landscaped gardens and the void deck where I sat a decade ago was still filled with odd, battered chairs that had been donated, I presumed, by the residents. Everything about the estate still felt rudimentary.

Moreover, in recent general election campaigns, the PAP has often played hardball, telling voters that the estate will only be upgraded after those under PAP control have been spruced up. In other words, if you do not vote PAP, you do not get an extensive makeover. Yet the admirable Potong Pasir residents, young and old, still believe the glass is half full in their estate. Ignoring the enviable building work across the street, they proudly focus on the upgraded "speaking" lifts and the freshly painted blocks and, most important of all, the fact that their MP offers an alternative voice in Parliament. He still does. Three months after I visited my old home, the admirable people of Potong Pasir returned Chiam to Parliament with a slightly increased majority in May 2006. Political pride had triumphed over material incentives once again.

Quickly stepping down from my soapbox, I headed over to the lift lobby of Block 220 to visit my formidable old landlady. I was certainly apprehensive. The woman was now in her late seventies and I had written about her tendencies to flash her boobs and her penchant for verbally battering the neighbours before. In fact, her antics had become well-known in certain circles and I owed her quite a lot. When I knocked on the door, I half expected her to laugh and knock me out with a swift left hook. Instead, a Filipino girl answered. She told me that the flat had been sold several years ago to an old Chinese couple. "That big-sized Indian lady" had moved somewhere else, but had left no forwarding address. For some inexplicable reason, I was deeply saddened by the news. One of the most entertaining, and most memorable, chapters of my life had finally closed. I had told stories about the old woman for years and was eager to say "cheerio" (the appropriate one) to her before I left Singapore.

But I knew that wherever my old landlady was, some other poor soul was now enduring the odd nipple in the eye. Strangely comforted by that surreal image, I meandered over to Lorong 7 to see Victor, one of my oldest Singaporean friends. Just a few days before Christmas in 1996, he allowed me to use the fax machine in his photo-developing shop—for free—so that I could send off my résumé to an English speech and drama school. Victor and I became friends, I got the job and, a decade later, I found myself asking him to take me on an unusual, and slightly macabre, tour of his neighbourhood.

Adrian Lim was one of the most infamous people Toa Payoh has ever known. On the morning of 25 November 1988, he was hanged for his role in the ritual child killings that had taken place seven years earlier. In 1981, the bodies of a 9-year-old girl and a 10-year-old boy were found outside an HDB block in Toa Payoh. Lim was soon arrested at his home in Lorong 7 and the subsequent High Court trial of 1983 became one of the most sensational in Singapore's history.

Singaporeans were stunned to learn that Lim was a self-styled spirit medium, who lured women of all ages to his flat. Using cheap tricks and simple gimmicks, Lim claimed he possessed supernatural powers. The charlatan said he could cure young women of their various ailments through the guidance of the sex gods, which invariably enabled him to commit unmentionable sexual acts on women who usually consented. Lim, a thoroughly despicable and evil man, preyed on the weak and the mentally disadvantaged, who flocked to his home in Toa Payoh, willingly offering money or sex in exchange for a little attention from the gods.

Rituals included covering crucifixes and Hindu and Taoist idols in blood, dispensing tranquillizers and applying electric shock treatment. At the trial, it was revealed that one of Lim's mistresses had allowed her husband to suffer the electric shock treatment to get rid of evil spirits. It killed him.

From his "altar" in his flat, Lim told his mistresses that he needed to offer human sacrifices to the gods. They obliged. The heinous crimes committed against the young girl and boy before they died do not bear repeating here.

Victor was around the same age as the victims, when the bodies were found around Block 11 in Lorong 7. Victor lived in Block 9. He was terrified. "It was really bad. Couldn't go out and play," he recalled. "I used to play at the playground where they say the women looked for children to take back to Lim. And the church. They went to my church, too. I always used to say I was a potential victim. I lived in the flat next door and I was the same age as those kids who died. I was a potential victim. Ask anyone in Toa Payoh, they'll remember Adrian Lim."

That is why we stood outside the apartment block where the killer had once lived. Almost every Singaporean knows Lim's name. The dead man has become an omnipresent monster, the country's pantomime bogeyman, the ghost who can be called upon to scare children to sleep. Singapore's Jack the Ripper. Throughout the 1980s, parents could order their children indoors at the mere mention of his name. Yet he was arrested in 1981 and hanged seven years later. Why is the name still so familiar in Singapore? Because he is the only one. There has only been one Adrian Lim. There have been other murderers of course, but none so reprehensible.

In Britain, there can be two different murders involving children in a single week. It happened shortly after I met up with Victor. Over seven days, I read about two teenage girls being stabbed and shot. Only one survived. That was followed by a story highlighting the "happy-slapping" phenomenon, whereby teenagers pay warped homage to Stanley Kubrick's *A Clockwork Orange* by assaulting innocent strangers and recording the beatings on mobile phones, which are subsequently posted online. In one attack, a young barman was kicked to death. Although the details of both cases were published in the national newspapers, I can no longer recall any of the individuals involved. In Britain, there have been countless Adrian Lims, to the extent that their identities are now indistinguishable. And monsters are only forgotten when there are too many to remember.

CHAPTER 4

Singapore's Mass Rapid Transit (MRT) train system is the finest in the world. It is cheap, efficient and inexpensive and never suffers from the union problems that dogged the London Underground when I was growing up. The MRT is a public transport network that Singaporeans are rightfully proud of. It has only one minor fault. What happens if the curry you consumed the night before suddenly decides to bid your bowels a fond farewell while you are waiting on the station platform? Has that thought ever crossed your mind? It certainly crossed mine as I dashed off the train at HarbourFront Station, making more noise than the brass section of the Singapore Symphony Orchestra. When there is too much broccoli and cauliflower in my vegetable curry, I can usually mimic the trumpet on "All You Need Is Love" the following morning.

But there were no toilets on the platform. Opened in June 2003, HarbourFront is part of the ultra-modern, $5-billion North-East Line (NEL) operated by SBS Transit. NEL takes Singaporeans from the new towns of Sengkang and Punggol into the business district and transports tourists to Little India, Chinatown and Sentosa (via HarbourFront). The trains are futuristic, fully automated and driverless contraptions with TV screens and bright bucket seats in every carriage. But if you need to pee, you are buggered.

Of course, most MRT stations have toilets above ground and I only made the HarbourFront's public amenities with seconds to spare. Any longer and I might have left a trail. Like most of the MRT toilets, this particular one had just been cleaned. The floors were still wet (I had been in the country for months before I finally realised that most public toilets are cleaned every few hours. I thought Singaporeans were peeing all over the floor). The cleaners were busying themselves around the sink. I closed the door and ruined all their hard work in an instant. Then I listened in on the conversation. There is nothing like eavesdropping while you are sitting on the throne.

"Cannot *tahan* already, the *chee bye,*" one of the cleaners said. Do not hold back, mate. Say what you really think.

"Yah, I know. What to do?"

"He take any small thing and make it into a big thing. I tell you, any small thing, he want to make it into a big thing. So I fuck him, lah."

They were criticising their supervisor, I believe, but the dialogue could equally have detailed a gay romp they had enjoyed the previous night. I opened the cubicle door cautiously, hoping not to find them both smiling and pulling up their trousers. But they were still cleaning their taps so I left them cursing and headed for the tourist attraction I have visited more times than any other in Singapore.

The prevailing attitude towards Sentosa in this country has always intrigued me. Say to most Singaporeans that you are off to the island at the weekend and it is usually greeted with a hollow laugh followed by a litany of reasons why the place is "so boring". Some are almost embarrassed by the fact that next to one of the world's busiest and most famous ports is a resort that is not Disneyland, or Universal Studios, or Dream World or Genting Highlands. It is not even close.

But therein lies its charm. The island won me over when we first met in 1997, precisely because it was so schizophrenic and difficult to categorise. Sentosa had beaches, but it was not a beach resort and Bali certainly had nothing to worry about. There was rainforest and nature trails, but it was hardly a walk on the wild side of Borneo. There was a water slide park and the odd simulator, but it was not a theme park. There was Images of Singapore, but the place was not a metropolis of museums to rival New York. There were golf courses, but these only appealed to a minority. And there were food courts and restaurants, but both were more expensive and less plentiful than on the mainland. In essence, many Singaporeans felt it was everything to nobody.

For a few bucks, however, the island provided a bit of nature, some greenery, decent beaches, a couple of football pitches, an escape from the millions swarming around Orchard Road and a half decent light-and-laser show to round off the evening; that is all I am really looking for from these kinds of places. But it was not enough. Unlike the Singapore Zoo, many of Sentosa's visitors were tourists and attracting locals back to the place was proving difficult. So a theme-park specialist who had worked on setting up Tokyo Disneyland was hired. Shortly afterwards in 2002, an ambitious $8-billion revamp was unveiled to drag Sentosa into the 21st century before destinations such as Hong Kong Disneyland swallowed it up altogether. By 2010, the island aims to attract eight million visitors a year. Take a moment to process that extraordinary figure. It is double the population of the entire country, and Sentosa is only a 500-hectare resort.

That explains why my wife's parents found the quaint island rather enchanting in 1998 and why my mother was none too impressed when she visited it in 2004. By that stage, Sentosa was nothing more than a glorified building site, with the Merlion offering panoramic views of half-naked Indian construction workers hanging out their washing. Indeed, my favourite attraction, the water-based theme park Fantasy Island, had been transformed into a car park. So many attractions were being closed and new ones opened that it was difficult to keep up. But Singapore can rebuild an entire island quicker than Londoners can rebuild Wembley Stadium and I was eager to see Sentosa's progress and find out why over five million people were still flocking to the incomplete resort every year.

I returned to the island the same way I had first visited it in 1997. On foot. This proved to be an infuriating experience. Turning right out of HarbourFront (which was not even there in

1997, we had taken the No. 143 bus from Toa Payoh), I headed down Gateway Avenue to walk across the bridge. The area was a mess. The spectacular VivoCity project, which will be the country's largest shopping centre (because Singapore really needs another one) with over 350 retailers when it opens at the end of 2006, was not finished and I was beginning to think I was being pursued across the country by a team of deep sea drillers. Overhead, the Sentosa Express, a $140-million light rail system, was also being hammered into shape. When it is completed, the Express will run along the top of the bridge above the cars and coaches. But I could not even get onto the bridge. A security guard checked my path.

"Where you going?" he asked, none too pleasantly.

"I'll hazard a guess and say Sentosa."

"Cannot."

"I cannot go to Sentosa?"

"No, you cannot walk across the bridge. It's closed to the public. They're doing upgrading work. Take the bus."

I muttered my consent, but I had no intention of taking the bus. A Singaporean cyclist had just whizzed past, taking the very bridge that was supposedly closed, followed by a Singaporean jogger. And the security guard had stopped neither. The bridge to Sentosa was not closed. It just was not open to those fresh-faced tourists from Changi Airport. Taking them from the HarbourFront Bus Interchange directly to the island's arrival centre meant they could bypass the dusty building site and all those scary construction workers and head for the sanitised world of Sentosa.

But I sneaked over the bridge and immediately regretted it. I saw at the counter that there was only a combined bus and entrance ticket. But I had not taken the bus. Indignant, I approached a member of staff at the turnstile.

"Excuse me, how much should I pay because I didn't take the bus. I walked over."

"You walked over. Are you sure?" He spoke to me like I was dribbling and wearing a bib.

"Yeah, I think so. I was there."

"But how did that happen? Who allowed you to cross the bridge? Who allowed you to get through?"

I felt like Papillon on Devil's Island. The corrugated iron fences dotted around the ferry terminal reinforced the feeling. A quick makan at the Sentosa Food Centre would have cheered me up but that was boarded up, too. Oh, this trip was turning into a barrel of laughs. There were a few construction workers hanging around outside the place and I asked what had happened to the food court.

"Must close. Gonna build casino here. Make more money than a food court," one of them said, laughing.

It was true. After months of deliberating over what the entire country already knew to be a foregone conclusion, the government gave the green light to an "integrated resort" (the government avoids using the word "casino" for fear of offending religious sensibilities). The family-oriented integrated resort will be sold to the highest bidder and then coach parties will come from across the continent for a bit of blackjack. I had only been on the island 15 minutes and I already wanted to leave.

So I got on my bike, a rented one, that is, from the northern corner of the island and made a valiant attempt to circumnavigate Sentosa by pedal power. After speeding past the rather artificial and rather lame Lost Civilisation and Ruined City, I savoured some splendid scenery as the trail ran along the edge of the island with the sea immediately beneath me. Labrador Park stuck out in the far corner of the mainland and passenger ferries bound for Indonesia's Batam Island sped up and down Keppel Harbour. I praised the island's planners for building such a picturesque bicycle trail. Then I cursed them when the trail ended abruptly behind Underwater World and I nearly went over the handlebars and headlong into a bloody fence.

As I got off the bike, there was a rustling in the undergrowth. Not the rustling of a skink or a gecko, but the rustling of something that eats cyclists' feet for breakfast. Taking three tentative steps, backwards, I spotted the head of a monitor lizard sticking up above the grass. As reptiles go, it was a big old brute. From forked tongue to tail, it was around 1.3 metres in length. Indeed, it was only a couple of metres from my feet, and stumbling upon it so abruptly had clearly made us both nervous. Then something extraordinary happened. Something I will tell my grandchildren in a pitiful attempt to sound like an intrepid explorer. The beast edged cautiously down the rocks and then slipped into the sea. The sea! Not some pond, lake or reservoir at a nature park but the open sea. A day trip to Sentosa had turned into a National Geographic documentary. The water was quite choppy, but the lizard swam beautifully, keeping its bobbing head above the waves. It drifted out about 20 metres and, as it turned left, it dawned on me what the clever little bugger was doing. There was a tiny beach to my left, no more than 10 metres across, which was adequate for a fleeing lizard. After swimming an arc of about 50 metres, the cunning reptile stopped about 2 metres from the shore to check that the coast was clear. Satisfied, it effortlessly paddled the rest of the way before slinking off up the beach and back into the undergrowth.

It was a beautiful moment, more so for its irony. The wild encounter occurred behind the entrance of Underwater World, an adequate, if expensive, attraction with an 83-metre-long tunnel for visitors to stroll along while sharks and stingrays swim overhead. I had visited Underwater World three times, but not one of those occasions compared to my close encounter with Godzilla. No artificial environment, no matter how realistic, can ever compete with observing wild animals in their natural habitat.

I headed into the optimistically titled Jungle Trail. Sentosa is no jungle, but the secondary rainforest has proven to be remarkably resilient, considering the British military and then Japan's occupying forces cleared most of it, using the wood for fuel in the 1940s. According to an information board, Sentosa is part of a regional archipelago that is home to one of the richest plant communities on Earth, with over 2,300 species. I had no time to count them all, so I took their word for it. Snakes with fancy names like the oriental whip snake and the paradise tree snake also hang out along the nature trail, but it is those buzzed winged beasts you have got to look out for in the equatorial rainforest. A sign warned: "Watch out for the giant black bees and the orange hornets, they may hurt you, but only if offended." How do you offend an orange hornet? Do you go up to it and say, "I'm not being funny, but orange really isn't your colour. When it rains, and my God it never stops in this place, you look rusty."

I passed a rain shelter and noticed a young Indian chap and a Malay woman engaging in a little jungle boogie. Their hands were all over each other and their tongues were more active than the monitor lizard's. They thought they were alone until an infantile *ang moh* went racing past singing Marvin Gaye's "Let's Get It On". About 15 minutes later, I paused for a drink and allowed the mosquitoes around my thighs to do likewise. As I sat under a rain shelter, the young couple sauntered past holding hands. They were both smiling and he was smoking a cigarette. It was good to know Sentosa still offers some attractions not found on the island map.

From young lovers to married couples, the island catered for all. At Siloso Beach, a bride and groom posed for their wedding photographer at the water's edge. They were not the only newly-weds having their pictures taken at Sentosa that day and I have often found their choice of venue slightly surprising. No matter how skilled the photographer, certain photos will inevitably feature some 50 container ships queuing up on the horizon. Unless your husband is Popeye, it is difficult to understand why a bride might favour such a cluttered backdrop.

Siloso Beach provided a clear indication of Sentosa's future direction. There were more eateries and the introduction of "surfer, dude"-type beach bars, something I do not recall the island having 10 years ago. There was the obligatory 7-Eleven, naturally, which is housed under the new Beach Station, one of the stops on the Sentosa Express. As much as I miss the quaint, discontinued monorail, the new station was impressive. Stopping just metres away from the beach means pampered travellers will step into their air-conditioned bubble at the bridge leading to Sentosa, trundle across Keppel Harbour, cut through the island and alight at the water's edge. I suppose that is a good thing.

The beach had been transformed. It still had that animal show, the one in which the domesticated monkey cleans up all the rubbish (a tad annoying as long-tailed macaques are native to the island and belong in the trees behind the amphitheatre, not picking up Coke cans for applauding tourists), but the beach and lagoon had clearly been spruced up. They were packed with teenagers of all ages playing various sports. Of all races too. Watching a beach volleyball match, it suddenly dawned on me that there were Chinese, Malay, Indian and Caucasian teenagers playing together. It is rare to see such natural integration (rather than integration gently enforced by schools, the church or the workplace or even the product of some patronising racial harmony campaign). After a while, though, I was not sure if I was watching the match to celebrate its racial harmony or to ogle at the thongs that some of the young women had opted to wear. A trifle concerned, I got back on the bike and pedalled off to Tanjong Beach.

I wanted to see Tanjong Beach simply because I had never been there. Hidden in the southern corner of Sentosa, Tanjong Beach comes after Siloso and Palawan beaches and is therefore the least crowded. If Tanjong and Siloso represented the "before" and "after" stages of redevelopment, then Palawan was the "during" stage. Portaloos and piles of sand greeted me as I hurried through. Other than that, there was nothing to see.

Tanjong Beach provided the perfect getaway, not only from bustling Singapore, but from the Palawan Beach building site. Being further off the beaten track, the beach hosted just a handful of Singaporean teenagers playing football. Otherwise the beach was deserted. Currently a peaceful, beautiful retreat, Tanjong Beach awaits redevelopment with baited breath. Until then, enjoy the soft sand, the clearish lagoon and the gentle sea breeze before the coach parties that currently stop at Dolphin Lagoon move a little further along the coastline.

CHAPTER 5

After biking around Sentosa, I wanted to explore Pulau Blakang Mati. I came across the obscure island when I met the inimitable Cliff. It was mid-November 2004 and I was standing outside the Smithsonian National Museum of Natural History in Washington, DC, waiting for it to open. I was there on a writing assignment and had some time to kill. Cliff was there because he needed to pee. A jovial, ruddy-cheeked elderly chap, he ambled up and asked, "Are you English? Because I really need to pee."

"Are the two related?"

"No, I asked another chap where the nearest toilet was and he didn't speak any English and I really do need to pee."

"Well, I think there's one in the museum, which opens in a couple of minutes."

Not a moment too soon for poor old Cliff. With the cold wind exacerbating matters, he appeared to be turning blue. To take his mind off his sprinkler, I enquired why an elderly Englishman was travelling alone around Washington. His story was both amazing and humbling. After his wife died, he signed up for the Heroes Return programme, a noble travel package financed by British lottery money that allowed World War II veterans to revisit the countries where they had once served, some 60 years after VE Day. Cliff had never served in Washington, but he had family there and was recharging his batteries before heading for Australia, New Zealand, South Africa and Asia. The brave, resolute man was 81 years old and still eager to conquer the world. I praised his fortitude and wished him bon voyage. Six months later, the phone rang in my Toa Payoh apartment. The voice was initially hesitant. Then it boomed down the line.

"Hello? That you, Neil? I'm standing in some place called Clifford Centre and I really need to pee."

It was Cliff. In the flesh, in Singapore and still in urgent need of a urinal. I had given him my business card in Washington and thought no more about it. From the American capital to a food court beneath Raffles Place, Cliff had tracked down one man but could not locate a public toilet.

"Hey Cliff, how are you, mate?"

"I'm fine, fine. Wondered if you wanted to get that Tiger Beer we talked about. Still tastes the same after all these years, you know. I've borrowed this phone from a lovely woman, who's standing next to me ... You really are nice to let me borrow your phone, love. You don't mind me talking to my friend, do you? Thanks, love. We met when I was looking for a toilet in Washington."

We spent an unforgettable day together in Singapore. Cliff served in the British Royal Navy during World War II as a signals yeoman and was stationed near Penang. He joined the navy at 15 because he assumed it was an easy way to meet women.

"But you ended up worrying about the men," he said, sipping a Tiger Beer at Boat Quay. "When we were in the Malacca Straits, the bloke in the bunk above me kept reaching into my hammock. And he wasn't after my bloody boot polish, I can tell you."

In September 1945, Allied forces left Cliff's ship off the Penang coast and set foot on Malayan soil for the first time since the Japanese Occupation. On 12 September, Admiral Lord Mountbatten accepted the Japanese surrender in Singapore, thanks to Cliff and his brave band of brothers. This man was not just entertaining company, he was living history.

After the war, Cliff stayed on in Singapore for a few months, working in naval communications. Over 60 years later, my wife and I took him back to the Padang to pick out all the places he remembered: the Fullerton Hotel (then a post office), the Victoria

Theatre clock, St Andrew's Cathedral and the Supreme Court. But one place eluded us.

"I'm trying to get over to Blakang Mati," he told me and I nodded. But I nodded in that slightly patronising way. Like you do when your grandmother points at the television and you say, "Yeah, nan. That's right. It's called a t-e-l-e-v-i-s-i-o-n. You can press this thing here. It's called a remote control. It changes the channels so you watch different programmes."

"Fuck off, funny boy, I want to watch *Desperate Housewives*."

The name sounded familiar and I knew I had heard it before. Perhaps he meant Bukit Merah.

"Ah, you mean Bukit Merah? Little estate in the south, not too far from Queensway?"

"Were the Allied forces stationed there after World War II?"

"Don't know. But I think IKEA is there if that helps."

Of course, he was right and I was wrong. A few months later, dear old Cliff wrote to me and said that he had visited Pulau Blakang Mati, although he had barely recognised the place. Because Blakang Mati no longer exists—it is now called Sentosa. I had not put the two together at the time, but as I stood in front of a machine gun post overlooking Siloso Beach, I thought about dear old Cliff.

The post was called a machine gun pillbox and its location was ideal. Hidden within the dense foliage, the lookout had an unblocked view of the sea. Built between 1936 and 1940 in anticipation of rising Japanese militarism, the pillbox once housed two Vickers machine guns and most probably two extremely bored soldiers. Because, as we all know, while they played pocket billiards with each other, the Japanese came through the Malayan jungle and across the Causeway, invading Singapore from the north. Some of them came over on bicycle. By the time the poor bastards in the south around Labrador Point and Blakang Mati knew what had hit them, it was too late.

All of which makes Sentosa's relaxed setting today rather ironic. Even its name (Sentosa is Malay for "tranquillity") is at odds with its history. With pillboxes every 550 metres along the coastline, the island once formed a strategic part of the overall beach defence plan. The island had been a peaceful fishing village before it became a military fortress, first for British forces and then for the occupying Japanese. After World War II, the British used the island as a military base once again, which was when Cliff stopped by. Some of the troops, including my late Uncle Johnny, knew the place as the "Island of Death from Behind".

My Uncle Johnny was desperate to return to Blakang Mati before he died but he never made the trip. In 2004, my mother paid pilgrimage on his behalf and was left deeply disappointed. She expected sombre, touching tributes to the members of the Allied forces who had defended and protected the country from here. Instead she found a poor man's Disneyland—an island dotted with half-finished attractions, piles of rubble, fenced-off building sites, incessant drilling and crowded beaches with inadequate facilities.

Fortunately, that is changing. The superb Fort Siloso has been upgraded considerably since my previous visit. Not only does the tour take visitors around Singapore's only preserved coastal fort, but it has been thoroughly updated with life-sized replicas and interactive exhibits to give a taste of what life was like here for men like Cliff and Uncle Johnny. And rightly so. The history of Blakang Mati, both botanical and political, is there but it needs to be hunted down. The nature trail provided information boards detailing the role the dense forest played for the military and a surprising number of machine gun posts have been preserved along the coastline. Hidden among the 7-Eleven stores, the surf shops and the bistros, they were subtle reminders that even though Sentosa is evolving by the week, Blakang Mati will never be forgotten.

After a glimpse of the past, I had a quick peek at Sentosa's future. It is called Imbiah Lookout and offers several new attractions. There is the Sentosa 4D Magix, which is one of those cinemas that involves all your senses by spraying water in your face and tickling your feet, while the Carlsberg Sky Tower is Singapore's tallest observation tower (131 metres), from which you can see the surrounding Indonesian islands on a clear day. No doubt the tower will be followed by the Coca-Cola Roller Coaster and the Maggi Mee Merlion.

The Imbiah Lookout provided some splendid views of the mainland and the port, which is one of the world's busiest (a fact you are constantly reminded of in Singapore), but it also had its Coffee Bean, Subway and a pizza place, making it a little too anywheresville. But the place was crammed with tourists and locals who seemed happy enough to gorge on mediocre pasta in the midday sun.

But I was here to try the new Sentosa luge, which operators proudly claim is the first in Southeast Asia. Now, might I be so bold as to suggest that that is a rather strange boast to make. You can imagine an elderly couple from Middle America discussing where to stop off on their luxury world cruise:

"So, which is it gonna be, Ella May? Singapore or Sarawak?"

"Well, you know how much I been wanting to meet an orang-utan, don't cha?"

"I sure do, hon'. But wait, says here, this place called Sentosa has got the only luge in Southeast Asia. It's one-half go-kart, one-half toboggan and one whole lotta fun."

"Really, dear? Well, then, screw it. Put me down for the luge."

I sat down for no more than two minutes to determine where I was going when a bird left its mark on my Sentosa map. It had the entire stretch of pavement on the Imbiah Lookout to choose from but, no, it chose my island guide. Birds should focus their efforts on more deserving targets. Like anyone wearing a Hawaiian shirt.

Fortunately, the luge was only a short distance away so I threw my map away and grabbed a crash helmet. I did not get very far.

"Have you driven a luge before?" the young luge assistant asked me as I struggled to squeeze my gangly frame into a vehicle that was clearly designed for ewoks.

"No, this is my first time. Do I need to pass a driving test first?"

"Of course not, it's very simple."

And he proceeded to reel off a list of instructions that must have been lifted from a NASA flight manual. The luge was like a small plastic bike, with no visible wheels or pedals. To start the luge rolling, I had to lift the handlebars and push them forward slightly. If I did not push them hard enough, the luge refused to budge. If I pushed them too hard, the brakes came on. It was incredibly complicated. As I sat there, motionless, jerking backwards and forwards like a hormonal teenage boy, children barely out of nappies whizzed past me, shrieking at the fact that they had managed to get the hang of the luge faster than the dopey *ang moh*. I was ready to burst into tears. Eventually, after further intervention from the giggling assistant, I managed to push the handlebars forward to the correct millimetre, and I was off down the slope.

Right, I thought, I will soon wipe those grins off their grubby little faces. Using my additional weight, I gained momentum and found myself hot on the heels of the Evel Knievels from kindergarten. One more bend and I would zoom past them with a wave of the hand and a deep, theatrical laugh. But these contraptions were not built for me. Probably for Mini-Me, but not me. Scrunched up in my luge, I turned the bend too sharply, the vehicle veered dangerously to the left and my right knee came up and whacked me in the cheek. Dazed, I had no choice but to concede defeat to the nappy gang.

Undeterred, I vowed to take my revenge. I had three more goes, but those pesky, little brats caught me every time. I felt like the villain in *Scooby Doo*. If I am honest, though, I used the children as an excuse to keep going back on the luge. I loved it. But caution is advised if, like me, you have the inside leg measurements of a giraffe.

Before leaving Sentosa, I felt duty-bound to visit the old Merlion. The tourism symbol of Singapore, it is a strange creature whose origins are dubious to say the least. Surely, it can only be the offspring of an escaped African lion that had sex with a mermaid at the edge of the Singapore River. Perhaps that is what Sang Nila Utama really saw back in 1299. According to the *Malay Annals,* the Sumatran prince spotted a strange animal, possibly a large cat, running into the forest. As tigers had lived across Southeast Asia for thousands of years, he naturally assumed the animal was a lion. No one said he was a smart prince. So he called the island Singapura, which is Sanskrit for "Lion City". I prefer my interpretation of events but I have no idea what the Sanskrit is for "Lion Caught Shagging Mermaid City".

But their love child was in a dreadful state. On its left, sweaty construction workers were busily finishing off the Merlion Station, part of the new Sentosa Express. The station platform was practically in the beast's mouth. Can visitors really not walk anywhere anymore?

The dust from the building site had clearly taken its toll on the concrete hybrid. There was a sizeable brown stain down one side of the Merlion's chin, suggesting it had been eating fish head curry. But I am sure someone will have wiped its chin with a handkerchief and it will be accompanied by a gleaming train station by the time you read this chapter. And when you do visit, behave like a child and go and play in the Merlion's tail. I always do; the water pools and mini-fountains are much more fun than the Merlion itself.

I thought I had better have a polite look around a gift shop before I left. My God, I hope Sentosa's upgrading programme incorporates its gift shops. I have never seen so many things I did not want or need (except my books of course, well done Sentosa!). A souvenir shop inside the ferry terminal sold a toy poodle money bank, for what I believe was $22.90! Are they expecting Paris Hilton to pop in?

My favourite Singapore souvenir was a computer monitor cleaner that was shaped like a Scottie dog. Why are they selling such a household product? Surely every home on the planet already has one? Get one of those little beauties wrapped up and you could solve your shopping woes at a stroke. Return home from Sentosa and say, "I couldn't decide on the 'Singapore is a fine city T-shirt' or the cheongsam. In the end, I realised they don't really sum up what Singapore is all about. They don't encapsulate the mood of the people or the city's modernity. Fortunately, this computer monitor cleaner shaped like a Scottish terrier does."

Realising I was a credit card swipe away from buying every Scottie dog in the shop, I headed for Mount Faber.

CHAPTER 6

I knew I had forgotten something. How could I leave Sentosa without watching its light-and-laser show, with musical fountains, dancing fountains and a fiery Merlion shooting green beams out into the night? And best of all, the show was free.

The attraction has certainly come a long way since 1997, when I recall it was nothing more than a few fountains swaying to classical music, with a few green laser beams thrown around. In the realm of entertaining technology, it was about as futuristic as an Atari—that enthralling tennis game in which each player was represented by a stick and every time the ball struck the stick, it made realistic beep and boop sounds. That was how hi-tech the old musical fountain show was at Sentosa.

The new version was clearly geared towards the Playstation generation. On a wall of water, images of balletic dolphins were projected dancing into the air before splashing back into the ocean. Robots shuffled along the water and beautiful women did some weird, supposedly exotic, wooing at the audience. The older spectators "oohed" in all the right places and the children appeared sufficiently entertained. Although it was not exactly a ride on a roller coaster.

But the show's storyline must have been written by someone high on LSD. The MC, who served as a conductor for the musical fountains, was energetic to an alarming degree and possibly in need of psychiatric help. To spice the show up a bit, Kiki, an animated green monkey, turned up and invited the MC into his "world".

Appearing on a video projected onto the wall of water, the two of them explored the deep seas surrounding Sentosa. Then a beautiful princess rose above the surface and Kiki, the monkey boy, declared his love for Princess Pearl, who, I think, was supposed to have pearls in her hair. On closer inspection though, they looked like inflated condoms. The infatuated pair blew kisses at each other, the Merlion shot his green laser beams all over the island and, suddenly, the lights came on and the show was over. It was like an acid trip. If I understood the story arc correctly, a hyperactive MC chased a green monkey into a dark tunnel, but the primate was not interested because he had the hots for Miss Condom 2006. Try telling that bedtime story to your five-year-old. Distracted by the images of a randy, animated monkey, I left for Mount Faber.

When Scott and I first arrived in Singapore, David selflessly accepted tour-guide duties. He drove us around the city in the early hours of the morning: three young men looking for some action. This was before hubs and all-inclusive societies were the order of the day. Singaporeans still went to New Zealand for their bungee jumping, 24-hour party people belonged in Bangkok and bar top dancing remained a wet dream. So we drove to Mount Faber to watch young couples have sex. Not literally, of course. We did not intend to peer into car windows and give marks out of 10 for length and longevity; we merely drove past rocking cars pretending to be undercover CID officers.

I thought Mount Faber was fabulous. As it rises to around 117 metres, it provided an arresting vista, with Sentosa and the old World Trade Centre on one side and the skyscrapers of Raffles Place and the Orchard Road hotels on the other. For the first time, Dagenham seemed like a long way away. From the top of Dagenham Heathway, a man-made hill built to allow the District Line Tube service to run underneath, the only visible landmarks were hundreds of red-tiled rooftops and the Ford Motor Company's car plant. At Mount Faber, the twinkling lights of an Asian metropolis sparkled in every direction. It looked like Manhattan. If you squinted. But there was no one there. On foot at least. There were a lot of cars rocking to the Kama Sutra on the way up, but Faber Point at the summit was deserted. I had always believed that the 56-hectare site had been underutilised by a government famous for developing and cultivating its land to the nearest square inch. But apart from providing a quiet place to have sex, Mount Faber offered little else other than a cable car station to take dissatisfied tourists back to Sentosa. Something had to be done.

It was. And my sitting on a No. 409 bus bound for Mount Faber proved that. The bus service leaves the bus interchange beside HarbourFront MRT Station every half an hour after 6pm on weekdays and only recently came into existence. The loop route around Mount Faber Road was established to serve The Jewel Box (a spiffy new restaurant and bar for the more discerning diner), part of the $8-million makeover the old hill has enjoyed. There was also a bistro, which offered a panoramic eating experience that would cost at least twice as much around City Hall.

I got off at Faber Point and was pleased to see that I was not alone, even though it was almost 9pm. But I was the only single person there. Countless couples huddled together on benches holding hands, with bulges in all the right places. They had only one thought on their minds: I wish that leering *ang moh* would get lost. Trying to avoid stepping on a saliva-sharing couple was difficult. Faber Point was a minefield of randy men and women. There was a signboard with a labelled photograph highlighting all the visible landmarks from Faber Point, but I could not get near it because a pair of young lovers were leaning on it and eating each other. At one point, the girl almost had his head in her mouth. It was like one of those crocodile shows in Bangkok. Pornography might be illegal but, at Mount Faber, you get a great view and a free live show.

I lingered around the signboard because I really did want to pin down the Marriott Hotel at the corner of Orchard and Scotts roads. From there, I would be able to make out Toa Payoh. But I was crossing the line from being an interested tourist to becoming a dirty *ah pek*, so I went downstairs, where there were some fine sculptures by an artist called Sim Lian Huat that depicted Singapore's history. They kicked off with the country's humble beginnings as a 14th-century trading settlement and progressed to the arrival of Stamford Raffles in 1819. Now, I have a question about old Raffles: Why is he so often portrayed in the same pose? You know, the one where he is folding his arms and tilting his head slightly to his left. The other sculptures displayed all the usual suspects: the arrival of cheap immigrant labour from China and India in the early 1900s, the Japanese Occupation, the PAP's quest for self-governance and the racial harmony bit, which, to be honest, gets a bit wearing after a decade or so.

With another 20 minutes before the No. 409 returned, I took a slow walk down Mount Faber Road. Dozens of bats flew overhead and I instinctively ducked every time one came near me. My wife always laughs at this. Behind our old block in Lorong 1 Toa Payoh was an underpass that provided a welcome short cut to the bus stop on Thomson Road. But the underpass was also a popular hang-out for bats and I was convinced that one of them would eventually fly into my face.

"Why do you keep ducking? The bats won't come anywhere near you," my giggling wife would say.

"That's easy for you to say, midget. But some of them are swooping to within 2 metres of the ground. They could take my head clean off."

"God, you really are stupid, aren't you? Bats have got echolocation. They send out sound waves, which hit an object and bounce back. The bats know where you are long before you even see them."

"All right, David Attenborough. I'm telling you, they get complacent in Singapore as everything bounces off shorter people like you. No one's almost 2 metres tall like me. The bats don't expect to encounter someone as tall as me here. When their sound waves bounce off me, they think I'm a tree."

And I swear that is true. Asian buses are not ready for me. The buttons inside lifts never expect me to be so tall and MRT trains misjudge my height. A flying mammal will eventually do the same and I will end up with a bat in my belfry. So I will continue to duck, thank you very much.

I came across another old bat at Mount Faber. She was a Caucasian woman (a number of expats live in the Telok Blangah area around the hill). Wearing ill-fitting Lycra leggings that Caucasian women of a certain age tend to favour when they are exercising, she marched towards me. She was one of those power-walkers who are taking over the planet. Have you seen them? They storm across nature parks and town gardens like demented gamekeepers and you feel compelled to shout, "Either walk like a normal person or run because you look bloody ridiculous."

This woman looked particularly menacing because she wielded ski poles. I am sure they have a technical term among the power-walking fraternity, but they were essentially ski poles, which she used to plough her way through the difficult terrain that is the smooth tarmac of Mount Faber Road. She looked really, really cool. When she passed me, she breathed that heavy, theatrical sigh popular among overtaking power-walkers. It was a real effort not to kick away one of her ski poles.

With time to kill, I wandered down to the Marina Deck Restaurant, which was shaped like an old, timber-built sailing vessel. It looked nice and nautical but was largely empty and strangely eerie. The upper platform had no lighting and I heard whispering voices moving around behind me. This is it, I thought. I have been here before. I know the signs. Whispers in the shadows inevitably lead to me being left out of pocket. I moved to Singapore after being mugged twice in England and, after spending 10 crime-free years in the country, I was about to complete an unwanted hat-trick.

Then I heard a female voice giggling. I turned reluctantly to discover yet another courting couple fumbling around in the dark. For heaven's sake, Mount Faber was developing into a retreat for the matchmaking Social Development Unit. Don't these people have homes to go to? Of course, they do, but they are invariably packed with parents and siblings. Space is at a premium in Singapore.

So is sex. The government is obsessed with the country's ageing population, the falling birth rates and its future labour force. Ministers claim Singaporeans are not reproducing fast enough. Well, all I know is, it is not for the want of trying.

CHAPTER 7

When I was young, I wanted to be Samuel Pepys. You must have heard of him. He is quite a significant figure in British history. He was an English diarist who wrote for the *Dagenham Post* every Wednesday. Hidden among the teen pregnancies and the drug busts was a weekly column that talked about, well, not a lot. Old Pepys chronicled his shopping trips with his wife and other such intrepid adventures such as buying a new car or visiting his relatives around Dagenham. A columnist who wrote about his mother every other week? That will never catch on, I thought. But his inane musings about life in Dagenham proved strangely addictive and the elderly readers of the newspaper could not get enough of him.

Then I visited the Monument one afternoon in the City of London. Designed by Sir Christopher Wren, the Monument stands as a tribute to the rebuilding of England's capital following the Great Fire of London in 1666. The historic site notes that the Great Fire, along with the terrible Plague that had preceded it a year earlier, was recorded in the detailed private diary of one Samuel Pepys. Not only was Pepys a key administrator under King James II and a Member of Parliament, he also played a pivotal role in establishing the British Civil Service. And yet he still found time to write a weekly column for the *Dagenham Post*. What a humble guy.

Imagine my devastation, then, when I discovered that old Pepys had died in 1703, which would have made it almost impossible for him to write about getting the spark plugs in his Ford Cortina changed at a Dagenham garage in the 20th century. The *Post* writer was using a pseudonym. Borrowing the name of the most famous diarist in English history. How dare he? I never quite recovered from the shock.

So when the street sign Pepys Road leapt out at me as I trundled along Pasir Panjang Road on the No. 143 bus, I knew that it was the very stop for me. My plan for the day was to take a gentle amble through Kent Ridge Park, cut through the National University of Singapore (NUS), take a break in Clementi Woods because it sounded like a location from *The Blair Witch Project* and finish off with a sunset over West Coast Park.

But I got sidetracked. Heading down Pepys Road, I glimpsed a sign for a national heritage site called Reflections at Bukit Chandu, a World War II Interpretative Centre. It was at the edge of Kent Ridge Park, which I had visited before, but I had never noticed the museum. Oh well, I could always spare 15 minutes for a national heritage site. I stayed for over two hours.

This exhibit was truly one of the National Heritage Board's hidden gems and a compulsory visit must be included on the curriculum of every Singaporean student. With the exclusive address of 31K Pepys Road, the old colonial house was the only one left around Bukit Chandu, an area that forms part of Pasir Panjang on the west coast. Bukit Chandu, by the way, means "Opium Hill" in Malay and possibly refers to a British-owned packing plant that was located there in 1910. Yet another proud legacy of the old empire. The house had been charmingly restored and served as a deeply poignant tribute to one of the most heroic acts of bravery recorded in Singapore's military history. Notice I say Singapore's, and not British, because most of the men came from the 1st and 2nd Battalion Malay Regiment. The soldiers were mostly Malay Singaporeans, not British, or even Australian. They fought not for a Union Jack, but for a land that was their birthright.

As most Singaporean students will tell you, the invading forces of Japan took just 55 days to overrun Peninsular Malaya and had reached Johor Bahru by 31 January 1942. The Japanese eyed Malaya, known as the "Dollar Arsenal" of the British Empire, because it had produced half of the world's supply of rubber and tin since the beginning of the 20th century. Expecting an attack from the south, the British forces were pushed back quickly as the Japanese poured in from the Causeway and Pulau Ubin. In desperation, the guns that faced out from Labrador Point, along with the ones that I had visited at Siloso Beach, were dramatically turned inwards to fire on their own country.

But it was all in vain, of course. Local forces retreated to Bukit Chandu and prepared for their last stand. The battle should have been a formality. As most of the soldiers at Bukit Chandu were from the Malay Regiment, they were considered to be less experienced and battle-hardened than their Western officers. They were outnumbered and running out of ammunition but they simply refused to yield. The bloody battle at Bukit Chandu on 14 February 1942 was essentially a battle for Singapore and the odds were insurmountable. When the Malay soldiers ran out of ammunition, they resorted to hand-to-hand combat, displaying immeasurable valour in a battle they knew they could not win.

The British surrendered the next day, but the Japanese were reportedly so outraged by the indomitable spirit of the Malay Regiment that they took revenge in the most savage and cowardly fashion. They stormed the nearby Alexandra Hospital. Being used as a British military hospital, there were around 200 injured soldiers and civilian medical staff there. An unarmed British lieutenant rushed out to meet the Japanese soldiers, waving a tragically pathetic ad hoc surrender flag—a hospital bed sheet. He was mercilessly bayoneted to death.

In the hospital, doctors, nurses and civilians were stabbed. According to one survivor, the Japanese entered an operating theatre and murdered all the medical staff in the room, before bayoneting the patient lying on the operating table. This went beyond collateral damage. This was mass murder. A handful of survivors were herded into a small room and locked in with no food or water. Some were taken out later and executed, others died in the night through medical neglect (most were injured in the first place). Of the 200 who were attacked in Alexandra Hospital, no more than five survived to ensure that this monstrous act would never be forgotten. There is now a memorial to commemorate the tragedy at the hospital.

Singapore's government, particularly its old guard, is forever reiterating the importance of remembering and respecting the country's past. I could not agree more. Singaporeans are spoilt today. Children of the "maid generation" barely know how to make instant noodles by the time they go to university. They have never ironed a shirt, washed their school uniform or mopped their bedroom floor. There is little, if any, appreciation of the suffering that paved the way for their pampered existence. I am not sure they even care. While I wandered around the fascinating Bukit Chandu museum, a group of students, all around 15 or 16, were ushered in to watch an informative video about the Malay Regiment's courageous final stand and the massacre at Alexandra Hospital. Some looked bored. There was fidgeting and the occasional glance at a branded watch. I find that infuriating, particularly in a country that barely has a recorded history. The "maid generation" does not need to regurgitate every relevant fact about the island since the 14th century, but it must recognise that Singapore's history does not begin in 1959.

After lunch, I headed up the steepish slope outside Reflections at Bukit Chandu and into Kent Ridge Park. It was only 47 hectares, but its ponds and natural vegetation, including rubber wood, wild cinnamon and those sturdy *tembusu* trees, made it an unusual park stuck in the middle of the concrete labyrinths of the National University of Singapore and the Singapore Science Park.

There was also the superb Kent Ridge Canopy Walk, which was not here when I last visited. Built at a cost of $1.3 million, the 280-metre-long boardwalk opened in November 2003 to link the Reflections at Bukit Chandu museum with the park. And what a graceful combination of nature and history it was. The walk was a breezy stroll among trees that were helpfully labelled until

I reached its centrepiece—the site of the actual battle between the Japanese and the Malay Regiment. A blown-up photograph allowed me to pick out Alexandra Hospital between the trees and it seemed almost incredulous that such a serene setting marked Singapore's plucky last stand in 1942. Plant nurseries now occupied the old battleground. Somehow that seemed appropriate.

As it was a Monday afternoon in the middle of February (coincidentally, the same week that Singapore had fallen to the Japanese 64 years earlier), I had the Canopy Walk all to myself until a teenager swaggered towards me, singing aloud to whatever he was playing on his iPod. His headphones were bigger than a couple of Belgian buns and he favoured those massive aviator sunglasses that I thought had gone out of fashion with *Magnum, P.I.* When he got closer, I realised he was not only singing to himself, he was also talking to himself, which is a rare feat for those of us not living in a padded cell.

"Excuse me, mate," I asked tentatively. "Is NUS this way?"

"Yeah, man," he replied, still bouncing along to his iPod. "Keep going straight, man."

"Thanks. Are you a student there?"

"What? Hey, no way, man. No way."

He looked disgusted. I had apparently insulted his intelligence. A university education was clearly beneath him. But then if he spent all day talking to himself, he would always be first among equals.

Kent Ridge Park had one of those signs that the conscientious guys at the National Parks Board diligently provide at their green havens across the garden city. It simply read: "Lookout Point". Because if the sign was not there, you would not know, would you? The sign smacked of a fledgling garden city trying too hard. I think I speak for all park visitors when I point out that if I am standing at the top of a hill that provides unblocked vistas of the southern islands, I can deduce for myself that it is a lookout point. What is more, signs such as this one are meaningless because they offer no information. A lookout point for what? Pink dolphins? A sinking Chinese junk boat? Crazy Horse dancers jiggling their boobs?

The phenomenon of pointless signs is not isolated to national parks either. Take a walk around any shopping centre in Singapore and follow the signs. The first one will say "shops". And the second? "More shops". Well, that is informative, isn't it? And here I am thinking that I will turn a corner in Suntec City Mall and find myself confronted by an escaped rhinoceros.

In Britain, shopping centre signs sensibly inform the shopper that Woolworths and Boots are on the left and Marks & Spencer and The Disney Store are on the right. It is not a complicated system. I remember Scott, an architecture graduate, being fascinated by the lack of information when we first toured Orchard Road. He would stand under a sign in Takashimaya Shopping Centre and shout, "Here Neil, you'll never guess what they've got down there on the left?"

"What?"

"More shops! And on the right, they've got, now this may come as something of a surprise, more bloody shops! How the hell did they build such a modern mall and then fail to provide the most basic information to the shopper?"

Perhaps the fad culture is to blame. With fashions and crazes coming and going faster than you can make a cup of bubble tea, shop turnover rate is high. Retail units at Far East Plaza, for example, appear to change every week. Signs that indicate the location of Hello Kitty, cinnamon bun, 10-minute haircut and *luohan* fish shops would need updating frequently. Maybe it really is easier to simply say "more shops".

After spending a few minutes at what was indeed a splendid lookout point, I jogged down the steps that led to the two ponds in the park. Unfortunately, the native wildlife was conspicuous by its absence. The team of drillers digging up the path around the pond did not help matters. By now, I was convinced they were tracking me around the country. Reluctantly, I trudged back up the steps. It was about to rain; the humid air was oppressive and my damp clothes were stuck to my skin. And I had climbed the wrong steps. A gentle ramble around a park had somehow turned into a never-ending trek up a troublesome hillock. Then I spotted a turnstile at the top of the steps. Rather fortuitously, I had stumbled upon a side entrance to NUS, where an air-conditioned food court waited for me. Or so I thought.

"Woah, woah, woah, woah! Where you going, ah?" shouted a sprightly Chinese chap in his sixties, striding up the steps behind me. How the hell had he caught up with me so quickly?

"You got a pass? Must have a pass. If you don't have a pass, cannot go in. No, cannot go in without a pass. Must have a pass." I had not uttered a word. The man was having a heated argument with himself.

"I'm going out on a limb here, but am I right in saying that I must have a pass? I need a pass just to walk through the university campus grounds?"

"No, no, no. This not the university. No, no, no. This is private property. University not here."

"Then where is the university?"

"Don't know. Not here. See the sign. This private property."

"I've just walked up a thousand steps to get here. Why wasn't the sign at the bottom of the steps instead of at the top? Is there any way I can get back into Kent Ridge Park without going all the way back down the steps?"

"Kent Ridge Park? Where's that, ah?"

"Where's Kent Ridge Park? It's there! Right beside you! You see that huge forest right next to you, full of trees, bushes and plants? That." I wanted to kill him.

"Oh, follow *longkang*, go by *longkang*, *longkang*. You want *longkang*, *longkang*."

And he was gone, through the turnstile and into his private property. And I was left wondering whether he was repeating himself or calling me a *longkang*, or drain.

On the way down, I was accompanied by a younger Chinese man who left the mysterious building as the uncle went in. Wearing an expensive shirt and a sharp tie, he obviously did not clean the *longkangs*.

"If it's not NUS, what is it?" I asked, as I wrung out my sweaty, soaked shorts.

"We're called DSO," he replied, rather hesitantly. "It's a research company, defence and stuff."

"Wow! You work for the government. Singapore's answer to James Bond. What are you working on at the moment?"

He laughed politely as we continued to walk down the steps together. But he did not reply and the penny eventually dropped. I was dumbfounded.

"You're really not going to tell me, are you?"

"Better not, lah."

So he did not and we parted ways at the car park. I later discovered that I had chanced upon DSO National Laboratories in Science Park Drive. DSO is Singapore's leading defence research and development organisation. According to its website, it essentially strives to improve national security, working to increase the operational effectiveness of the Singapore Armed Forces and create cutting-edge defence technology. I was lucky I had not been shot.

But some perspective is also desperately needed here. The last time I watched one of his films, James Bond was not a lanky, red-faced *ang moh*, wearing sweaty shorts and moaning about "these bloody steps". But that is life in Singapore. Self-censorship has become a reflex action from the bottom up. How many times have you opened a newspaper and read about an interviewee who has refused to give his full name, even though his comments are usually inane? Indeed, it is quite common to read paragraphs such as: "An eyewitness, who only wanted to be known as Mr X, said, 'I stood on my balcony every evening, watching the dramatic events unfold. I eventually realised that when the sun goes down, the moon always comes up.'"

Some Singaporeans are so conditioned to regulate their own thoughts that, in some instances, it has become detrimental. In 2005, the country was shocked by a series of revelations concerning the National Kidney Foundation. One of the most respected and wealthiest charities in Singapore, the NKF has benefitted countless dialysis patients over the years with its vigorous fund-raising programmes. Truly commendable stuff. Until it became apparent that its top executives had helped themselves to first-class travel and luxurious business trips while staff members had received numerous increments in a single year and run up inflated expense accounts. The final straw came when an independent audit revealed that only 10 cents of every donated dollar actually went to the people that mattered—the kidney patients.

But it was what came out afterwards that really struck a chord. Subsequent stories hinted that one or two NKF employees had been concerned for some time that extravagant spending was going on, unchecked, in high places, but had opted to say nothing for fear of the repercussions their allegations might have had on their "rice bowl". One extremely courageous soul within the NKF had questioned the wasteful spending via an e-mail but was soon slapped into place by a lawsuit in 1999. There is too much deference given to figures of authority here, particularly in the corporate world. It is such a shame. Look through the country's short history and it is exceedingly difficult to find an Erin Brockovich, the woman who successfully waged war against a national American gas and electric company, or a Dr Jeffrey Wigand, the insider who took on the American tobacco industry.

Always wise after the event, there were repeated calls at every level after the NKF scandal for more Singaporeans to speak up when they suspect any wrongdoing along the corridors of power. Now the island is expected to become a nation of four million whistle blowers. But it is not as simple as that. For over 40 years, most Singaporeans did not even know they had a whistle.

CHAPTER 8

Scott and I had never experienced such domestic bliss. Our dear friend David had moved us into his late grandparents' five-roomed flat in Toa Payoh just in time for Christmas in 1996. I thought the tiled floors in every room added a touch of opulence. We had never lived in a climate warm enough to accommodate living without carpets. If you sat on a tiled floor in a Manchester flat in the middle of February, you would require the services of a welder to prise your frozen backside off the floor. Our new Toa Payoh abode was palatial in comparison. With its marble tiles and whitewashed walls, the HDB flat resembled a Mediterranean holiday villa. A couple of Grecian urns, a six-pack of San Miguel and Sky Sports playing on cable in the background and it could have been a family jaunt to Tenerife.

Just 12 months earlier, Scott and I had been living in the most decrepit terraced house in the north of England. On the positive side, our Victorian hovel was close to the University of Manchester. But then, so was the local park. And on most nights, its benches were warmer than our living room. Rising damp was a perennial problem. In the bathroom, the wall turned black every month. The landlord solved the health hazard by painting over it. By the end of the year, the paint on the wall was an inch thick. The box bedroom beside the bathroom was even worse, with a bubble the size of a pillow emerging in the centre of the ceiling after three months. But our penny-pinching Fagin followed strict health and safety regulations. He burst the bubble and painted over it.

Walking up Kent Ridge Road now reminded me of those hard times. We were not destitute by any means in Manchester, but we rarely had any money and lived in a crumbling dump fit for demolition. Singaporean students, on the hand, are a pampered lot. They should be. Studying for one's future takes precedence over everything else here. They should not be preoccupied with fiscal concerns, inadequate housing or a Fagin-like landlord, such as ours who sincerely believed that a washing machine was a superfluous consumer durable (sad, but true). I spent most of my second year in Manchester's fine John Rylands University Library. Not because I was the university's most conscientious student, but because the library was much cosier than that hovel.

In comparison, the accommodation at the National University of Singapore looked more like jaunty seaside chalets. I felt the slightest pang of envy when I strode past King Edward VII Hall. With the sea as their backdrop, the students' rooms were modern, uncluttered blocks, similar to the holiday retreats at Pasir Ris. As I followed the winding, precipitous road, a sulphur-crested cockatoo let out a distinctive loud screech as it flew over my head and landed in the tree above. Lucky bastards, I thought. Those students attend a first-class university (NUS was ranked 22nd in the world's best universities, according to the *Times Higher Education Supplement* World University Rankings in 2005. That figure attracts just as many raised eyebrows here as it does plaudits), the accommodation is top-notch, the institution is surrounded by the greenery of Kent Ridge Park, Clementi Woods and West Coast Park and they are visited by confused wildlife mistaking the place for Darwin.

But they do not have a bar. I still find that incredible. Sitting in a food court at Yusof Ishak House, I was surprised to see a sushi restaurant and a bakery on campus, but no pubs. Some of the guys have already carried a gun through the Pulau Tekong jungle during their National Service, but they cannot wield a pint at university. As I had been struggling up Kent Ridge Road earlier, a pizza delivery boy whizzed past me on his scooter and it now occurred to me: Why did anyone on campus need a pizza? No one was drunk.

Singapore boasts more gamblers than serious drinkers, yet NUS undergraduates cannot have a beer together at a student bar on Friday night but gambling addicts will soon have two gleaming casinos to choose from, at Sentosa and Marina Bay. The irony is bewildering. But then, if student bars provided over 30,000 jobs, attracted coachloads of tourists and contributed billions to the economy, then I am sure they would be springing up all over the country, too.

At the food court, I took out my trusty street directory to determine whether or not Clementi Woods was within walking distance. As usual, I found myself distracted by the street names. Just a little further north was Dover Road, with Folkestone Road, Maidstone Road, Sandwich Road and Deal Road branching off. I could not believe it. They are all towns in the English county of Kent, where my mother now lives. Deal is one of the family's favourite seaside towns and my brother goes to Sandwich Technology School (where they told my mother during induction week that the curriculum was based on the "Singaporean model"). I had been here 10 years and had no idea that there were such poignant reminders of my family back in England. To Singaporeans, this small enclave was tucked away behind the Transview Golf and Country Club and had little significance. But to me, almost every street name represented a memory.

I took a bus down Clementi Road, missed my stop and ended up walking back down Commonwealth Avenue West, passing some schoolchildren messing around at the fitness corner of their HDB estate. Then I crossed over into Clementi Road, passed some Singapore Polytechnic buildings, turned into Dover Road and overtook some giggling teenagers from New Town Secondary School before finally reaching Folkestone Road.

And I stepped back into the 1920s. The tiny street had a charming, rural setting. Trees sheltered the houses, which were almost identical. Detached, spacious whitewashed colonial residences with black window frames were complemented with lovely gardens, swimming pools and space for two cars, which were typically Lexus, Mercedes-Benzes and BMWs. Why are rich people so shockingly unoriginal when it comes to their choice of car here? Why do they never say, "Screw it, I'll have a 1959 pink Cadillac?"

The palatial homes were aesthetically pleasing, but strangely incongruous beside the HDB estates that I had only just left in Commonwealth Avenue West. Perhaps it was not the houses, it was the people. There were no Asians. A young British girl came out of one house riding a scooter, overtook me and then knocked on the door of a house further down the same street, where other British children played on a trampoline that was bigger than my living room. At another mansion, a female British voice shouted instructions to her children and I saw another small group of my fellow countrymen playing in the back garden.

I am sure there were Asians living in "Little Kent" but, on this particular day, I only saw three—an old Chinese uncle cutting a front lawn, a young Filipina who was walking her employer's dogs and another, older Filipina who gave me a warm smile as she closed the gates of one of the houses. Everyone else was white.

It was a shock to see my culture in such an unusual environment. Every race has its favoured enclaves in Singapore, whether the government chooses to admit it or not. And everyone knows that Caucasians frequent Holland Village, River Valley Road and Cairnhill but I had never realised that bastions of Little Britain remained within HDB estates. It was extraordinary, as if several streets had been airlifted from the real Kent in England and replanted here. I could not have been more surprised, even if Somerset Maugham had wandered across in a white silk suit and enquired if I fancied joining him for a pink gin and a chinwag on the wonders of Raffles Hotel while the ladies showed off their charleston steps on the veranda. I later discovered that "Little Kent" was once a housing estate called Medway Park for British officers, who named the streets after the English Channel ports in the county. Singapore has been independent for over 40 years, but little has changed at Medway Park. When they are stationed in Singapore, naval officers still occupy some of the black-and-white mansions and the area remains a thriving expatriate community. Now, I do not begrudge the expatriates who occupy these houses. I am sure the head of every household contributes to global security or oversees a multinational corporation that generates zillions towards Singapore's GDP and generously patronises an arts scene desperate for every cent. But as I walked briskly along Commonwealth Avenue West trying to escape a cheerless shower, I noticed those schoolchildren again. They were still playing on a cycling machine at their fitness corner. Many of the gardens around the colonial residences in "Little Kent" were bigger than the fitness corner that served an entire HDB estate. Somehow, it just did not feel right.

Clementi Woods was a bit of a disappointment. There was actually nothing wrong with the park. Indeed, it was a pleasant little town garden, with the usual fitness corners, acacia and *tembusu* trees, a children's playground and a closed-down seafood restaurant. But its name had suggested I needed a miner's helmet with a torchlight. I had expected country bumpkins to stroll over from the village pub, look up at the sky and mumble, "Stay on the path, yah? It's a full moon." Or, at the very least, three disparate bears moaning that someone had eaten their porridge. But no, the atmosphere was all too convivial and laidback so I made the short walk over to one of Singapore's finest parks.

West Coast Park is easily one of the country's best-kept secrets. Residents who live in the area use it frequently and smile knowingly when they pass each other, as if they are masons walking across sacred ground, the keepers of a natural treasure. The rest of Singapore, of course, goes to East Coast Park. I have got nothing against the East Coast, even if it is a mite overrated. Indeed, when I first arrived in Singapore, I followed the expatriate dictum: You are an expat. You will go to the East Coast. You will eat its seafood and pretend you understand why everyone makes such a fuss over it. You will cycle up and down its congested paths. You will hire Rollerblades and make a complete tit of yourself. Okay, I did everything except the last part. You must draw the line somewhere.

But it was eight years before I visited West Coast Park, and even then it was not intentional. Part of the reason it is overlooked is its size. The park is only 50 hectares, a fraction of the East Coast's 185 hectares that stretch over 20 kilometres. But therein lies the attraction. With the exception of its filthy beach (which was in the process of being cleaned up by the town council), West Coast Park offers everything the East Coast offers: green spaces for sports, sea views, a bird sanctuary, more wildlife, barbecue pits and, most important of course, a huge McDonald's. And to think it all stands on the sea. The park was built on reclaimed land back in 1979 and redeveloped in 2000.

When I got there, a football match occupied the sizeable fields. Nineteen men who clearly could not count made up two teams of plump, have-a-go footballers. It was marvellous. I stood on the sidelines for 5 minutes and never witnessed a tackle. The game was played at a walking pace, which contrasted sharply with the social football at Dagenham's Parsloes Park when I was a kid. Crop-headed types with massive sovereign rings kicked the hell out of each other for 90 minutes. As the old joke goes, 10 minutes before the end, a game of football broke out. Indeed, I once observed a full-scale brawl. There was screaming and shouting and the fists finally flew when someone shouted, "Why don't you mind your own business, you fucking nosy cow?" And they were the footballers' wives and girlfriends watching from the sidelines! It was unforgettable. As the tackles flew on the pitch, the peroxide partners abused each other on the touchline. When the women began pushing each other, and this really is true, I debated whether I should intervene and play the noble peacemaker. But I shaped up the situation by examining their brawny partners. Then I looked down at my partner. I was a 13-year-old walking skeleton and my partner was a poodle puppy called Bruno. Well, it was none of my business really.

No chance of a brawl with these guys at West Coast Park. They lacked the energy. I left them to their gentlemen's game and crossed the Marsh Garden Boardwalk, which led to a pond popular with ornithologists. I was delighted to spot a purple heron, a bird more commonly found around Kranji. I knew it was a purple heron because it looked dead. This bird stands still for so long that it begins to blend into the reeds around it and you begin to think it is a model. Then just as you are about to complain to the National Parks Board for pulling such a cheap trick, the heron suddenly stabs its beak into the water and comes up with a fish stupid enough to mistake the heron's legs for reeds. And that is exactly what happened here.

I was having trouble savouring the experience though because mosquitoes were chomping through my calf muscles. Irritated by their persistence, I took out my insect repellent, bent over my legs and engaged in a petulant spraying frenzy. Then I heard a cough and the distinct phrase "*kan ni na*". That was an extremely unpleasant Hokkien vulgarity, I thought. Still bent over, I glanced through a gap under my armpit just in time to see the last of a substantial cloud of insect repellent float into a seething teenager's face. That was most unexpected. I had not realised she was there. Standing on the other side of the viewing platform, she rubbed her eyes repeatedly while her boyfriend comforted her and contemplated throwing me into the pond. With my chin sheepishly tucked into my chest, I had little choice but to exit stage left. I was eager to avoid causing a scene at the Marsh Garden Boardwalk. And I had run out of insect repellent.

CHAPTER 9

There is an unwritten rule that owners of landed properties in this country must own a dog. Not a cuddly canine that hangs off Paris Hilton's cleavage, but a drooling, snarling, brutish creature that spends most of its days locked in a dungeon with its testicles tied up with barbed wire. The dog has only one purpose—to sniff out the poorer classes and bite off any swinging appendages. And should an unknowing stranger inadvertently stray past the capacious cavern owned by its master, the beast's testicles are unleashed and it flies at the gates, sensing proletarian blood.

I know. It happened to me. I was wandering down Pasir Panjang Road, admiring the private houses, when I walked past the garage gates of one particularly lavish property. In a split second, I glimpsed the dog. Suspended in mid-air. Going for my jugular. Although I did not catch its name tag, it looked like an Alsatian, but could have been a lion for all I cared. This startling image sent me reeling backwards. His bark almost threw me under a bus. Only divine intervention prevented me from a vicious mauling. That and the garage gates.

In Singapore, the bigger the house, the bigger the dog. It is a rather transparent status symbol. HDB flats only permit small dogs. When I amble across the garden beneath my Toa Payoh block, I always check my shoes to make sure there is not a squashed sausage dog underneath. Some of them are no bigger than a toilet roll and have that scrunched-up face that suggests they have chased one parked car too many.

But no such regulations are in place to deny the landed property folk. They want the world to know where they live and a slathering, farting savage apparently does the trick. Walk around some of the wealthiest private estates off Sunset Way and you will discern dogs bigger than their owners. Honestly. When they take Digby for a walk, it is like a scene from *Honey, I Shrunk the Kids*. You can almost hear the owner saying, "Yeah, I know. It's an Afghan hound. Big, isn't it? Wouldn't get that in an HDB flat, would you? No way. I've got three of them and they've all got their own maid. Yep, I know what you're thinking, my house is *that* big. Now, as the notice on my driveway clearly states, members of the working class will be exterminated, so piss off."

I actually had no plans to even be in Pasir Panjang Road. I had been on a Clementi-bound bus when I saw the entrance to Haw Par Villa, with a banner advertising the attraction's free admission. That surprised me. I thought Haw Par Villa had closed down years ago, and so did some of its neighbours. When I got off the bus, I double-checked with a teenager to see if that really was the old villa up ahead.

"Yeah, that's Haw Par Villa, but you sure you wanna go there?" He appeared to find me amusing.

"Well, I was hoping to. Otherwise, I'm just a weirdo asking strangers to point out national landmarks for me."

"Well, cannot visit this one. Haw Par Villa shut down already. Been closed for years."

I was not amused. Having narrowly avoided losing my reproductive organs to a flying Alsatian, my fractious mood might not have tolerated a No Entry sign. But, to my pleasant surprise, Haw Par Villa was open and admission was free. Yet a teenager who lived no more than 400 metres from its entrance was adamant that it had been closed for years.

That is not as strange as it seems. Haw Par Villa enjoys a bizarre love-hate relationship with Singaporeans and even though I had lived here for a decade, I had never had an overwhelming desire to visit. No one has ever approached me and said, "Oh, you must visit Haw Par Villa." East Coast, yes. Sentosa, yes. The four floors of whores at Orchard Towers, yes. But never Haw Par Villa, even though its history is full of eccentricity, spontaneity, egotism and philanthropy; colourful quirks that are rarely encountered in this country.

In the mid-1930s, Aw Boon Haw was one of Asia's wealthiest businessmen. An entrepreneur ahead of his time, he had a flair for marketing, ensuring that his Tiger Balm ointment was the ointment of choice all over the Malayan peninsula. It still is among the aunties and uncles. Whether you have got a mosquito bite, a sprained ankle or gonorrhoea, they will slap some Tiger Balm on the affected area before you can cry out, "Ow! That stings. Shouldn't we be using live yoghurt instead?"

With his fortune secured, the charismatic Aw woke up one morning and decided to purchase a site to build his brother Boon Par (hence the name) a house. But not just any house. Oh no, this had to be a dome-shaped mansion on the top of a hill, with six rooms, sea views in every direction and sprawling gardens containing hundreds of statues and tableaux depicting traditional Chinese myths, customs and virtues. I was impressed. I only got my brother an iPod for Christmas.

With no expense spared, the lavish villa was finally completed in 1937. Visitors flocked to the place and the surrounding Tiger Balm Gardens became one of the most photographed sites in Singapore. Although there was hardly any competition back then. Sentosa was a British military base and there is only so many times that you can take a picture of Raffles Hotel.

Of course, time waits for no tableau and Haw Par Villa began to lose its lustre. Tourists were being drawn to the Singapore River, Sentosa was slowly taking shape and Singaporean children were having more fun in Genting. The appeal of standing in front of a statue of a laughing Buddha had worn thin. The park fell into disrepair, forcing the government to intervene. The macabre and the horrific became the order of the day. Some $80 million was reportedly spent remodelling the place, with lots of electronic gadgets to jazz up the fading statues. The operators employed budding actors to work as ghosts and ghouls. There was even a boat ride and fancy indoor theatres to rehash Chinese folklore. All that was missing was an ice show.

But it came at a cost. When Haw Par Villa reopened in October 1990, the admission ticket set adults back $16. And it was another 10 bucks for the kids. Now that is a lot to fork out for the privilege of standing in the baking sun to look at a few statues. After an initial upswing, attendance eventually took a tumble, the park haemorrhaged money and it closed in 2001.

I did not even know it had reopened. But here it was in front of me, clearly desperate for any kind of patronage. It was Saturday morning, but the park appeared to be empty. This did not seem like a good idea. I was already castigating myself for my impudent behaviour when a souvenir stall owner beckoned me into the park. He practically pleaded. Oh well, I was here now. I would buy an ice cream I did not want from him and take a respectful, but hasty, walk around Haw Par Villa.

Well, it exceeded all my expectations. True, I never had any. And I will not pretend that a trip to Haw Par Villa equates to a week in Las Vegas. But the place was so damn bizarre, so eclectic and so disorganised in a country that is renowned for being none of those things that it felt like I had temporarily left Singapore and jumped into a Lewis Carroll novel.

Like every other visitor to Haw Par Villa, I headed towards the 10 courts of hell. I passed quite a large gift emporium, one of those period costume shops where you can dress up like a member of the Tang Dynasty and have your photograph taken and a coffee shop. All three were empty and the employees of each were sitting together at a table reading the Chinese newspapers. They virtually begged me to "come inside, take a look", so I compromised. I patronised their toilet.

Patronise is the right word because outside the toilet, someone had left a money box with the handwritten message "Toilet paper, 10 cents" scrawled on the side. That is not uncommon in Singapore.

But we were not talking a sealed packet of tissues here. These were individual sheets of paper torn from a roll and folded into pretty little patterns. If the guy's days as a toilet paper crook are numbered, he will always have a future in origami. I know Haw Par Villa needs every dollar it can get, but 10 cents for a couple of sheets of ripped toilet paper seemed a touch cheeky. Exorbitant, really, and it was not even absorbent.

The toilets themselves were surprisingly trendy, with smartly tiled floors and a few potted plants around the sink. Everything said modern, except the empty toilet-roll holders. Someone is making a mint here. There is probably a toilet-roll baron living off his ill-gotten gains in a colonial bungalow over in "Little Kent".

After drying my hands, picking my ears and blowing my nose to make sure I used up every last sheet, I handed over a token $1 admission fee and headed into the 10 courts of hell. The signs proudly stated that terrified children once ran out of this exhibit screaming. Which just goes to show that children were stupid in those days.

The 10 courts of hell depict what will happen to us after we die, according to Chinese mythology. The courts are controlled by Hu Fu Shi Zhe, who manages the ghosts and devils in an executive capacity, and guarded by Ox Head and Horse Face. Their grotesque 2-metre-tall statues reminded me of the bouncers who once stood outside Hollywood's Nightclub in Essex, the nocturnal dive of choice when I was a teenager. I felt most at home.

The first court of hell is judgement day, where a dead person's deeds are reviewed. The good guys are sent over the golden bridge to paradise, where there is no poverty or famine and West Ham United win the Champions League every season. The bad guys are told to stand before the mirror of retribution. With heads bowed and bottom lips sticking out, they are sent to the nine torturous courts to atone for their sins. And the exhibit has created a freakish tableau for each of the courts.

Do not go looking for subtlety in the 10 courts of hell. There is red paint splattered all over the place. Evildoers are thrown head first into volcanoes, drowned in filthy bloody ponds, tied to a tree of knives and crushed by a large stone. The lucky ones, who probably stole half a slice of stale bread or something, merely get their hearts removed. Rumour-mongers have their tongues pulled out, a fact I gleefully passed on to my wife and mother-in-law later.

Each court seemed to be progressively more violent than the last and it did get a bit repetitive. There are only so many times Chinese children can be told to be good otherwise they will get their heads cut off with a sharp implement before it gets tiresome. When I was little, I was informed that if I misbehaved, Father Christmas would not drop off a VHS copy of *The Karate Kid*. Here, they tie you down, rip your tongue out, cut out all your vital organs, stamp on your heart and throw you into a volcano. It did not seem fair really.

At the 10th court, the sinners are taken to the pavilion of forgetfulness, presumably with their head, limbs and organs all in a basket, to determine whether they will be reincarnated as a human or an animal. Just for the record, I would like to come back as a sloth.

After the blood and gore of the 10 courts of hell, I stepped back into the daylight and studied the bare breasts of the virtues and vices tableaux. Essentially a list of dos and don'ts, each scene depicted a vice or a virtue and its repercussions. The most controversial tableau championed the importance of filial piety. It was more gruesome, and certainly more distasteful, than anything offered in the courts of hell. I suppose there are many ways to demonstrate filial piety: by carrying grandmother's shopping perhaps, or cleaning her windows, cooking her food and sweeping her floor. I am sure you could come up with your own example but I bet it would not top Haw Par Villa's. They had a young woman feeding her elderly mother-in-law, from her own breast! I have never seen anything like it and I have visited Desker Road in the twilight hours.

Rather than being shy about having a boob thrust into her face, old mother-in-law apparently could not get enough of the good stuff. The milk actually dribbled down her chin as she suckled on the nipple. It was a real Freudian nightmare: a pornographic horror movie.

The other tableaux were a bit of an anticlimax after that and I have not had a glass of milk since. But the sheer eclectic range of statues made the park intriguing. There were crabs with human heads, a human band with animal heads, a miniature Statue of Liberty and, my own particular favourite, a family of oversized gorillas eating fruit under some trees. Anyone mad enough to put a statue of King Kong in his brother's front garden is all right by me.

I liked Haw Par Villa because it was essentially pointless. It is highly unlikely that such a daft project would ever get commissioned in Singapore today, when almost every landmark, green space, heritage site and tourist attraction must have a purpose, a function and a revenue target. The old villa and the surrounding Tiger Balm Gardens owe their existence to the eccentricities of one flamboyant Chinese philanthropist. In 1937, that was reason enough. There was no tourism task force required to set visitor attendance and profit targets. Just one guy who woke up one morning and said, "Yes, I see it now. A tableau of a brass band, where each band member is a human being but has the head of a cat, duck or monkey, and statues of beautiful young women with exposed breasts. Have someone build that in our garden immediately."

I left Haw Par Villa a happy man. After spending a third of my life here, it was reassuring to know that Singapore could still surprise me.

CHAPTER 10

I do not like technology. Or rather, I am not overly keen on people who do like technology. Usually because they are indescribably dull individuals who naturally assume that everyone around them is equally tedious. If buying the latest gizmo and gadget simply because they have not got it is not irritating enough, they feel an irrepressible urge to share their contraptions with the world. Unfortunately, there are a lot of these people in Singapore. Far too many really. You cannot move in the office without someone saying, "Have you seen my new handphone?"

"Well, I have now, seeing as you've just thrust it under my nose."

"Yah. It can take pictures of 50 pixies and store them at the bottom of your garden with the fairies. Because it's hands-free, I can call someone, play Europe's "The Final Countdown" from the MP3 and take a huge dump without getting up from the toilet."

"You are a deeply boring man."

"Yah, but I'm gonna trade it in next week. They've got an upgraded model. It's purple and has Swahili ringtones."

"That's just marvellous. Tell me something, have you ever kissed a girl?"

And they are all such experts, aren't they? In a rare moment of weakness, do not ever reveal you have succumbed and invested in an incomprehensible piece of technology. It will always, always, be the wrong model, bought at the wrong price.

"You've bought a phone made by *knock-off?*" they will say, in a voice that is so loud and so theatrical that you will find yourself ripping out their trachea. "No, you should've bought a phone made by *semen*. That'll never go down on you. Why didn't you come to me first?"

"Because you're extremely sad and annoying."

"Yah, that may well be the case but I could've got you one for half of the price. Where did you get it?"

"Far East Plaza."

"Should've gone to Sim Lim Square."

"I was joking. Of course I got it at Sim Lim Square."

"Should've gone to Far East Plaza."

"Fuck off."

I encountered a tech lover on the platform at Clementi Station. He caught my attention because he was holding his child in one of those rucksack baby carriers and sitting beside his wife on a bench. The couple, in their early thirties, were both showering their child with attention, lots of cooing and giggling. It was a heartwarming sight. There was no maid. It is becoming increasingly difficult in Singapore to spot a middle-income family without one.

The father took out his mobile phone from the rucksack to entertain the child. He switched on the MP3 player and treated the entire platform to a burst of that '80s pop classic "Forever Young" by German band Alphaville. If you are of a certain age or, better yet, of a certain taste, you might have been spared this ghastly song with lyrics that demonstrate English clearly was a second language for the band. "The Final Countdown" sounds like the work of Philip Larkin in comparison. But it is an *ah beng* anthem here, played a couple of times a week on mainstream radio. I had never even heard of the song until I came to this country. But then, I had never heard of the Danish band Michael Learns To Rock either. There are no push factors related to my decision to leave Singapore. But Michael Learns To Rock comes close.

The country's fascination with, dare I say it, '80s music has long fascinated me. In that particular decade, some fine bands, including Madness and The Police, came to the fore in the music world. But they seldom get airplay here. No, Johnny Hates Jazz,

Rick Astley and Sheena Easton are the order of the day. It has taken me 10 years but, thanks to Singapore's radio stations, I now know every word to that James Bond classic "For Your Eyes Only".

There is nothing wrong with nostalgia. One of the most popular radio stations in Britain is Capital Gold, which plays hits predominantly from the 1960s and 1970s. But its popularity generally derives from the sheer quality of its selections, from The Beatles to Motown. Gold FM plays similar music here. But Singapore must be the only country left in the civilised world where a mainstream, contemporary radio station still plays Kajagoogoo's "Too Shy, Shy" with a straight face. The music is safe and conservative and the lyrics repetitive and simplistic. It is pre-Beatles bubblegum pop set to synthesizers. This particular brand of '80s music is benign and non-threatening, which could explain its longevity despite its overwhelming blandness. Either way, Singapore finds itself stuck in a musical Groundhog Day, where the nation wakes up every morning to the tune of "Brother Louie, Louie, Louie/Oh, she's only looking to me". The band behind "Brother Louie", Modern Talking, is no longer modern and no longer talking. But those German musicians, like their compatriots Alphaville, will always be forever young in Singapore.

I got off the train at Queenstown. The western town is famous for being the oldest housing estate in Singapore, predating even the birth of the Housing and Development Board in 1960. Indeed, the first blocks in Queenstown were initiated by the same chaps who built Dagenham—the British! The Singapore Improvement Trust was established in 1927, after the British colonial government finally recognised that the kampongs were crumbling and citizens deserved decent, affordable housing. The Trust drew up the initial plans that finally came to fruition, thanks to the more efficient HDB, in the 1960s. Toa Payoh proudly took the prize for being the first complete estate constructed by HDB planners, but Queenstown did, in fact, come first.

For a while, you could tell. When I began visiting the area around Tanglin Halt Road and Stirling Road on a regular basis in the late 1990s, some of the blocks were in a dreadful state. The climate had taken its toll; the paint was peeling and the apartments had taken on a dirty, greyish colour. Pavements were cracked and pockmarked, window frames were rusty and gardens were virtually non-existent. Many of Singapore's poorer families, and I have to be honest here, a high proportion of whom appeared to come from the country's minority races, lived in the Queenstown area and it was difficult not to conclude that these residents were getting a pretty raw deal.

That has all changed. The town council must be commended for breathing new life into Singapore's oldest municipal estate. Almost every block has been upgraded, with the additional room at the back, and most of the paths, void decks and corridors freshly paved. The estates, particularly around Tanglin Halt Road, now enjoy landscaped gardens that are actually being used. In Toa Payoh, it is rare to spot children around town after 6pm. They are mostly at home drowning under a sea of textbooks, tuition timetables and the *kiasu* demands of their parents. And that is just the pre-schoolers. But as I meandered around Queenstown, children were doing something quite unusual; they were playing. Dashing in and out of corridors, void decks and each other's ground floor units, some eight or nine children played hide-and-seek. Perhaps it was a coincidence, but they were all Indian and Malay. They certainly looked very happy.

And I was in Queenstown to return to a place that once made me very happy. Well, two places actually, but we will come to the Commonwealth Avenue coffee shop later. I was here to revisit Queenstown Stadium. In 1998, my wife and I decided to take the plunge and rent an entire apartment. We were craving space. Our Indian landlady already had us packed into one small bedroom and two Filipinos in another when she decided to sleep on the sofa and rent out her third and final bedroom. The prospect of seven adults, four languages and a woman lying on the sofa with her enormous boobs hanging out was a bridge too far. So we rented our first home, a three-roomed flat in Lorong 1 Toa Payoh from the affable

Uncle Kong. After signing the contract, he asked, "You're English, ah? You like football?"

"Of course. I support West Ham United."

"Never heard of them. Anyway, if you like football, go meet my daughter, Christine, at Queenstown Stadium. You can help her, tell her you know all about Manchester United."

"It's West Ham United."

"Never heard of them. Go see Christine at Queenstown."

And that is how I got involved with Tanjong Pagar United Football Club, which was then one of the best S-League sides in the country. I met the overworked and underpaid Christine (a familiar tale for Singaporeans working in sports administration) and she asked if I would help out with the fan club and write the odd piece for the club's newsletter. It was enormous fun, even if Christine had a habit of talking up her new *ang moh* assistant. I remember at one of Tanjong Pagar's matches, she took me to a half-time reception and introduced me to the S-League CEO by saying, "This is Neil Humphreys. He's joined us from West Ham United."

The closest I ever got to becoming part of the administration at West Ham came at the age of 12 when I joined the fan club and was taken on a stadium tour. We went onto the pitch, visited the dressing rooms and had a look at their trophy collection. The last did not take long.

Coincidentally, and I cannot take any of the credit for this, the year 1998 proved to be the most successful in Tanjong Pagar's history. They won a cup double, lifting the Singapore and FA cups, finished second in the S-League on goal difference and picked up the S-League Fan Club of the Year title at the end of the season. And there were some genuinely memorable matches that season watched by up to 5,000 fans. English clubs in the lower leagues cannot guarantee such attendances on a regular basis. Tanjong Pagar played to packed stadiums almost every week and was clearly destined for bigger things.

Today, the club no longer exists. At least in a footballing sense. After several years of walking a financial tightrope, the club's management eventually threw in the towel after the 2004 season. They dropped out of the S-League, citing debts reported to be around $600,000. They vowed to return but they played no part in the 2006 league season and the silence coming from the club's management remains deafening. A club that once had strong roots in Singaporean football, beginning life as Tiong Bahru United in the 1970s and producing several national players along the way, has gone.

I saw the banner sign above Queenstown Stadium's entrance. "Home of the Jaguars" it proudly boasted. Tanjong Pagar's nickname was the Jaguars. Like a Jaguar's coat, the sign was once striking with its red, black and white stripes. Now, it was faded and pathetic. After two years, no one had even thought to take down the "next fixture" window box that provided details of the upcoming match and it remained stuck to the wall beside the turnstile. A ghost town would be the obvious analogy, but for the fact that there were three guys sitting on the kerb outside the stadium. Red-eyed and surrounded by empty Tiger Beer cans, they were gently swaying from side to side in that harmless, intoxicated state, while trying to hold and read a newspaper. What the hell were they doing here?

But, of course. Inside the stadium stood the S-League's greatest legacy—a Singapore Pools betting outlet full of punters boning up on the evening's Premiership fixtures. The football club may have gone, but the gambling will always endure. Legalised football betting on the S-League and the Premiership was introduced to provide additional revenue for the likes of Tanjong Pagar. But the S-League was nothing more than national service. The English Premiership was the real cash cow and still is.

I drifted along the running track and up the concrete terrace to see the old Tanjong Pagar fan club and admin office. It was still there, but only just. The Portakabin (the management could not accommodate a permanent office inside the clubhouse; the space was reserved for the jackpot machines) was covered in rust and moss stains, suggesting its days were numbered. If anyone can actually be bothered to knock it down, that is.

With nostalgia getting the better of me, I sat in what was once my favourite spot in the empty stand. It was Saturday evening and there used to be over 3,000 people crammed in this stadium. Now there were just two joggers; one an elderly chap, the other a disturbingly tanned fitness freak, pounding the track around the pitch. HDB flats still look down on the stadium. On match nights, neighbours watched from their windows. I loved that. It reminded me of the tower blocks that overlooked West Ham's Upton Park. When we were young, my friends and I each promised to buy one of the East London flats so we could watch Tony Cottee and Frank McAvennie for free every week.

Then I sat in the press box, the name of which always was a bit of a stretch. It was nothing more than a row of plastic seats with a wooden work top laid across the top and a crackling phone line that had probably been installed by Alexander Graham Bell himself in 1876. From that seat, I once composed scintillating prose for those *Straits Times* readers dying to know what had happened between Tanjong Pagar and Balestier Khalsa. There were only about 3,000 of them, I suspect, and they were already sitting with me in the stadium. I am sure sports readers would have been preoccupied with far more important news that day, such as David Beckham getting his head shaved.

But in some respects, the perilous state of Tanjong Pagar United sums up the state of professional football in Singapore today. It is a dead S-League football club with a packed betting outlet. And no one really seems to care.

After visiting the ghostly Queenstown Stadium, I needed cheering up a bit. So I strode purposefully over to a Commonwealth Avenue coffee shop to find arse man. In keeping with time-honoured traditions nurtured at West Ham United, Tanjong Pagar matches were often complemented with supper at this particular coffee shop, which was popular with both fans and players. I always found that aspect of the S-League fascinating. You would have to go back to the days of the maximum wage in English football to see West

Ham fans and players sharing a table at a pie and mash shop in Green Street. But I was not here to spot Jaguars, I had come to ogle another man's buttocks.

Arse man worked, I seem to recall, at a Western food stall, although I could be wrong. He had two visible distractions that rendered all other memories hazy. In a certain light, the stall assistant could have been Singapore's answer to Cliff Richard. He wore large aviator glasses and had the same big hairstyle once popular with the Bay City Rollers, the one that middle-aged Chinese men inexplicably favour. But it was his shorts that made him a minor celebrity and earned him a photograph on the front page of *The New Paper*. They were once jeans, I assume, that had been cut down to shorts. But these things had been massacred. They made the famous Daisy Duke hot pants in the *Dukes of Hazzard* look like flared trousers. When this guy turned the other cheek, everyone in the coffee shop saw it. The shorts were cut at least one inch above the groove between bum and thigh, showing off the pale white fleshy parts. When he bent over, the little hairy brain was almost visible. No one ever ordered his chicken frankfurter.

His bizarre ensemble was rounded off with a pair of wellington boots, which, in my mind's eye, are yellow but that could be attributed to Phua Chu Kang. He was certainly a sight to behold. With the aviator glasses, the wellies and the exposed crack, I had always hoped he would suddenly throw down the plates and give us a quick verse of "YMCA".

I checked every stall, but he obviously was not there. He is not a man who is difficult to pick out in a crowd. The Western stall where I thought he worked was closed, so I asked the neighbouring stall holder about him. Now, this was a difficult conversation.

"I'm looking for a guy who worked at this coffee shop. I think he worked at the stall next door to you."

"Sure thing, man. What he look like?"

Now, how was I supposed to answer this question? He was a Chinese man in his 30s who looked like Cliff Richard and mooned all his customers.

"Er, well, he's Chinese, wears big spectacles and likes to wear, er, shorts, you know? Short shorts."

I demonstrated their cropped length and the old uncle smiled. He knew who I meant.

"He's not working today. Doesn't work weekends," he laughed. "But don't worry, he still works here."

That was good to know. Singapore's oldest housing estate needs a little continuity. Its S-League football club may have gone, but there are compensations. Arse man is still around. May he bare his chiselled buttocks to all and sundry for many years to come. Feeling strangely uplifted by that thought, I ambled back to Queenstown Station humming "Forever young! I wanna be forever young!"

CHAPTER 11

At this point of my farewell tour, I decided to take a detour. I planned to visit Singapore's sprawling empire. Like neighbouring Indonesia, Singapore has a number of islands under its flag. Indonesia has over 13,500; Singapore has Kusu Island and St John's Island. Yes, all right, I am being flippant. Singapore has tens of islands it can proudly call its own but they are not serviced by a ferry on Sundays. Kusu Island and St John's Island are. These two islands form part of the Southern Islands, which are located about 6 kilometres off the coast of Singapore. Until the Sentosa Leisure Group started providing regular ferries to both islands, visitors had to rely on old sampans and bumboats. But we are spoilt now; all I had to do was be at Sentosa Ferry Terminal by 11am.

Inevitably, I was 2 minutes late. Still stuck in the stubborn mindset that I can reach anywhere within half an hour, I left Toa Payoh at 10.20am and fully expected to be 10 minutes early. I took the train from Braddell Station, changed at Dhoby Ghaut, alighted at HarbourFront, ran like a madman who never exercises to the bus interchange to catch the Sentosa feeder bus, then grabbed a poor teenage member of staff wearing the bright orange Sentosa shirt and ordered him to send a message to the ferry terminal. But I was so out of breath I could barely speak.

"Tell ... them ... wait. Don't shoot off ... I coming ... over ... John ... right now." The boy looked scared.

The bus got caught at some traffic lights as the clock on board read 10.59am. At the Sentosa arrival counter, I made the same plea before dragging my shaking legs and nauseous stomach off to the ferry terminal. I looked at the clock on the wall. It was 11.02am. There was no ferry. At the counter, the sign read "Next ferry: 1pm". I suddenly felt faint.

"Next please," said a far too chirpy girl working behind the counter. She got a shock when she saw a sweaty, blotchy-faced *ang moh* desperately trying not to vomit over her counter.

"Has the 11am ferry gone already?"

"Yes, sir, it left right on time." I looked up and down Keppel Harbour but could not see it.

"Excuse me, is it a ferry or a rocket-propelled speedboat? It's completely disappeared?"

"Ooh, it's very fast. Always leaves on time."

No, it does not. After spending the next two hours in an oxygen tent, I returned to the ferry terminal promptly at 12.50pm and was the first person on the bright orange ferry, which boasted agreeable air conditioning and comfy plush seats. We did not move for what seemed like an eternity.

"What's the time, mate?" I asked a Malay chap next to me.

It was 1.05pm. I was not pleased. And I really should start wearing a watch. The ferry's captain sounded the horn for departure then stopped to allow three extremely handsome and giggling young German couples to board. It was 1.07pm. Cheeky bastards. I have nothing against Germans, you understand, I am just deeply suspicious of any nation that sends David Hasselhoff to the top of its music charts.

Finally, after I had visualised several ways to drown six young Germans at Kusu Island without being caught, the ferry zoomed away. The counter girl was right. It was a fast vessel.

Like many Singaporeans, I first visited Kusu Island during the ninth lunar month (which falls between September and November, according to the Lunar Calendar). Cheap ferries take across thousands of devotees for their annual Kusu Pilgrimage to pray for health, peace, happiness and the winning 4D numbers. I go to stock up on cheap Buddha statues for my mother. You cannot move in her house for laughing Buddhas with fat bellies. They giggle at you from the living room, the dining room and even the back garden. It is certainly an interesting blend of cultures. My mother lives in a semi-detached house in Kent. She loves to tell the story that her son braved the elements in an old sampan to visit a remote, cloud-topped island in the South China Sea. There, the indigenous people spend many months mining for precious stones before handcrafting beautiful delicate Buddha statues, a tradition that has been passed down from generation to generation. In reality, of course, I boarded a packed ferry during the ninth lunar month and bought three statues for $10 on Kusu Island.

I do like Kusu Island (Kusu means "tortoise" in Chinese). Tortoises loom large in the island's legends because there is a similarity in shape, hence the island's name. According to one legend, a magical tortoise transformed into an island to save two shipwrecked sailors, a Malay and a Chinese, which sounds plausible enough. Just 5.6 kilometres from Singapore, Kusu is only 8.5 hectares in size, giving it a cosy, intimate feel. At its centre are the turtle lagoon and a Chinese temple called Da Bo Gong (God of Prosperity). The temple was built by a wealthy businessman in 1923 and is where the Chinese come in droves during the ninth lunar month. I had a polite look around. Unless you have a penchant for looking at pythons locked up in a cage with a donation box stuck on one of the bars, there really is not much to see. But I was desperate to escape from the insufferable midday heat.

The tortoise sanctuary outside the temple has always intrigued me because it is usually full of turtles. On this particular day, there were dozens of turtles splashing around in the concrete bay and just a couple of tortoises thrown in to ensure that Sentosa Leisure Group does not fall foul of the Trade Descriptions Act. I spent several minutes watching an elderly tortoise do nothing. Is there a more boring animal on the planet than the tortoise? A gathering of tortoises is not an exhibit; it is a tableau. A couple of Chinese teenagers took several photographs with the tortoise sanctuary behind them. Why? The backdrop is not going to change. You will never hear a tourist say, "Quick, Alfie, stand still. I want to get you and the tortoise in the same shot ... Damn it, the tortoise just ran off."

The tortoise sanctuary was certainly a more pleasant experience out of season. The coming of the ninth lunar month is the death knell for most of the defenceless animals. I visited one evening a couple of years ago and watched a cleaner sweep up half a dozen dead turtles. He said it was a daily feature of his work, but not a surprising one. Idiots grabbed the turtles to pose with them for photographs, turned them over and poked them to satisfy their morbid curiosity or, worse yet, handed them to their small children to play with. Of course, pick up any creature and it will react. Admittedly, a turtle hardly has the reflexes of a cheetah, but the reptile's head suddenly withdraws and its stumpy feet stretch out. This reaction invariably leads to some ditzy teenager screaming and throwing it across the sanctuary. When this happens, the food chain's hierarchy has to be seriously questioned.

I ambled round the back of Kusu to my favourite part of the island. It is nothing more than a beach really. But it is an undisturbed, pristine one. The sand is soft and always clean, the blue lagoon is generally pellucid and a decent spot for some rare snorkelling and the splendid scenery includes Singapore's Lazarus Island on the right and Indonesia's Batam Island way off on the left. And I usually get it all to myself.

I sat down under one of the many beach shelters to remove my sweaty socks and allow the red ants to eat my toes when I spotted my German friends again. With the entire lagoon to themselves, they were picnicking, sunbathing and snorkelling. Behind them was a rugged hillock with a Malay shrine of three *keramats* (holy shrines of Malay saints) at the top, which added a touch of Asian exotica to the setting. There was even a lifeguard on duty to ensure the German tourists did not drown. The beach setting was so tranquil, so perfect, I am surprised Alex Garland has not written a novel about it. Rock stars are always bitching about travelling to the far ends of the Earth to find an exclusive beach in the Caribbean to escape the paparazzi. Nonsense. Come to Kusu Island. Privacy is always guaranteed. No one will ever find you.

And what about Singaporeans? In contrast to the golden sands at Kusu, East Coast Park and the Sentosa beaches are crowded at the weekend, even though they offer dirtier beaches and certainly fewer snorkelling opportunities. And cleanliness is a given here. I noticed three cleaners sweeping the paths and beaches and there could not have been more than 50 people on the entire island. Kusu's beaches may be few, but they are immaculate compared to those at both Bali and Phuket and you will not be bothered every five minutes by locals asking to braid your hair or massage your back.

The cost of an $11-ferry ticket provides Singaporeans with a secluded location for a few beers with poly mates, safe beach shelters and a lagoon where you can ogle your girlfriend's white bits and perhaps even squeeze one or two of them. Suggest a weekend trip to Kusu Island to most Singaporeans, however, and they will laugh. But they will never have the last laugh. That is reserved for the German tourists who had a stunning blue lagoon to themselves on a glorious Sunday afternoon.

I had high expectations for St John's Island as I had never been there before. The island is 6.5 kilometres south of Singapore, making it the southernmost point of my valedictory tour. And I was fascinated by its modern history. It is generally agreed that in his search for a post to protect British trade in the region, old Raffles came to Singapore in 1819 and anchored his fleet of eight ships off St John's Island. You would think there would be a plaque to commemorate this event on the island, but if there is one, it is well hidden.

The island's history then gets juicy. In 1874, the island became a quarantine area for cholera-stricken Chinese immigrants. By the 1930s, St John's had achieved the proud status of being the world's largest quarantine centre, screening both Asian immigrants and pilgrims returning from Mecca. Now, why isn't that little-known fact included in the Singapore Tourism Board's guidebooks? The country is always looking for opportunities to be the world's biggest or best. Best airline, best airport, best container port and best cholera quarantine centre. Why not? The day after I visited Cholera Cove, I mean St John's Island, there was a coordinated attempt at all the golf clubs in the country to set a new world record for the biggest simultaneous golf tee off. And the story made the prime pages of all the national newspapers. That is, unfortunately, one of the drawbacks of living in a comparatively crime-free, corruption-free country. You have to endure unbelievably humdrum news stories from time to time.

But a former cholera colony sounded so exciting. I half expected the ghosts of the victims, with sunken eyes and wrinkled skin, to float between *tembusu* trees and throw coconuts at unsuspecting visitors. But alas, all I encountered was a sun-burnt German tourist. Clearly agitated, he paced up and down the jetty three times before re-boarding the ferry. Perhaps he knew something I did not.

It is not just Raffles and cholera though. In the 1950s, St John's Island also hosted political detainees, including the late Devan Nair, who went on to become Singapore's third president (1981–1985). The island then enjoyed a spell as a rehabilitation centre for opium addicts before some bright spark decided to turn St John's into a resort for holidaymakers in 1975.

The fruits of that labour were self-evident as soon as I stepped off the ferry. Construction workers were putting the finishing touches to a bridge that connected St John's with Lazarus Island. The Sentosa Leisure Group now controls the Southern Islands of Kusu, Lazarus, Seringat, Sisters and St John's and plans to join them all together by ferry or walkway.

Even without that connection, St John's is a 39-hectare hilly island that has long been touted as a premier nature haven. So I followed a path past the Holiday Bungalow, which was basic and rustic but in dire need of a lick of paint, and into the little forest that remained. There was a distant, spooky hum. Paranoia might be to blame but I was convinced that it sounded exactly like hundreds of cholera victims groaning all at once. I was also aware that I was completely alone. I continued along a path that led to the Tropical

Marine Science Institute, where one of those threatening signs that are so common in Singapore warned that all trespassers would be hung, drawn and quartered.

Not wishing to retread the same path, I stumbled around in the forest for a bit only to encounter broken, concrete staircases that suddenly stopped halfway up the slope or paths that ended abruptly at a fence. I appeared to be going round in circles. Wherever I looked, there were crumbling staircases or remnants of brick walls lying in the undergrowth. Thick tree roots dramatically protruded through cracked paths at regular intervals. Naturally, my foot found the biggest root and I managed to execute a near perfect forward roll while wearing a rucksack. Like the film tag line once said: "In the forest, no one hears you scream, 'Bloody bastard of a tree!'"

This is it, I thought, as I pulled the spiders' webs out of my hair and examined the scratches on my leg. This is where I am going to die. I had no idea where I was and I had drunk the last of my water hours ago on Kusu. I was hungry, increasingly sunburnt and had just ruined the home of an irate black-and-yellow spider the size of my hand. Although St John's Island had a certain ring to it, as John is my middle name and the name of my father, it just was not glamorous enough. If I had to die prematurely in Singapore, I hoped to be knocked down by a hot *mamasan* in Chinatown's Neil Road. That is almost poetic.

This, on the other hand, was a shambles. Eventually, I completed one big circle of nothing in terms of places of interest and ended up back at the ferry terminal. Kusu Island was a weekend on *Temptation Island* in comparison. I headed off down another path and walked past a tired-looking basketball court that was fenced in and surrounded by rolls of rusty barbed wire. In obsessing over finding something of interest in the forest, I had been oblivious to an obvious feature of the place. The island was surrounded by high fences and barbed wire. In every direction. There were even watchtowers. It felt like a childhood holiday to an old Butlins Holiday Camp in England, where once you had paid your admission fee, the barbed wire was employed to keep you from escaping.

I had another look at the map of St John's and noticed, to my surprise, that the island did at least have a cafeteria. And it most certainly did ... but it was closed. Being on a hillock, however, it did offer me sweeping views of the nearby fences and watchtowers. If you substituted the Raffles Place skyline for that of San Francisco Bay, this could have been Alcatraz. When I returned home, I discovered that, in 1999, a part of St John's Island had been sectioned off to detain illegal immigrants. Now, doesn't that sound just the ideal destination to take the kiddies for a game of beach volleyball?

On its website, Sentosa Leisure Group says its redevelopment plans for the Southern Islands will eventually include "residential, resort, and entertainment facilities", but is rather short on details. Whatever the plans are, execute them quickly. St John's Island offers little attraction because it has no focal point. There is no real reason to come here. Kusu Island has its temples and beaches, Bukit Timah has its summit and nature trails, East Coast has its seafood and water sports and Pulau Ubin has its nostalgic kampong lifestyle. St John's has barbed wire and watchtowers.

Dehydrated and exhausted, I sat at the jetty and waited for the last ferry back to Sentosa. I was early, but there really was nowhere else to go. Apart from a handful of Malay fishermen, I was the only person there. Low, dark clouds accompanied by thunderclaps suggested a downpour was imminent and the whole island now looked gloomy. In the distance, I spotted about 10 birds of prey hovering somewhere behind Lazarus Island. Through my "geeky" binoculars (so christened by my wife), I realised they were white-bellied sea eagles. Common off the coast of Singapore, it was still unusual to see them in such numbers. Considered to be the biggest bird of prey found here, they glided effortlessly across the sky using the warm air currents to float upwards. It was an impressive sight. But as the drizzle started, St John's Island looked increasingly eerie behind me as the huge eagles continued to soar ominously overhead. For some strange reason, the ferry could not come quick enough.

CHAPTER 12

There are certain things I have never understood about Singapore. I have never figured out why the elderly slap an empty seat on a bus before they sit down. It is most bizarre. They shuffle along the bus looking every inch the benign auntie or uncle, spot an empty seat and promptly go ballistic. Acting as if the seat offended them on a previous trip, they lean over and give it a damn good thrashing. Innocent bystanders are generally confused by the violent and unprovoked attack because it achieves nothing. No dust ever flies up and there is no physical altering of the seat. But still, they slap away like a demented sadomasochist before finally deeming the seat acceptable for their ageing buttocks.

Second, I have yet to be given a satisfactory explanation as to why two parents sitting at a dinner table require the services of a maid to feed their own child. Is it too much for them to feed themselves and their child at the same time? Will their arms fall off if they shovel spoonfuls of rice from two plates instead of one? Or maybe it is the complexity of the procedure. After all, it is a complicated task, cutting up fish balls and rolling them into the screaming brat's mouth.

And finally, I have never fathomed why Westerners and Western wannabes are so enamoured by Holland Village. Apparently named after Hugh Holland, an architect and early resident of the area, Holland Village is touted as Singapore's Bohemia, a little enclave of eateries, bars and art galleries. That may be the case, but Manhattan's Greenwich Village has nothing to worry about. In

10 years, I have not visited the area more than a dozen times and just cannot recognise its attraction. Believe me, it is not through want of trying.

When I arrived, Singaporean and foreign colleagues said, "Oh, if you want a good place to hang out, you must go to Holland V. It's a great place for chilling." Be deeply suspicious of anyone who feels compelled to use the word "chilling" in everyday conversation.

"It's called Holland V? What's the V stand for?"

"Oh, it means 'village'. But I always call it Holland V."

"Why? Is there something wrong with you?"

Whenever the modern marketing weapons of short forms, abbreviations or acronyms are deployed in a desperate attempt to sound hip and clued in, I reach for the snooze button.

But I was an eager tourist back then, dutifully following any direction offered so I took a leisurely stroll around Holland Village one afternoon. Yes, I set aside an entire afternoon. The tour was completed in 10 minutes. I spent more time in my Dagenham minimart when I was young, sneaking peeks at the big and bouncy magazines on the top shelf. I seem to recall a handful of restaurants, some banks and, by Singaporean standards, a tiny, colourless shopping centre.

The only memorable evening spent at the bustling Bohemia (it makes me laugh just typing it) came after a last-minute victory for Tanjong Pagar United when I celebrated with one of the players at Wala Wala Bar. We were watching a 1998 World Cup match when I felt something tickle my feet. I looked down and saw a confused, baby rat trying unsuccessfully to find its way back to its burrow. My suriphobia made it exceedingly difficult for me to return after that. But the rat encounter was eight years ago and nothing stands still in Singapore.

Holland Village had changed, quite dramatically in fact. It was an orderly shambles. In other words, the shopping enclave was marked by yet another building site, complete with cranes and those industrial, deafening drills that apparently need to bore their way through to the Earth's core to allow the new MRT Circle Line to trundle underneath Holland Village in 2010. In the stifling midday heat, I stepped off the bus and the dust in the still, humid air was everywhere. How the poor shop owners put up with these noisy, irritable conditions I will never know. The construction site was surrounded by a 2-metre-high corrugated iron fence right in the heart of Holland Village. Visitors had to negotiate a narrow walkway with the obstreperous drilling on the left and dusty shopfronts on the right. I am sure in the evenings, when dust hopefully gives way to dusk, shopping here is a more agreeable experience, but it is bloody awful in the early afternoon.

The shops in Holland Village were the usual haunts frequented by expatriates and younger Singaporeans: one or two European restaurants, the odd grille, The Coffee Bean and a Burger King. The two-storey shophouses offered fake branded goods, some Singaporean souvenirs and the odd dentist. Intriguingly, there were also a number of motorbikes parked in Lorong Mambong, behind Holland Road. It felt like a dislocated Bali. In effect, Holland Village was Bali without the beach. More so when I visited, with all that bloody dust providing an uncomfortable substitute for sand. Picture a few tanned Scandinavians in sarongs, a group of elderly locals massaging the feet of fat *ang mohs* and some grungy old German hippy running a bar along Lorong Mambong and Holland Village really could be Bali.

Perhaps that is why the buzzing Bohemia does not quite work here. It is out of place. If the entire village could be lifted and transported wholesale to the East Coast, I suspect it would be a massive hit with backpacker types from all over the world. The setting would certainly match the clientele. Holland Village has everything Bali or Koh Samui offers: bars showing Premiership football, restaurants offering decent international cuisine, fast food outlets, cheap clothes, postal services, banks, bakeries and reasonable parking for scooters and motorbikes. On a much smaller scale, Holland Village does offer the young Singaporean, the tourist, the backpacker and the expatriate all of the basic essentials of a bohemian lifestyle, except sand, sea and sex, that is, which tend to be the most important ingredients. Concrete is no substitute for sand and sex on a building site just does not have the same ring to it.

But the little shopping parade is not without its plus points. The long-established newspaper and magazine stall offers publications from just about every major country in the world. Although it comes at a price. I do not doubt for a second that the *Mail on Sunday* is not a quality weekend read, but I am not sure it is worth $12.50. The windmill on the top of Holland V Shopping Mall is quaint and you cannot complain about the breadth of cuisine offered here. German, Lebanese and Mexican restaurants are all close to each other and there was even an eatery offering "Brazilian". I was not even sure what constituted Brazilian fare and the restaurant's façade did not give much away. There were no photographs of dishes in the window so I had a closer look. There were several shots of women's legs and the word "WAX" featured prominently on the walls. There was a "male menu" but its offerings should only appeal to Olympic swimmers, Tour de France cyclists and those who frequent Orchard Towers on Friday nights. An employee in the shop glanced up at me and smiled. I almost fell over my hairy legs to get away. That was all I needed. I could have popped in there for a little plate of Brazilian and come away with a giant walnut between my legs.

But I was neither hungry nor in need of a German newspaper, so there was little else to keep me in Holland Village. I took a bus to Buona Vista and then a train to a spiritual haven that has made me far too superstitious for my own good.

Scott and I were in a really good mood. And not because we were lying on a bed together in our boxer shorts. It was 4 December 1996 and I had just signed a two-year contract as a speech and drama teacher. Scott already had a job as an architect in the bag and the next day was my birthday. After three weeks of job hunting and almost no sightseeing, we could finally drop the former and do a little of the latter. Besides, we had to get out of the apartment. We were sleeping in the same bed, cooking for each other and generally turning into Toa Payoh's version of *The Odd Couple*. In a certain light, Scott was beginning to resemble Jack Lemmon and I found him rather fetching in his tight, cotton boxer shorts. We desperately needed fresh air, a temporary escape from instant curry noodles and a chance to mix with fully clothed people again. After much deliberation, we settled on visiting the Chinese Garden. Not because we were particularly fond of pagodas and stone lions, but because it was cheap and beside the MRT station of the same name.

The Chinese and Japanese Gardens afforded us our first glance of the country that existed behind the housing estates. Ironically, the green spot was cultivated in the mid-1970s to serve those very housing estate workers and residents, but it was our first glimpse of the garden city. Until then, we had only seen the city. The 14-hectare Chinese Garden and the 13-hectare Japanese Garden were beautifully landscaped and, like most Western visitors, we were impressed with the traditional features of Chinese gardening art, particularly the seven-storey pagoda modelled on the Ling Ku Temple Pagoda in Nanjing, China. The only viewing tower we had encountered so far was in the Toa Payoh Town Garden and that really was a limp erection in comparison.

We stopped for lunch at the Bonsai Garden because the cheese slices in our sandwiches were melting. In a conversation I will never forget, we sat there for at least an hour, plotting our spectacular ambitions for the following year in Singapore. Some we achieved, some we did not. Scott could not fulfil the easiest and most important ambition—to stay in the country. Thanks to those incomprehensible civil servants at Immigration (although there is another, more adequate description of their profession beginning with "c"), Scott had his employment pass application rejected three months later. There was no explanation given. Treated like a criminal, he was ordered to leave the country within seven days. I have never forgiven the immigration authorities for their inexplicably draconian, heavy-handed behaviour. For the record, Scott is now an accomplished architect living in Hertfordshire with his wife and son and is reaching most of the targets he laid out while eating sweaty cheese sandwiches in the Chinese Garden a decade ago. Well done, Singapore Immigration. You really made the right decision there.

On my birthday the following year, I took my partner back to the same spot at the Bonsai Garden for lunch, told her about the conversation with Scott and we inevitably ended up discussing our plans for the next year. Being a creature of habit, I have returned to the same spot on the same day almost every year since. At the risk of sounding like a pretentious wanker, the annual trips feel quite spiritual. If I go alone, I analyse the year that has passed and lay down what is realistically achievable in the next 12 months. When I am alone, I find myself muttering aloud although I am not sure why, or to whom. On one occasion, I failed to notice that a cleaner had wandered in to sweep the footpath. He spotted a lanky lunatic eating a cheese sandwich and giving a sermon on the mount at Bonsai Garden and nearly fell into the pond. I may not be able to turn water into wine, but I can almost always make cleaners fall into the water.

There was one birthday, somewhere in my late twenties, when I had to travel to England for an extended writing assignment and missed my annual pilgrimage to Jurong. The following year did not go quite according to plan. It was probably a coincidence and I may well be talking rubbish, but I have not missed a year since.

One of the advantages of visiting the Chinese Garden today is that it is free. Like Haw Par Villa, Sentosa, Holland Village and countless other tourist attractions around the country, the Chinese Garden was currently in the midst of redevelopment and most of the Japanese Garden had been fenced off. The operator rightly assumed that it would be presumptuous to charge visitors for the privilege of admiring piles of sand, No Entry barriers and the exposed backsides of foreign workers.

Do you think there will ever come a time when the upgrading ceases in Singapore? Can you ever envisage a day when the hammering in your neighbourhood stops? Let's dream of a day when some bright spark at the Urban Redevelopment Authority eventually stands up in front of his colleagues and cries, "Let us put down our drills, step down from the cranes and tear down the fences. Let's stop digging holes in the country today!"

"But what would we do with all that corrugated iron fencing?"

"Bury it on Pulau Semakau for all I care. I've had enough."

"But you know the economic threat Singapore faces. What about China and India?"

"All right, bury it there then. Along with the drills, cranes and concrete mixers. Let's just allow the country and its people a five-minute respite to breathe a little."

"Sure, Chu Kang. Whatever you say, mate ... Can we get a straitjacket, please? Now, lie back and close your eyes. You'll just feel a little prick."

The seven-storey pagoda was closed. I was quietly pleased. Had it been open, I would have been compelled to climb it in the oppressive heat. Instead I popped into one of the most noticeable beneficiaries of the ongoing upgrading—the public toilets. Clearly modelled on the Night Safari's original and highly successful concept, the toilets had a rural, open-air feel, with no wall to separate the trees and plants from the sinks. This was rather startling. From the urinal, I noticed a middle-aged Caucasian couple strolling along the footpath towards the toilet. If I could see them, they could almost certainly see me. And no one is getting a glimpse of my pagoda. How did the planners overlook the obvious fact that male visitors can be peeped on while peeing? Admittedly I am taller than most Asians, but the sinks are low enough to affect just about everybody. Unless Snow White's pals fancy a day trip here, every other man will feel embarrassingly exposed.

The site of my spiritual home in the Bonsai Garden was also closed. I was bloody apoplectic. The main gates to the Japanese Garden were also locked. This was getting ridiculous. As appealing as it may sound, I did not fancy dissecting my year at the nearby "live" turtle and tortoise museum that was now housed within the Chinese Garden. I might mutter to the occasional cleaner, but I draw the line at talking to a turtle.

At least the smaller twin pagodas were open. I climbed the spiral staircase to the third storey and surveyed Jurong Lake. From one vantage point, it was easy to pick out all of the basic ingredients of Singaporean living: a reservoir with an accompanying town park, HDB estates and condominiums fighting for the best view of the lake, MRT trains trundling over a canal, a golf and country club, a stadium, a community centre, a shopping centre and the faint outline of an industrial estate. If a foreign visitor wanted a visual microcosm of life on this island, a trip to the top of the twin pagodas would suffice.

I strode through the magnificent main archway of the Chinese Garden, crossed the white stone bridge and thought about the delectable Cleopatra Wong. In 1978, not long after the Chinese Garden had opened, the superbly cheesy martial arts flick *They Call Her ... Cleopatra Wong* was released throughout Southeast Asia. A sexy, deadly secret agent, Wong was Singapore's answer to James Bond who, through wit, ingenuity, lots of sex and a crossbow, took out currency counterfeiters from Hong Kong to the Philippines. It was exploitation film-making at its most surreal, cashing in on an industry that had been kickstarted by Bruce Lee. But the film turned Wong into Singapore's first and only international movie star to date. The actress now lives a quiet life in Katong but, in 1978, half of Southeast Asia wanted to sleep with her.

I watched a grainy print of the movie a couple of years ago at a film festival and was genuinely surprised by its cinematic legacy and its impact on contemporary pop culture. Wong's striped leather costume and matching crash helmet, her motorbike, her martial arts and her sassy persona were all thrown into Quentin Tarantino's melting pot to create Uma Thurman's assassin in *Kill Bill*. The debt Tarantino owes Singapore's only international superstar is considerable, but sadly the link between *They Call Her ... Cleopatra Wong* and *Kill Bill* is seldom made by anyone outside of Tarantino's circle of friends, so I am more than happy to do it here.

I thought of the sexy siren now because there is a wonderful scene in the film that is so daft that it could only come from a film dating to the 1970s. Never one to miss a trick, the Singapore Tourism Board must have had a hand in the film's production because every attraction the country had to offer back then features in the movie at some point. And there clearly were not too many. Fleeing from the bad guys on what I believe is Sentosa, Wong jumps into a cable car. There are several shots of her looking behind nervously at the villains in the cable car behind. This goes on for quite a while. Looking terrified, she glances over her shoulder as the snarling scoundrels close in, smiling as their prey appears to draw closer. Now, how is this possible? They are both in bloody cable cars. They are travelling at the same speed and the cars are equidistant on the same cable line.

Refusing to let science get in the way of a good cops-and-robbers chase, Cleopatra Wong flees the cable car and dashes to her Mercedes at what looks like Mount Faber. And not a moment too soon because the pursuing villains are, well, just as far away as they were when they were in the cable car. Wong floors the accelerator at Mount Faber, turns left and crosses the stone bridge that leads to the main archway at the Chinese Garden! From the southern tip of the country to the west with just one turn of the wheel. Cleopatra Wong was one classy act. Of course, the Chinese Garden was not the Chinese Garden but the secret, reclusive home of Asia's most dangerous criminal. It took Interpol's finest secret agents half the film to track down the hideaway because an extravagant Chinese mansion that size would be nigh on impossible to find in Singapore. Scott and I found it in less than an hour.

Delighted with our impressive sense of direction, I now strode purposefully down Chinese Garden Road trying to picture Cleopatra Wong astride her motorbike in her skintight leather suit. But it was an exercise in futility. I could only see Scott astride an armchair in his boxer shorts.

CHAPTER 13

My mother loves to walk. Some of my earliest memories are of my little sister and me being dragged out of the house to "go for a walk". We strolled to markets on Sunday, shopping centres on Saturday and distant beaches on our Clacton-on-Sea holidays. Clacton, by the way, was once the popular destination of choice for the working classes of Essex and East London. Think Batam with fewer palm trees and more "kiss-me-quick" hats. My mother always led the way, guiding us past A-roads, speeding juggernauts bound for Dover, salivating dogs and the occasional motorway so we could find a distant Essex beach away from the sunburnt hordes. We would walk for hours to locate the beach, sit down for 15 minutes before she would say, "Come on, we can't waste a day sitting here, can we? Let's go for a walk." And we would be off to another mystery destination that was after Clacton, but before Land's End.

My mother still does it now. We barely have the chance to drop our suitcases in the hallway before she cries, "Come on, you haven't come all the way from Singapore to spend your time in the hallway, let's go to Deal! Then on to Sandwich, Broadstairs, Cliftonville and back to Ramsgate. Then we can have some breakfast. Right you lot, follow me!"

I have spent entire holidays in England when I have only ever seen the back of my mother's head. It usually disappears over a grassy hillock and reappears at the next seaside town. It stops occasionally to reprimand us for "walking too bloody slow" and to berate Bruno for "pissing up the side of that baby's buggy". Bruno is the family's pet poodle. He is not an incontinent uncle.

My mother's fondness for long ambles through the city streets and country lanes of England is matched only by her impatience at bus stops. Now that is a sight to behold. When I was young, many a sunny afternoon was spent walking 5 miles home from a distant shopping centre because my mother's fidgety feet had taken charge.

"Come on," she would say to my exhausted sister and me. "We can't stand here all day waiting for a bus that's never going to come. Let's walk to the next bus stop."

"Mum, we've only been here for 37 seconds."

"Yeah, but by the time it does get here, we could be home."

"But this is Romford. Dagenham is 5 miles away. My feet ache and Jodie's managed to fall asleep standing up."

"Oh, stop moaning. Jodie, wake up! We're walking home. Come on, follow me!"

Of course, we would walk 50 metres and the No. 174 bus would go racing past. My mum would pretend not to see it while I would mutter some half-baked complaint under my breath and then duck really quickly. My oblivious sister never saw the red double decker, having perfected the art of sleepwalking years earlier.

"That's the trouble with buses here," my mother would say an hour later as we stumbled through the front door. "You wait for ages and they don't come. Then when you start to walk home, what happens? Fifteen come at once. And they never stop where you want them to stop. Might as well bloody walk home ... Neil, what kind of brother are you? Go and carry your sister up to bed. Can't you see she's tired?"

I planned to follow in my mother's footsteps and take a heroic saunter from the Chinese Garden, along Yuan Ching Road, past the former Tang Dynasty City, turn into Jalan Ahmad Ibrahim, amble over to West Coast Road and then push on to Pandan Reservoir. I got as far as a food court opposite Tang Dynasty City. It was rather pitiful, but the scorching sun was relentless. You could have fried an egg on my forehead. Both starving and parched, I ordered mushroom noodles and received what can only be charitably described as spaghetti and shiitake mushrooms drowned in Campbell's mushroom soup.

After my mediocre makan, I found a bus stop outside the former Tang Dynasty City on Jalan Ahmad Ibrahim. The bus services in Singapore are truly outstanding. I was standing in the middle of a highway, the street was deserted and the area was more industrial than residential, yet the No. 30 bus picked me up and dropped me beside Pandan Reservoir. Commuters are so well served here and I think their occasional gripes in the newspapers lack perspective at times. Buses in Singapore are generally frequent and inexpensive and there really is no need to walk 5 miles to your destination, unless you really want to. Of course, that did not stop my mother when she visited Singapore for the first time in 2004. She was a visitor whereas I lived here and yet I spent most of the fortnight following the back of her head. It was most peculiar.

But at Pandan Reservoir, however, I turned into my mother for several draining hours. Have you ever been to Pandan Reservoir? It is bloody huge. According to an officer at the Public Utilities Board, the reservoir was completed in 1975 and boasts a track that is 6.2 kilometres in length. Cyclists and joggers adore this place and speak lovingly about the sun rising above the reservoir as they fly around the gravel track every morning. The lake is also available now to canoeists and rowers for the odd tournament. But they all have one advantage; they are fit. I, on the other hand, had turned up at 7pm already exhausted from my trip to the Chinese Garden. But the cooler, dusky air made a walk around the reservoir deceptively inviting so I thought, "Since I'm here ... "

I trotted briskly along the gravel path that separated the narrow Sungei Pandan from the main Pandan Reservoir. Surrounded by water, I savoured the gentle breeze and quietly cursed every fit bugger who dashed past me without having broken into a sweat. Then, as I turned a bend and found I had the entire reservoir to myself, night happened. There was no warning. It just happened.

The sun dropped behind the housing estates of Jurong and Bukit Batok and it was suddenly pitch black. There was no dalliance with greys or dark blues. The sky simply said, "That's it, I've had enough. Make it night. Now! Let's scare the shit out of that *ang moh* below who has decided to walk around an entire reservoir after 7pm. Idiot. Right, here we go then ... let it be night!"

No one had thought to light the path around the reservoir because no one had thought that anyone would be daft enough to go for a stroll after dinner. I quickened my pace by imagining my mum was ahead of me shouting, "For goodness sake, Neil, hurry up, it's almost dinner time. And you've got to go to the fish and chip shop."

Then I was attacked. It was my own fault really. No one should head off on an impromptu trek into an unlit area after dark, even if it was on property controlled by the Public Utilities Board. I felt a minor blow to the back of the neck, then another to the side of the face. The aggressors were unmistakable—midges. They pounced from every angle until there was a sizeable cloud of them permanently above my head. From a distance, I must have looked like Roger Moore in *The Saint*. The tiny flies flew into my ears, my eyes and my mouth, often all at once. One kamikaze midge even flew up my nostril, where he was quickly drowned in a reservoir of snot.

In a fit of temper, I threw my rucksack down onto the ground, grabbed the insect repellent and sprayed like a madman in every direction for a good 30 seconds. My random, uncontrolled spraying stung my eyes and I petulantly screamed, "Bloody midges!" An action I immediately regretted. There was no need for such uncouth, uncivilised behaviour. I am sure David Attenborough does not scream "Bloody midges" when he is in the Amazon. He would know the exact breed of insect he was cursing.

I sprayed my hair, my neck, my cap, my rucksack and all my clothes but the swarm pursued me right around the rim of Pandan. I could have surrendered. I could have waved a white flag and stepped down from the path and onto Jalan Buroh, a main road that ran alongside the reservoir. However, I stubbornly persevered, determined to complete the circuit. If I could walk from Romford to Dagenham at the height of summer when I was 11, I could perambulate the boundaries of Pandan Reservoir. Besides, the view from the other side of the lake was quite spectacular. The lights of the housing estates reflected off the water and, from where I stood, it all looked rather serene. Of course, I hardly saw any of this because I had a street directory stuck to the right side of my face. With the wind blowing towards me, the swarms of midges were splattering into my cheek. The street directory provided a temporary respite from the persistent little bastards.

But I completed Pandan Reservoir and, feeling that momentum was now on my side, decided to push on further west. So I shook the dead midges out of my hair, wiped them off my street directory and strode off into the darkness of Jalan Buroh.

I thought I had made a mistake at first. I walked for hours. Wandering through the deserted Jurong Industrial Estate at 10pm felt like a cross between *The Hills Have Eyes* and *Wolf Creek.* Although the area was not unsafe, there was still a perceptible sense of uneasiness. I know that Singapore is one of the safest countries in the world, but the dark, eerie atmosphere still lent itself to the remote possibility that drunk fishermen could jump onto Jalan Buroh Bridge, rip my eyeballs out with a fishhook, garrotte me with a filament line and leave my carcass to the packs of stray dogs that patrolled the area.

Jalan Buroh was an endless line of factories, dotted with the occasional piece of vacant land, the long grass of which provided an unkempt shelter for the strays. I rarely saw the dogs, but they were there. I could hear them running through the grass and occasionally howling at the moon. Almost every factory was labelled in the street directory. Except one. No. 51. It was just marked as a sizeable pink square, indicating it was a public or commercial building. This told me nothing. It could have manufactured anything from condoms to concrete. The property was certainly spooky. The security post was empty and its windows were broken. Grass and weeds grew through the fence, around the gates and up the security post. In the distance was a lone lorry parked in front of a dark warehouse that had its shutters raised high enough for employees to go in, but not high enough for casual observers like myself to see what was going on inside. But the strangest part was that there were no signs anywhere. Not one. This is Singapore for heaven's sake, a country that indicates lookout points at the top of a nature reserve. Nevertheless, here was a property sitting on quite a chunk of prime industrial land and it was not labelled. And it was deserted. I did not spot a single employee and I stood there for several minutes. In the distance, I could hear a faint, rhythmic pounding. Someone was clearly banging an object repeatedly, slapping it down on a table, turning it around and hitting it again.

Of course. No wonder the guys inside wanted to maintain a low profile. They must have been playing mahjong. It was an illegal gambling den. I expected the police to arrive on the scene and drag out a mahjong table, hundreds of packets of instant noodles and a dozen middle-aged aunties. Then I made out the tiniest of road signs that said "Jurong Abattoir". Ah. That made more sense than an illegal gambling den run by triads, even if it was far less glamorous.

A couple of days later, I called the Agri-Food and Veterinary Authority (AVA) and asked for the exact address of Jurong Abattoir to satisfy my curiosity. The conversation would have been less conspiratorial had I called the Internal Security Department instead.

"Ah, hello. I'm just calling to check if 51 Jalan Buroh is the address of Jurong Abattoir," I asked an AVA officer in my best telephone voice.

"Why do you want to know where Jurong Abattoir is?" That was indeed a very good question. Other than being a nosy bugger, I did not really have a reason. So I made one up.

"Well, because I'm standing outside it right now," I replied from the sofa of my Toa Payoh apartment. "And there are no signs outside. I'm looking for a factory in Jurong and I don't want to walk into an abattoir by mistake because I'm having pizza later."

"Oh I see, then yes, No. 51 is Jurong Abattoir. That's where we slaughter pigs."

Ah, touchy subject. Hence the secrecy. Checking the map again, however, I noticed that the property next door at No. 53 was marked down as a pet hotel. A bloody pet hotel! Imagine getting those two buildings mixed up. It was not as difficult as you might think; one of them was not even signposted. I hope no one ever uses No. 51 as a short cut to get to No. 53. That would be one short hotel stay for poor Lassie. A bellboy would not be much help, but a taxidermist might be of some assistance. The street directory calls No. 53 a pet hotel, but the AVA prefers the term "Jurong Animal Quarantine Station". Naturally.

The closer I got to Jurong Pier Flyover, which is the turn-off for Jurong Island, the quieter the street became. By the time I had reached an SPC garage, I was venturing into the land that time had forgotten. Indeed, the garage could have been a saloon from an old western. It just needed a pair of louvre doors for me to push open. There were no customers, only a couple of elderly employees sitting on a wall stroking a dog. The snarling canine was golden in colour, but its breed was difficult to ascertain. Its perpetual drooling suggested it was born in a test tube in South Korea. As I headed towards the petrol pumps, the eyes of the two men and their salivating pet followed me across the garage forecourt. I fully expected one of them to spit out a toothpick, kick over a spittoon and, in a slow, Texan drawl, say, "Where might you be goin' stranger? You better git goin' real soon or little Clint here will bite yer bawls off. And if that don' work none, I'll set the dog on ya."

But instead they kindly pointed out the toilet to me. The dog, however, was far less welcoming. It barked at me incessantly and I was forced to walk in a big arc to avoid it and get to my temporary refuge. I locked the toilet door but it had those slats at the bottom for ventilation and I could clearly see the dog sitting just a couple of metres away. It was waiting for me. That much was obvious. I had no idea what its plans were, but I had no problem relieving myself, I can assure you. The two uncles made half-hearted attempts to calm their mad dog but were far more enthusiastic discussing their supper plans. I had already spent five minutes locked inside the cubicle and it is generally not a good idea to hang out in a men's toilet in an empty garage in a deserted industrial estate at 11pm. The loneliness of the long-distance lorry driver is well-known. But the prospect of being dragged past the petrol pumps by a mongrel of dubious origin did not really appeal either.

In the end, the compassionate uncles came to my rescue. They whistled and Frankenstein's monster returned to its masters and sat by their feet. When I saw through the door slats that they had grabbed its collar, I took my cue. Red faced and perspiring heavily, I flung the toilet door open, dashed across the forecourt and hared off down Jalan Buroh.

Almost five hours after arriving at Pandan Reservoir, I reached my final destination for the day—the lookout tower at the top of Jurong Hill Park. Just 100 metres from Jurong BirdPark, the observation tower and its accompanying restaurant provided cracking views of the private Jurong Island nearby. Opened in 1970 for residents living in the increasingly cluttered industrial area, the tower was built at the top of a 60-metre hill and resembled one of those circular car park ramps, with extremely wide walkways. Having struggled along from one end of Jalan Buroh to the other, it was a bit of an effort to get to the top, but I could hardly quibble with its wheelchair-friendly design. Despite its size and prominence, I actually had trouble finding the damned thing initially and walked aimlessly down Bird Park Drive for several minutes. Then I realised a few cars and vans with young couples inside were driving up a hill on my left. They were either going to the tower or heading to a mass orgy. Either way, their destination was well worth a peek.

Sure enough, the summit presented me with a view of a dozen canoodling couples. There was a middle-aged Chinese chap beside me pecking at the neck of an extremely young, attractive Chinese woman. They took a breather, probably to allow his pacemaker to recover, and had an animated discussion that lasted quite a while. Although they may have been ruminating about the hypnotic lights of the oil refineries twinkling under the starry sky, I suspect they were haggling over the price.

I took off my steaming shoes and sat on the concrete floor, staring out at the bright lights of the big city. Midnight was approaching, but the entire west corner of Singapore appeared to be lit up and blinking back at me. It really was beautiful and I no longer cared that my entire body ached. The walk through Jurong had been interminable at times, but one that was thoroughly rewarding in the end.

My old mum had been right after all.

CHAPTER 14

She will probably never speak to me again, but I must tell you this story. My mother visited Singapore for the first time in 2004 and, as a 50th birthday present, we also took her to Perth to look up some old friends and relatives. Knowing that mobs of kangaroos had overrun most of Australia, I was eager to see the marsupials in their natural habitat. We were told to visit Pinnaroo Valley Memorial Park, a cemetery famous for its kangaroo population. The place was big, grassy and secluded; the only visitors being those who came to pay their respects or to watch the kangaroos grazing. For a week, I had stubbornly insisted that we were not flying back to Singapore until I had been to "kangaroo cemetery", as it is known locally. My wife and younger brother were also keen, but my mum was a little uncertain.

"So you really want to go to this kangaroo cemetery, then?" she asked.

"Yeah, it'll be great. It must be amazing to see."

"I suppose so," she said, clearly not convinced. "I'm not sure they'll be that much to see and it sounds a bit morbid to me."

"It's only a cemetery, mum. Think of all those kangaroos we'll see running around."

"Running around? What are you going on about? They'll all be dead."

"No they won't. Who told you that?"

"You did. You said it was a kangaroo cemetery." Apparently, she had thought it was a pet cemetery for kangaroos! She insisted that "kangaroo cemetery" must be a place where Aussies gathered to bury their beloved, bounding friends. Fifty thousand graves, all filled with dead kangaroos. The headstones would certainly make for interesting reading: Here lies Joey. Son of Joey. He leaves behind a wife and a dozen children. All called Joey.

My mother's kangaroo cemetery came back to me as I respectfully observed a stray dog enjoying some shade. It was sleeping beside a grave near the back of Choa Chu Kang Chinese Cemetery. I had no plans to visit the cemetery. I was heading to Old Lim Chu Kang Road but the startling image of hundreds of graves, spread out in almost identical rows across the grassy hillside, had caught me off guard. It is not a common sight in Singapore, but it is if you grow up in Dagenham. Churches all over the parishes of Dagenham and Barking have gravestones going back hundreds of years. Dogs pee on them, vandals desecrate them and drug addicts leave their needles among the flowers. Even in death, peace is not always guaranteed.

But cemeteries are difficult to find in Singapore—they are not a popular place with the many superstitious folk. Coffee shop cynics will whisper that the *gahmen*, the affectionate colloquial term for the government, does not advocate burials and insists that the dead are cremated. This is not quite an urban myth but it is not entirely untrue either. In 2001, it was announced that the 26-hectare Bidadari Cemetery had to go to make way for housing projects. Well, naturally. The graves (around 58,000 Christian and 68,000 Muslim) were to be exhumed so 12,000 new high-rise homes could house 40,000 residents at the junction of Upper Serangoon Road and Upper Aljunied Road in central Singapore, not too far from my home in Toa Payoh. Most of the remains were eventually relocated here at the Choa Chu Kang cemeteries. But their descendants were not amused. The cemetery, one of the oldest in Singapore, opened in 1907 and 5,000 graves belonged to foreigners, including Australian and British servicemen who had died during World War II. Furious relatives from all over the world sent letters to the media, asking for the men who had once defended the country to be left in peace.

But obstacles to economic progress are easily sidestepped, so a few silent corpses did not pose too many problems. The exhumation project went ahead and was completed in 2006. Even in death, peace is not always guaranteed.

I know that land is scarce in Singapore. It is a mantra that is drummed into Singaporeans from their first history lesson at primary school. But again, I do wonder, and I always will wonder, how many apartments and shopping centres does a country actually need?

Contrary to popular belief, however, Singaporeans can still be buried in Choa Chu Kang Cemetery if they are willing to pay the price ($940 per adult, according to staff at the Chinese Cemetery). Behind the rows and rows of circular gravestones, often adorned with stone lions and pagodas, new plots had been freshly dug. Like the graves, most of the plots were dug in rows that sloped slightly along the hillsides off Lim Chu Kang Road. I was told this was to accommodate drainage during heavy downpours. Even in death, the authorities are stunningly practical.

The smell of incense was everywhere and charred paper money blew all over the place. Several graves were covered in burnt litter. They looked dreadful. Making sure dead relatives have cars, houses and money in the afterlife is most commendable, but some visitors neglect to consider the impact it has on the living.

I reached the end of Path 19 of the Chinese Cemetery. Had I ventured any further, I could have been shot. The reservoirs of both Poyan and Murai in the northwestern corner of the country are live firing areas for the Singapore Armed Forces. I noticed a couple of young Chinese guys digging plots while an older chap, possibly their boss, sat on the back of his van calculating sums on a notepad.

"Excuse me, do you work here?" I asked cautiously. He viewed me with the kind of suspicion reserved for tall, strange Caucasians carrying notepads around graveyards in the middle of the day.

"Yah, what you want?" Time for another story. And I am going straight to hell for this one.

"Er, a distant relative is sick and she wants to be buried here."

"Can, can. Still got plots. Look, can see. But not cheap. Each plot costs $940."

"But someone told me it's better to go for a cremation."

"You know why or not? The *gahmen* don't want burial. Cremation better. Where got space for so many burials? But if you know where to go, can still bury. No problem."

I thanked him for the advice and left but he called me back. He smelt a sale.

"Hey, you need burial or not? You got a contractor? Need a contractor to make the stone?"

He was the Phua Chu Kang of the graveyard industry.

"No, it's okay. But rest assured if anyone dies, I'll certainly come to you first."

He smiled broadly at the prospect of a death in my family. I had clearly made his day.

I had a quick stroll around the Muslim Cemetery which, if truth be told, did not suffer from the littering problems of the Chinese Cemetery. The graves were more pristine and far less cluttered. Then I crossed the near-deserted Lim Chu Kang Road, took a side turning called Lorong Rusuk and headed into the rustic solitude of Old Lim Chu Kang Road.

When I decided to embark upon a farewell tour of Singapore, I was keen to examine its underbelly and its darkest corners: I wanted to see the *ulu* bits. *Ulu* means "remote" in Malay. In Singlish, *ulu* refers to the distant four corners of the country where taxi drivers will not respond to calls and will not take a passenger there without moaning for the entire journey about how he will never pick up a fare on the way back.

Old Lim Chu Kang Road was lovely. Full of vegetable farms and undisturbed forest, the street had a timeless, old world feel to it. Singapore has evolved from a kampong community to a global city, but this rural estate has stood firm against rampant redevelopment. Wearing those wide-brimmed straw hats, workers still picked the vegetables by hand, just as they did 50 years ago. This was not just another time; it was almost another country, bearing closer similarity to the neighbouring Malaysian state of Johor than to the nearby HDB estates in Choa Chu Kang. Backpackers who still insist that Singapore is all stylish shopping centres and has no substance should come here. Now I know I do not want to sound overly whimsical and naive. It is backbreaking work in harsh, humid conditions for the farmers, whose efforts are largely overlooked in a city-state focused on rapid urban growth. But it is an alternative lifestyle and that is a rarity here. If you are lucky enough to come across anything that might be deemed alternative in Singapore, cherish it.

The right side of Old Lim Chu Kang Road was largely devoted to Singapore's military forces. Nothing particularly alternative about that. I ambled past Lim Chu Kang Camp I and noticed a Coke machine just inside the entrance. I asked the guard on duty if I could buy one.

"Sure, man," he replied. "That's what it's there for." Bless his little camouflaged cotton socks. I hurried out of the army camp as soon as possible though. The guard was politeness personified, but five pairs of eyes still followed my every move.

As I crossed Lorong Serambi, a middle-aged Chinese farmhand walked towards me. He worked at the sizeable vegetable farm I had just passed. It looked impressive, but they could have been growing marijuana for all I knew. He stopped for what my mother's generation calls a "crafty fag".

"What do you grow here?" I asked curiously as he blew smoke in my face.

"Everything really. Lettuce, spinach, *kailan* and *cai xin*. Got most kinds of local vegetable here."

But the kindly uncle was more interested in my welfare. It was getting dark and Old Lim Chu Kang Road was hardly a kaleidoscope of bright lights.

"Hey, where you going, ah?" he asked, genuinely concerned. "Getting dark, no taxis here. Only one bus. Nothing else to see, just got army camp."

"Yeah, I'm gonna have to get that bus before the ghosts come and get me."

I laughed. He did not. He just looked up at the moon and nodded thoughtfully. They still look up at the moon in Old Lim Chu Kang Road.

But the stargazer was right about one thing. Time was getting on and I was hungry. According to my street directory, there was a bus terminus at the end of Lim Chu Kang Road, with a jetty overlooking the Johor Straits. That sounded most inviting. I was just a short bus journey from a food court, maybe a respectable cluster of shops and some lookout points (signposted, of course) around the jetty.

Do you know what the Lim Chu Kang Bus Terminus consisted of? A lay-by. That was it. The buses pulled in, dropped you off, turned around and went on their merry way. There was more life at the cemeteries. I barely had time to step off the bus before the manic driver swung the steering wheel around and floored the accelerator. Until another bus pulled into the "terminus", I was stranded. And the place stank of rotting fish. I had a perfunctory peek at the so-called jetty. It was nothing more than a dozen wonky planks nailed together. They were also rotting away. I stood on them and they creaked loudly, threatening to give way at any moment. There was a locked gate at the end of the jetty. A sign ordered me not to proceed any further. It was hardly surprising as it was the end of the jetty. The government does like to state the bloody obvious at times. Had I proceeded any further, I would have fallen arse over tit into the sea. What next? A sign at the edge of the Bukit Timah summit ordering me not to take another step?

I did not linger on the jetty. There was nothing to see and I was under surveillance the entire time. The Lim Chu Kang Base of the Police Coast Guard was on my left and a policeman in a watchtower was observing my uncertain movements. I understood why. No one comes this way. Unless you are a fisherman, there is no reason to be here, particularly after dark. Then a beep went off and I almost dived onto the jetty with my hands behind my head. It was not a police sniper's rifle, but my phone welcoming me to Malaysia.

"I'm still bloody here," I screamed at the stupid contraption as it cheerfully informed me of the various cheap rates I could enjoy if I called friends and loved ones back in Singapore. My moaning caught the attention of the policeman on guard outside the Coast Guard Base.

"Is everything okay, sir?" he asked warily. There really was no reason for me to be in such a remote coastal area so late at night. And my fractious mood did me no favours.

"Not really, mate. No. I got off at the bus terminus for some makan and there's nothing here. Bloody nothing," I groaned. "I'm stuck in the middle of nowhere waiting for a bus and my crap phone is using a Malaysian network. I might as well be an illegal immigrant from over there."

I pointed over at Johor Bahru. He laughed nervously.

"And another thing," I continued crankily. "What the hell is that rancid smell?"

"It comes from the fish farms near by. We can't stand it either. Luckily for us, we eat all our meals inside."

The policeman was a lovely guy really. He kindly showed me how to switch my phone back to a Singaporean network manually (I already knew how to do it, but he had a gun). Then he suggested some eateries back in Choa Chu Kang and we talked Premiership football. When all other forms of communication fail in Southeast Asia, you can always fall back on the universal language of the English Premiership. Then things took a surreal turn. There was a concrete slab in front of the police post for visitors to stand on. While building up Liverpool's Champions League chances (the man with the gun was a Reds fan), I stepped onto the slab. A stray dog had been sleeping there. It did not appreciate being woken up. And it really did not like a white-skinned stranger intruding upon its territory.

As I flew off down the country lane like a firecracker, I reached the conclusion that Singaporean dogs do not like me. Every dog

I had when I grew up in England treated me benignly. They wrestled on the floor with me and occasionally farted in my face when the chance presented itself. But they were generally harmless. Around the quiet coastal towns of Singapore, however, myopic stray dogs appear to confuse me with a 6-foot bone. It is a tribute to the bravery of the Liverpool-supporting police officer that I did not end up in hospital. I sincerely mean that. He shielded my canine assailant from my tender calves for a good 10 minutes. But the dog refused to heel. It barked at me continuously and forced me to hide behind a policeman half my size. I only had to poke a little toe around either side of my human shield and the dog pounced.

We settled on a temporary uneasy truce. The black brute paced up and down in front of us. It never took its eyes off me and it never stopped barking. Between us stood the copper, about 5 metres from both of us. If the dog tried to sneak around him, the boy in blue raised a boot to cut it off. On one or two occasions, he had to physically push the snapping stray back and could have lost a couple of fingers in the process. Yes, it was that serious.

Then the bus arrived. The driver pulled into the lay-by and swung the vehicle around 90 degrees so it stretched across the road. Its inviting, open doors faced us in the distance. I screamed at the driver to wait. It was going to come down to a sprint—man against monster. With the bus on our right side, the copper shooed the dog away to our left. That was my cue. But the dog was not easily fooled. It moved before I did. There was no policeman between us now. The pursuing beast, and this is absolutely true, started snapping its jaws at my ankles. My justifiable terror got the better of my social etiquette.

"Get your gun out and shoot the fucker," I screamed. "It's gonna kill me."

"Cannot, cannot. Just keep running," the composed copper shouted back, still giving chase to the uncontrollable feral fiend.

"It's gonna catch me! Just shoot the bastard in the leg. Don't worry about negative publicity. I'm a journalist. I'll make you a hero. Shoot the bastard!"

Fortunately, the bus was just a couple of strides away and I heard the indefatigable policeman calling Blacky back. The mad mongrel never gave up the chase, but the copper's commands were enough to distract it. My leap onto the bus was so dramatic that the horrified driver raised his arms to break my fall. We almost ended up cuddling in the driver's seat. I slumped into the nearest seat and dropped everything on the floor: my bag, my phone, my notepad, my wallet. Everything. I struggled to pick up the slim notepad from under the seat. My hands and legs were shaking. Then my phone beeped. It was a message from my newfound friend and saviour. I had passed the policeman my name card just before the Asian werewolf in Lim Chu Kang had woken from its slumber. The message read "Glad you made bus okay. Sorry about the dog."

Can I just take a moment to declare my unfettered love and admiration for the Singapore Police Force? They go way beyond the call of duty to assist citizens and employment pass holders in their moment of need. My anonymous copper was courageous, selfless and utterly unflappable. But I still think he should have shot that bloody dog.

CHAPTER 15

The following morning I took the military express back to the farming estates of northwest Singapore. It was actually the No. 975 bus from Choa Chu Kang, but it served several army bases, a police academy and that bloody Coast Guard Base popular with murderous dogs. I was the only person on the bus not wearing a uniform. I wanted a gun just so I could fit in.

The No. 975 bus route has to be one of the most splendid public transport journeys in Singapore. It proceeds past the plant nurseries of Sungei Tengah, trundles alongside the cemeteries of Lim Chu Kang and turns into Old Lim Chu Kang Road (a silent country lane surrounded by vegetable farms and overhanging trees) before heading back down the near-empty Lim Chu Kang Road with its dense, forested areas and reservoirs along the coastline. Those who favour the sounds of silence over the city's cacophony really should venture out this way. Even those who collect gun magazines and have posters of tanks on their bedroom wall would like it here. You cannot move without seeing a tanned man in uniform. It was like a holiday camp for The Village People.

When I stepped off the bus beside Neo Tiew Road, I was confronted by a prominent red sign bearing a skull and crossbones. It was yet another live firing area for Singapore's military. But for one terrifying moment, I thought they were filming the sequel to *The Pirates of the Caribbean* here.

I strode purposefully up Neo Tiew Road. This part of Singapore was once home to much of the country's farming industries and rubber estates and I wanted to explore how much of it actually remained. When you think of rubber plantations and vegetable farms, you tend to think of Malaysia. Like rainforests and orangutans, anything tilled, cultivated or ploughed is usually associated with Singapore's cousin across the Causeway.

But that is not quite the case. According to a recent newspaper report, there are 114 fruit, vegetable, plant, dairy and fish farms in the Kranji area. To its credit, the Singapore Tourism Board has finally recognised that there is more to a country's soul than retail outlets and Sentosa and now actively encourages tourists (and local schoolchildren) to visit the *ulu* farms and nurseries here.

It is not an artificial experience. Many are long-standing, family-run working farms that predate high-rise housing and, dare I say it, the PAP. They are that old. And they are a damn sight more Singaporean than the Merlion. It is most ironic. Singaporeans lap up those short farm stays in Perth, complimenting the back-to-basics, rustic bliss of the simple life. Surrounded by haystacks, animals and Aussies, they welcome the escape from the grey drudgery of life in a sprawling metropolis, and rightfully so. But there is still a place here where they can amble around for hours, spot more wild animals than people, pick a ripe banana off a tree, walk in the forest, fish in a stream, eat an organic meal, drink the freshest milk and feed a goat. All within 30 minutes of their front door.

Neo Tiew Road was a slower, more congenial world than urban Singapore. Here, drivers in passing cars waved at me. Vegetable and fruit pickers shouted greetings in just about every Southeast Asian language. A fellow walker told me to have a nice day while several farmhands, and I know this resembles a scene from *The Waltons,* sang tunelessly in the sunshine. I passed cherry trees, African tulip trees and durian trees while the unkempt elephant grass towered above me in some places. I loved that. The grass outside my HDB block is not allowed to reach a height of over 5 centimetres before an alarm goes off at the Bishan-Toa Payoh Town Council and the legions of gardeners are deployed with their trimming weapons to take down the offending blades. Today, it is just a blade of grass. But tomorrow, it is a lawn.

I noticed a sign outside the Green Circle Eco-Farm encouraging visitors to pop in. With the merciless sun beating down, it certainly looked inviting. If nothing else, it had a roof. Calling itself Singapore's first biodynamic organic farm, Green Circle grows over 60 food crops on its premises, using no artificial pesticides or fertilisers. This is about as natural as organic food is ever going to get in Singapore. There was a middle-aged Chinese couple frantically completing orders, packing lettuces and other green vegetables into various boxes to be delivered. When they are not growing their own, as it were, the couple gives environmental talks to schoolchildren and conducts tours of the farm. I was suitably impressed.

"How do you guys do it?" I asked, awed by their dedication.

"It's hard work, must keep growing and selling to survive," replied the woman. She never stopped juggling lettuces. I was clearly in the way.

"But it's a 2-hectare plot of land. Why hasn't it been redeveloped by the government?"

Right on cue, the screeching sound of something airborne and armed flew overhead. It was an SAF fighter jet of some kind with luminous felt-tipped missiles and heat-seeking odour-eaters hanging beneath its wings. I am sure some boring bugger, who quotes lines from *Top Gun* and sleeps with an Action Man every night, will point out that the Singapore Armed Forces has recently received an order of a dozen condom-coated rockets to be attached to a pair of Blue-Tit Fat Fighters. But I really could not care less. Discussions on military hardware are right up there with the yardage of a golf course and the price of new cars.

When the man in his magnificent phallic symbol disappeared, taking his noise pollution with him, the lettuce lady glanced up at the sky and said, "That's why we're safe. We're surrounded by army bases so they can't build houses. Would you live here?"

There is irony for you. As long as excitable young pilots are tearing through the sky in their latest technological toys while soldiers dash through the forest shooting inanimate objects, the remnants of Singapore's farming culture can quietly go about its business of nurturing its peaceful sanctuary next door.

I had planned to find a shady bench somewhere to eat a rather austere packed lunch consisting of a bottle of water and a packet of crisps when I chanced upon a little dining delight. I had a vague recollection of there being a vegetable farm owned by Ivy Singh Lim in the area, but I had never expected this. A handcrafted sign shouted at me from across the road: "Bollywood Veggies: chicken curry, local delights, cold drinks and beer". Then I noticed a car park, an air-conditioned restaurant with a fruit and vegetable farm behind it and a decent-sized bungalow, all within one estate. The anomalous view was extraordinary. After ambling for several hours along a deserted lane surrounded by empty forest save for the odd farm, it was most bizarre to find a bustling restaurant with waitresses dashing around taking orders. The peculiar discovery was akin to floundering around in the sand of the Nevada Desert for days on end before finally stumbling upon Bugsy Siegel's Flamingo Hotel.

But Bollywood Veggies was not out of place. In fact, its location was ideal—a country restaurant in the country, with its homegrown food providing the ingredients for many of the dishes at its Poison Ivy Bistro. Half a dozen expat housewives and about 10 Singaporeans were eating inside. I was surprised. I had expected the eatery to be empty. Behind the bistro, a coach party from a special needs school was being given a guided tour of the Bollywood farm, which grows everything from papaya to avocados. Watching the enthusiastic guide stressing the need to protect the Singaporean countryside, I felt obligated to stay for a curry.

Then Ivy Singh Lim appeared. Married to a successful businessman, the indomitable, outspoken woman is a well-known socialite in Singapore. But you will never find her sitting by the pool berating the maid. A dogged campaigner for the Singaporean countryside and a staunch supporter of the local sports scene, she became president of Netball Singapore and turned the game into the most popular sport in the country for girls. In 2005, Singapore won the Asian Netball Championship. A media darling, she takes every opportunity to smack down the laborious, pen-pushing civil servants who have long dominated sports associations and government bodies in Singapore. I had met her only once before when I was a rookie reporter at *The Straits Times*. As she was being introduced to all the gathered journalists, she singled me out and said, "This *ang moh* doesn't know what to make of me, does he? He's been watching me the whole time with those piercing, cynical blue eyes of his."

And here she was, walking towards me wearing an army-style camouflage vest, khaki shorts and a pair of hobnailed boots. There was also a leather knife sheaf on her hip. Kranji's answer to G.I. Jane then noticed my Green Circle Farm leaflet on the table.

"Ah, are you part of the Kranji Association?" she asked. The Kranji Countryside Association was established by 10 farmers in 2005 to encourage more Singaporeans to visit and learn about the countryside. There are no prizes for guessing who the Association's president was. With an almost military bearing, she towered over my table.

"No, I just wanted to see some of Singapore's more *ulu* spots," I replied coyly. "I wanted to get away from the city for a couple of days. I'm, er, very impressed with what you're doing here."

"Well, just remember this," she said, with her hands on her hips for greater impact. "The baby gods may run the global city but Ivy Singh Lim runs the country."

I did not disagree. She had a knife.

I had intended to visit Hay Dairies Goat Farm, a few kilometres north of Bollywood Veggies, but the BBC came calling. Further along Neo Tiew Road was a sign that read "BBC World Service: Far Eastern Relay Station". Here I was in *ulu* land and all I had to do was take a lane called Turut Track and be confronted by the regional home of the greatest news service on the planet. I knew it was only a transmitting centre full of satellites and enormous aerials, but this was the BBC—the grandaddy of broadcasting. There were bound to be plaques, exhibits and blown-up photographs of Spike Milligan and Peter Sellers in *The Goon Show* and The Beatles performing at the BBC. Without hesitation, I made an impulsive, patriotic decision to savour a slice of my homeland in the middle of the Asian jungle. Delighted with my spontaneity, I marched off down the deserted country lane singing the only patriotic song I knew off by heart:

"Rule Britannia,

Marmalade and jam,

Five Chinese crackers up your arsehole,

Bang, bang, bang, bang, bang!"

I trudged along for a couple of kilometres, leaving a snail-like trail of perspiration behind me. And do you know what I encountered when I stopped outside the hallowed grounds of the BBC? Nothing. Bugger all. Just a dreary, boxy white building with narrow windows, the kind that was popular in Britain in the 1960s. The drab office block was surrounded by red-and-white pylons, all of which was fenced off. That was fair enough. But there was not even a plaque or an information panel to provide visitors with a brief overview of the BBC's role in Singapore, from the colonial days through to independence. They had even neglected to provide another human being, preferring one of those intercom speakers at the gate instead of a security guard. Feeling more than a tad fractious, I was tempted to push the button and ask for a double cheeseburger with no gherkins.

An hour later, I waved the white flag and threw myself at the mercy of benevolent truck drivers. I hitchhiked. There is no safer country in the world to do so and my legs refused to go any further. Besides, I did not fancy fainting in some ditch in *ulu* land and being left at the mercy of the stray dogs that wandered in and out of the forest. Somewhere along Lim Chu Kang Lane 3, I stuck my thumb out and, this really was true, the very first driver pulled over and picked me up. I scrambled up into his truck and slumped into the passenger seat. I almost dozed off.

"Aiyoh, look at you," said the shocked middle-aged Chinese driver. "Cannot walk in the sun for so long. Radio say it is 34 degrees now. Got no cloud and no rain today. You mad to walk in this heat. Where you going?"

"Hay Dairies Goat Farm. It's in Lane 4."

"Wah, with your face like that, you could scare the goats."

Hay Dairies Goat Farm is the only goat farm in Singapore. The Hay family built up a small fortune in pig farming, but the government decided in the early 1980s that pig farming was out, so the Hays invested in some alpine goats from Minnesota instead. Now they have got over a thousand and serve a niche market for Singaporeans allergic to cow's milk. I arrived at 3.50pm. As the farm was closing at 4pm, I rushed over to the lady at the counter and said, "Hello, Mrs Hay, can I buy a bag of your hay please, Mrs Hay?" She did not laugh either.

After a lightning dash around the goat pens, feeding as many goats as I could, I retired to a table for a drink. I felt a tap on the shoulder. A beaming Chinese chap in his mid-forties looked down at me while his pal collected a case of goat's milk from the counter.

"Where you from?" he asked.

"Toa Payoh."

"No, where are you *really* from? You don't look like you're from Toa Payoh."

This insensitive, anachronistic observation drives me mad, as I am sure it does the thousands of fair-skinned Eurasians whose families have lived in Singapore for generations.

"Really? What do people from Toa Payoh look like then?"

"No, no, sorry. What I mean is ... "

"I used to live in London." I let him off the hook. He was a decent guy really.

"Ah, I went to London in 1982 for business. I got an orchid farm. Used to sell one type of orchid to a big store. Called Mark and something. Mark and Son?"

"Marks & Spencer?"

"Yah, that was it. Mark and Stencil. We sold orchids to Mark and Stencil for three years, but then the contract suddenly stopped. Dunno why."

Probably because he kept referring to the store as "Mark and Stencil".

Shortly before sunset, I found myself stranded at the end of Sungei Tengah Road. On the map, the northern tip of the road was bordered by forest and surrounded by the streams of Sungei Tengah and Sungei Peng Siang. It certainly looked *ulu* on the map. It was. Too bloody *ulu*. On foot, the dense foliage was inaccessible to the most ardent of explorers, let alone someone who should have called it a day after Hay Dairies. Outside Seng Choon Farm, half a dozen foreign workers piled into the back of a truck. Rather melodramatically, I stepped hastily in front of the vehicle and pretty much demanded a free ride back to civilisation. It was presumptuous, but I was desperate. The Chinese driver found me so amusing he offered me a seat in the back. My fellow foreign workers, who were all Indian, gladly made space for one more sweaty body. Conversation was difficult as their English was about as proficient as my Tamil. But through a combination of hand gestures and guffawing, they managed to express their firm belief that despite coming from a country of over one billion people, they had never seen such big feet. I was outraged. India has elephants.

The guy beside me then took out a knife. That was an alarming, unexpected development and I was a trifle concerned. Then he produced a papaya, cut a slice and handed it to me. I was humbled by his generosity. We were all foreign workers on that truck, but I did not kid myself. Our Singapore stories contrasted sharply. Their wages are often appalling and their living conditions even worse. These poor guys are the country's invisible people—seen, but rarely acknowledged. They build Singapore's homes, offices and expressways and clean and paint the HDB blocks and hawker centres, but spend most of their time here in the shadows. We had almost nothing in common, not even a language. But for

15 minutes, we huddled together and enjoyed a breezy ride through the countryside, a glorious sunset and some papaya. The journey was bumpy, my entire body ached and I had to sit cross-legged all the way to Choa Chu Kang's town centre. And yet I had never felt more comfortable.

CHAPTER 16

Unlike almost every other male over 18 in Singapore, I have never fired a gun. Nor have I ever shared a bunk with another man. And I have never joined other young men in the jungle to paint helmets. National Service in Britain was abolished back in 1960, which means I am at a disadvantage in Singapore for several reasons.

First, I never get time off from work for reservist training. Singaporean male colleagues disappear from the office for the odd weekend jaunt claiming they are off to serve their country. I have no idea where they go, but they invariably return slimmer and tanned. I think they all go to health spas.

Second, National Servicemen are all fluent in bizarre Hokkien and Singlish phrases that mean nothing to anyone else. Approach a Singaporean woman and say "fuck spider" and she almost certainly will not clean your rifle. In the army, however, the spider refers to the dirt in a rifle during an inspection. Then there is the bizarrely sexual Hokkien rebuke often used by a superior officer to berate an idle subordinate. He might say something like, "Recruit, I told you to make your bed, but you just *kiao kah yo lum par.*"

For non-National Servicemen, *kiao kah yo lum par* roughly translates into "raise your legs and wiggle your balls". Now, I find it a mite peculiar that an officer orders a soldier to jiggle his genitals, but there you go. Like the masons, Singaporean men possess the ability to converse in an exclusive, members-only language. It is not Malay, it is not Singlish, it is not even Hokkien. It is Army Speak. If you do not know the language, you can go "fuck spider".

Finally, there is the big fish phenomenon. When three anglers discuss their respective catches together, the fish always get progressively larger. National Servicemen are the same. They have seen and caught everything in the jungle. They are *Buaya* Dundee. At times, you wonder whether Singaporean men carried out their Basic Military Training on Pulau Tekong or in Serengeti National Park. If you mention casually to a male colleague that you spotted a small monitor lizard in a canal at the weekend, he will nod slowly and then ask in a piteous voice, "How long was the lizard?"

"Well, it was about this long," you demonstrate proudly with your hands. "That, with the tail."

"Aiyah, when I was on night duty on Tekong, I saw a lizard so big I thought they were filming *Godzilla*. We needed a helicopter to get a leash around its neck. Couldn't send this one to the Singapore Zoo. Sent it to Universal Studios instead."

If you see a monkey, NS men have spent three months on Planet of the Apes. If you come across a wild boar on Indonesia's Bintan Island, they have lassoed a herd of buffalo with their own belt. If you spot a snake, they have wrestled an anaconda (and then probably wiggled its balls). In fact, they wrestled it, speared it, killed it, skinned it and ate it, using nothing more than twigs from a *tembusu* tree.

But one elusive beast remained. One rare creature that I knew guaranteed a certain cachet in masculine circles if I could find it. The deadliest predator in its environment, this guy's ancestors did not walk with dinosaurs, they ate them, to paraphrase the National Geographic Channel. This particular species is the largest reptile on the planet, found in northern Australia and across Southeast Asia. And at least one has been photographed roaming freely along the banks of Singapore's coast. I had spent five years trying to track it down, but to no avail. In desperation, I had asked the staff at Sungei Buloh Wetland Reserve to phone me if the reclusive reptile ever made a cameo appearance.

Then the call came. It lasted 10 seconds. "Hi, Neil, it's Andrew from Sungei Buloh ... Crocodile!"

"Right, I'll be there in 25 minutes."

I was there in 20. But the traffic along Kranji Road still suggested my desperate dash had been in vain. The estuarine, or salt-water, crocodile, the biggest reptile on the Earth, had submerged again. At low tide, the beast tended to appear on the banks of Sungei Buloh Besar, a stretch of fresh water, bordered by mangroves, that flow into the Johor Straits. But it came up only to allow the sun to roast its back. When it was overcast, the *buaya* (Malay for "crocodile") buggered off.

"You must be patient," said Andrew. "The crocodile bobs up and down every day. That's why we call him Mr Bob. When the sun comes out, so will he."

And in one sublime, unforgettable moment, Mr Bob's snout appeared above the murky water. To borrow a relevant phrase here, he was a beauty. His snout was long and brown, but he looked surprisingly benign. Crocodiles have been known to kill lions, bring down ungulates and attack sharks so I had expected to be exhilarated and petrified in equal measure, but I was just quietly respectful. Mr Bob glided effortlessly over to the water's edge to lie on the rocks, providing a stunning view of his entire body in the shallow water. His body was a muddy brown, with black, scaly squares down his back. This particular estuarine crocodile was not going to shatter any records, but he was still a respectable 2 metres in length. Toe to claw, he was longer than any human being on the island. But he was slenderer than most crocodiles, about 25 centimetres at his broadest point, and only a little wider than the fatter monitor lizards at Sungei Buloh. That could explain why he did not look fearful. (I must stress to Singaporeans and tourists here that there is nothing to be fearful of. You have got more chance of winning the Singapore Sweep first prize and then being struck by lightning on your way to the betting outlet to collect your fortune than you have of being killed by a crocodile in this country.) Instead, Mr Bob was a picture of serenity. Oblivious to the handful of gaping nature lovers who stood just metres above him on the overhead bridge, he was content to bask in the sunshine.

Then a suicidal fish brushed across his teeth, so he nonchalantly opened his mouth and ate it. That was a sight. His open jaws protruded out of the water like a jagged letter V as the witless fish wriggled around before they were quickly snapped shut. Clearly, Mr Bob had thought, "Look, I'm not hungry but don't take the piss. I'm one of the world's oldest predators and you're swimming in and out of my teeth. You wouldn't wiggle your arse in front of a heron's beak, would you?"

A little overcome with excitement, I became an impromptu, unpaid guide for the day. Whenever visitors passed, I pointed out Mr Bob (even though he was 2 metres long, he was still well camouflaged among the rocks) and stressed, rather manically, how lucky they were to catch a glimpse of him. A young Chinese couple peered down for five seconds, clearly unimpressed that they stood over Singapore's only known wild representative of a group of reptiles that can be traced back to the Triassic Period, roughly 230 million years ago.

"Oh, yah, it's a crocodile," said the bored 20-something woman. She could have hosted her own nature programme. "Not very big, is it?"

"How big would you like it to be?" I shouted after her. But the child of the American blockbuster movie had gone.

A couple of German tourists expressed their understandable shock at encountering such a prehistoric creature in a city-state. Lucky bastards. I spent a fortnight in Australia's Northern Territory and the closest I got to a wild crocodile was seeing a photograph of Paul Hogan in a glossy magazine.

Only an elderly Chinese couple matched my enthusiasm. Indeed, I am surprised that their excitable exclamations and constant jiggling did not trigger a bout of incontinence, particularly when I insisted that they check out Mr Bob. I was quite blasé about it by now. In fact, I had turned into a National Serviceman.

"Yah, there's a wild crocodile over there," I said, while casually flicking a piece of invisible fluff off my shorts. "It's been there about an hour now. Got very sharp teeth. Just ripped a fish's head off."

I neglected to mention that the fish was smaller than a tea bag.

"Wah, really ah," said the combustible auntie. "Where is it, ah? I mus' see. Mus' see. Where is it?"

"Where's what, sorry? Oh, the crocodile? That little thing? It's over by the rocks."

"Oh, yah. There it is. It's on the little island now. A crocodile! Look at its teeth! A crocodile!"

"That's a monitor lizard," I sighed. "The crocodile is still over by the rocks."

But the reptilian cousins did almost cross claws a little later to ensure the wild encounter ended on a memorable note. A prime candidate for a weight-loss diet, the fattest, most cumbersome monitor lizard in Singapore splashed around in the water under the bridge. With a bulging neck and an enormous body, the lizard wobbled and thrashed away, splashing everything around it. Including the crocodile. Mr Bob did not take too kindly to being disturbed by the world's stupidest creature. The sleek swimmer turned his periscope-like snout towards the blubbering embarrassment in front of him and dove under water. There was not even a ripple. Then that brown snout reappeared, just a whisker from the monitor lizard's tail. The stealthy Mr Bob had covered a distance of over 25 metres, undetected, in a matter of seconds. It was breathtaking, but worrying. The dopey lizard took an eternity to clamber onto the riverbank. At one point, the tubby twit stopped, presumably to ask its pursuer, "Now, be honest, Mr Bob. Does my bum look big in this to you? I've tried to exercise I really have but I just don't have the time."

The crocodile had positioned itself just behind the lizard, which had decided that now was the opportune moment to top up its tan. It was unbearable.

"Get out of the water, you silly sod," I found myself shouting. "There's a crocodile behind you and it's going to tear you in half. Move your fat arse!"

The unaware lizard looked up at the noise, as if to say, "What was that? Did someone say something then? Do you know,

I could've sworn someone said 'crocodile'. Silly me, that couldn't be right. This isn't Australia, you know!"

Finally, the dopey sod crawled off into the mangroves. According to the staff at Sungei Buloh, the crocodile was not hunting for its dinner, just protecting its territory. But that was irrelevant. As far I was concerned, Mr Bob pounced on Fatty, bit into its fleshy neck, performed the death roll and dragged it to the murky depths of Sungei Buloh. That is the story I will recount to my grandchildren anyway. I fancy even National Servicemen will have their work cut out trying to eclipse that one.

The Kranji Nature Trail was always going to be an anticlimax after meeting Mr Bob. But that is not to say it was not a splendid amble through grassland, secondary forest and mangroves. Divided into those natural habitats, the 2-kilometre-long trail, which is sandwiched between Sungei Buloh and Kranji Reservoir Park, provides visitors with fascinating examples of the mangroves' importance and subtly points out the damage urbanisation has inflicted upon the island. In the 1820s, when perspiring imperialists with superb sideburns were springing up all over the place, mangroves covered 13 per cent of the island. Now they cover only 0.5 per cent.

It is all a bit depressing really. Mangroves provide an island like Singapore with a natural coastline filter for all the flotsam. That is their purpose. Moreover, mangroves are also believed to absorb carbon dioxide emissions, generally blamed for being the major cause of global warming. According to recent media reports, a marvellous team of scientists from Singapore's National Institute of Education discovered that one hectare of mangrove forest can absorb something like 1.5 tonnes of carbon dioxide a year—the amount produced by one car in the same period of time. Consequently, the scientists appealed to the government to plant more mangroves around the island. I sincerely hope they succeed. And if you do not want to bequeath a lump of charcoal to your children, so should you.

Along the Nature Trail, the amount of crap caught up in the mangroves' roots was astonishing. According to a signboard, much of it is dumped from coastal kampongs along the Johor Straits. What the hell are they doing over there? Apart from the usual plastic bottles and odd shoes, I noticed truck tyres, a windscreen and a car seat. Are people driving their vehicles off the Causeway? It was most disconcerting.

I left the mangroves and took a short stroll down Kranji Way and headed into the reservoir park. It is not much of a park really, just a couple of old concrete benches, a dilapidated children's playground and a reeking toilet used mostly by fishermen to wash their rods. But Kranji Reservoir Park does boast the greatest sign in the country. Nailed to a bit of timber, the whitewashed board simply says "Warning! Beware of Crocodiles". And there is an awful, hand-drawn sketch of a crocodile above the stencilling. Even allowing for artistic licence, it looks more like an armadillo. Mr Bob would be most offended. But I wondered what the equivalent warning sign would be at Parsloes Park, my childhood park in Dagenham. How could it possibly match the exotic beastliness of a crocodile? After several minutes I came up with "Warning! Some kid has crapped in the sandpit". That was always pretty scary. I had suffered more wild encounters with fresh turds in Parsloes Park than with crocodiles in Sungei Buloh. Although they certainly added a spring to your step when you took part in the triple jump.

Kranji also hosted a major event in Singapore's short history that seldom receives the recognition it deserves. Amid the chaotic lack of communication, conflicting defence plans and general military neglect in the first two months of 1942, the sleepy, rural corner of Kranji could proudly claim to have temporarily succeeded where most of Malaya had failed—it scored a rare victory against the invading Japanese forces. On 8 and 9 February 1942, the Japanese Imperial Guard landed here to fight in what became known as the Kranji Beach Battle. But the aggressors landed at low tide and found themselves stuck in the deep mud. The enterprising 27th Australian Brigade, working alongside Singaporean volunteers, had earlier released oil into the sea. The Japanese were stuck in the oil slicks, which were then ignited. As a result, the attack was largely repelled. However, the British military command feared a Japanese landing in Jurong, so the exhausted troops at Kranji were ordered to withdraw south. This decision paved the way for the Japanese to land in greater numbers, take control of Kranji Village and consolidate in the north. It is a tragedy that such a bold stand ultimately proved futile, but that does not mean that it should not be remembered. There is a small, tasteful memorial dedicated to the ingenuity and resilience of the men who successfully defended Kranji in the middle of the reservoir park. But they deserve something more.

I sauntered along the shoreline for a bit, admiring the engineering marvel that is Kranji Dam. Have you ever been to Kranji Dam? It is a charming place. Ignore the dusty trucks bound for the farming estates and pay no attention to the tanned fishermen washing their groins at the public toilets and focus instead on the spectacular views. I stood on a grassy slope on the side that faced Malaysia to take in the stunning vista. The natural, breezy charm of Kranji Reservoir was on my right, the mangrove forest of Sungei Buloh behind me and the Johor Straits on my left. The tide had receded so the sea was a bit smelly, but that certainly did not detract from the splendid image of Malaysia's coastline. It is a familiar statistic, but one well worth repeating. The Johor-Singapore Causeway is only 1,056 metres long. Just 1 kilometre separates the two countries. Yet on a public holiday, it can still take four bloody hours to get across the Causeway.

I sat on a bench and peered over at the next door neighbour. The evening prayers at a coastal mosque drifted across the Straits. Condos, shophouses and the names of the Hyatt Hotel and New York Hotel were all discernible. Being rush hour, the streets were jammed with cars and lorries. From the tranquil setting of Kranji Dam, Johor Bahru was clearly a hive of bustling activity. The world of cheap seafood, discounted petrol and pirated DVDs looked quite inviting. So I decided to pop over.

CHAPTER 17

I set foot on Malaysian soil. But I was nowhere near the country. I was still in Singapore, in the train station at Tanjong Pagar, which is owned and operated by Malaysian Railways (Keretapi Tanah Melayu Berhad—KTMB). I took a bus to Keppel Road, darted through the dusty, grey building of the railway station and entered Malaysia, thanks to a crumbling empire. In 1918, the British colonial government allowed the grounds around the station and the line that runs through the heart of the island to be sold to the Federal Malay States with one caveat—they were only to be used for train services, not commercial development. Now we are not talking *ulu* land here, we are talking prime real estate: some 40 kilometres of rail track from Keppel in the south to Woodlands in the north, stretching to over 50 metres at its widest point, all owned by Malaysia. Not surprisingly, it remains a contentious issue on both sides of the Causeway. The dogged Singapore government has bought back segments of the land in recent years and asked its Malaysian counterpart to move the station up to Bukit Timah or, better yet, Kranji. But the Malaysians continue to stall on an agreement. I cannot think why.

However, the anomalous station's colonial history makes it a fascinating building. Its high, arched ceilings resembled several train stations in London and had the floor been delicately coated with pigeon shit, it could well have been the Waterloo and Victoria stations of my childhood. Stained glass windows depicted scenes of a nostalgic Malaysia, with men in traditional Malay costume working in a rural world that looked more like an illustration from a children's storybook than an accurate reflection of life over the Causeway. But then, the whole station had a dated, stale air about it. Faded posters of Kinabalu and Sarawak said many things, but visiting either destination was not one of them. There was a drab, Malay coffee shop, a magazine stand cum money changer and a few tatty souvenirs that only the most charitable of travellers would take a fancy to. There were a handful of backpackers and a few foreign workers; otherwise the cavernous station was pretty much empty.

I was nosing through the magazine racks when I realised, to my dismay, that I had less than five minutes to fill out my immigration form, clear Malaysian customs (at a counter positioned beside Keppel Road, it was so bizarre) and make the train before it departed at 10.30am. The immigration officers pointed out that forms could be completed and checked on the train. As that was not the case, I inadvertently spent the entire day in Johor Bahru as an illegal immigrant.

The train itself exceeded my expectations. I had taken a slightly, negative Singaporean view of the Malaysian train and anticipated an antiquated, non-air-conditioned carriage with lowly paid workers hanging out of one window and hens, goats and chickens the other. Instead, the air-conditioned train was modern, clean and comfortable and the wide windows offered expansive views of the journey. The carriage was about a third full with the usual foreign and local blue-collar workers and the omnipresent backpackers.

The train was ready to pull away when another pair of breathless backpackers jumped aboard. The 30-something woman had long, unkempt hair, à la Janis Joplin, and the 40-something man had blond-in-a-bottle hair, à la sad old git. He was one of those ageing, backpacking hippy types who gravitate to Southeast Asia for its bohemian lifestyle, eastern philosophies and naive, olive-skinned women. Less common in Singapore, they are all over the beach resorts of Pattaya, Phuket and Bali. They are usually in their mid-forties, tanned, but craggy from overexposure to the sun. The best ones favour ponytails to cover their bald spots and hang out at (or lease) beach bars and restaurants with Asian women half their age. Locals often view them as exotic, worldly travellers respected for their free-spirited values. Fellow expats often view them as wankers.

But men like the middle-aged hippy on the train have always intrigued me. Why hasn't anyone close to him ever discreetly pointed out that he looks bloody ridiculous? I genuinely do not know how someone in his immediate family has not said, "Shall we call it a day now, John? We recognise that you becoming a beach bum in Thailand is a brave protest against the jackboot of globalisation and the greedy consumerism of Western civilisation, but you're starting to look like Leonardo DiCaprio's grandad. Why don't we spend this summer in the real world, eh? So have a shave, get a job and leave the peroxide in the bottle."

The Malaysian train pulled out of the Malaysian station in southern Singapore and we were off. Well, the journey was delightful. The $2.90 one-way ticket to Johor Bahru provided a glimpse of rural Singapore that is impossible to see any other way. The tracks behind Bukit Merah were dotted with allotments, vegetable patches and handmade shelters and shacks. Knowing that the land on either side of the track cannot be redeveloped for commercial purposes, one or two squatters have moved in. Well, at least someone makes use of the land. We cut through the serious money of Singapore as we passed through the three-storey houses around Holland Road and Sixth Avenue. There were BMWs and overworked maids as far as the eye could see. Somewhere around Bukit Timah, a large sign indicated that KTMB was carrying out extensive renovations to improve the line between here and Woodlands. Then I spotted the industrious workforce—six pot-bellied Malaysian guys sitting on an unfinished track sharing cigarettes. Marvellous. The train raced alongside Bukit Timah Nature Reserve and, at one point, rainforest surrounded the carriage. Foreign visitors entering Singapore on the KTMB train must have an entirely different first impression of the island. The journey was so green. We went over a couple of railway crossings, the one at Ten Mile Junction at Bukit Panjang being the most unusual. For a few fleeting moments, we rejoined the more familiar environment of housing estates and shopping centres before re-entering the countryside once more at Kranji. Darting beneath the snaking queues at Woodlands Checkpoint was worth the $2.90 ticket alone.

Just 10 minutes later, I really had set foot in Malaysia. My passport still had not been stamped. I stood on the scruffy Jalan Tun Abdul Razak in front of the station. The air was stifling and the heat from the traffic almost unbearable. Johor Bahru, or JB, always feels claustrophobic. I scuttled from one shaded spot to another until I ended up in Jalan Wong Ah Fook. Running to the main highway out of Johor Bahru, this is the main street for shopping centres, markets, temples and money changers. I noticed a number of Western backpackers milling around. They have always been an integral part of the JB landscape whenever I have visited. The dusty town provides the perfect launch pad for the beach resorts of Malaysia and a ramshackle, laid-back alternative to the clinical, controlled island across the Straits. At least, that is the impression occasionally suggested in one or two guidebooks. And frankly, I find that hypocrisy abhorrent. Poverty Tourism is one of the most unsavoury by-products of globalisation. Trendy, young Brits or suburban American backpackers called Dwayne Eisenhower Teaspoon III love to come here to sample a little Asian exotica; the poorer, the better. Forget Singapore. It is an Asian city that has dared to emulate Western standards of living. How dare they? Try Cambodia or Vietnam instead. They have got great shanty towns. Some real shitholes. Snap a picture in front of a poverty-stricken auntie washing her clothes in a polluted river and put the framed photograph beside the baseball trophy and the signed 50 Cent album. How totally awesome is that?

But Johor Bahru is changing, even if the progress is slow. Tired of being labelled the poor Causeway cousin, there has been a discernible effort to spruce up the place. I recalled the square between Sri Mariamman Temple and the Sikh Temple being an untidy mix of market stalls selling souvenirs and the usual tat.

Now it boasted a smart town garden, with the usual array of potted plants, paved and covered walkways, mini fountains and a café in the middle. Do not repeat this too loudly but it looked suspiciously like an upgraded HDB town centre. I had a decent lunch in City Square, a shiny shopping centre that summed up JB's identity crisis as it struggles to refashion itself into a modern metropolis and shed its image of being a seedy, but exciting and cheap, coastal shanty town. Beside the impressive City Square was a decaying shopping centre where most of the shopfronts had their shutters down. Across the street was a rundown market and decaying shophouses with rusty zinc roofs. Indeed, in City Square's enormous shadow was a stall selling second-hand shoes and trainers. The footwear had been polished, with newspaper stuffed inside to give that brand new shoe shop look. It all looked rather pitiful really.

And then there were the toilets. If Malaysia's town planners commission the building of a colossal shopping centrepiece like City Square, then they must ensure that the public toilets inside are free. Making my way to the amenities on the third floor, I was stopped at the entrance by a convivial Indian lady who charged me 20 cents. That was acceptable. Then I went inside, locked the cubicle door and realised there was no toilet paper. That was not acceptable.

"Excuse me, but there's no paper," I barked at the poor woman. I went outside first. Please do not think that I shouted from inside the cubicle with my trousers round my ankles.

"It's 20 cents."

"I know it's 20 cents. I already paid the 20 cents. I gave you the money 2 minutes ago. Remember?"

"That was for the toilet. Give me another 20 cents for the tissue paper."

My impatient bowels were in no position to argue, but someone somewhere is taking the piss. When I washed my hands afterwards, I realised there was something unusual about the person at the next sink. She was a woman! And a young attractive one at that. The cleaner pointed her detergent spray nozzle at the sink while an indifferent Malaysian chap pointed Percy at the porcelain just a few feet away. In Singapore, I have occasionally encountered an intrepid auntie mopping the toilet floor while moaning about how long I am taking to tinkle, but I have never witnessed a young woman cleaning the sinks beside the men's urinals. Not a confrontation with the opposite sex one would expect in Malaysia.

I surrendered to the oppressive heat and took a taxi to "Little Singapore" in Jalan Dato Sulaiman, a few kilometres further north. It is nothing more than a shabby, faded shopping centre called Holiday Plaza, but it rivals Toa Payoh Central for the number of Singaporeans shopping there at the weekends. If you are after anything pirated, copied or fake, Holiday Plaza is the place to go. The basement and the first floor are generally populated with shops staffed by *ah bengs* whose outrageously dyed hair suggests they sit blindfolded in a barber's chair and throw darts at a colour chart to determine their latest shade. Each shopfront promises all the latest DVDs. But that is all it is—a front. There will be a handful of copies of the genuine article on dusty shelves, their token gesture of legality for the benefit of officialdom, but the real stuff is found behind a locked door at the back of the shop. Being the only *ang moh* browsing around the basement, I became the prime target for Ah Beng and his Technicolour Haircut.

"Hey, John, come this way," a young Chinese guy said, beckoning me into his illegal emporium. I have been called John a few times and it is a little disconcerting. I know it is only a figure of speech, but it also happens to be my middle name. I am never quite sure if I am dealing with an *ah beng* or a clairvoyant.

"You want DVDs, John?" he continued. "I got the best price in JB."

"And some say Batam?"

He did not laugh either.

"Come, come. I take you into my special VIP room. Only you can come in here, I never open this VIP room to anyone else."

"Only me? You'll open the VIP room just for me? Wow, that's really kind of you."

The same guy had ushered me into the same room on a previous trip to Holiday Plaza six months earlier. Inside the VIP room were floor-to-ceiling shelves of DVDs, including titles not due for cinematic release in Singapore for another three months. I was left in the capable hands of two younger *ah bengs*. They were hilarious. It is not politically correct, but there is something endearing about the incessant sales patter of an *ah beng* selling illegal DVDs in Johor Bahru. They never give up, they never get offended and they will say anything to keep you in the VIP room.

"Hey, do you guys deliver?" I asked, feigning interest.

"Can, no problem. We deliver anywhere. JB, Singapore, anywhere."

"Anywhere? Well, I want to get them delivered to a place called Ramsgate. My mum lives there."

"Can, sure, no problem. Where's that, ah?"

"Where's what?"

"That place ... Ram's Head?"

"Ramsgate? It's in Kent in southern England. About two hours from London."

"Oh, that one, ah? Can, no problem. We deliver to Ram's Head all the time. You buy plenty, we give cheap delivery."

"But what if some of the discs don't work. Then how?"

"No problem, John. Each one got a 10-year warranty."

Although I could have listened to them all day, I pushed on, promising to revisit the VIP room with my mother from Ram's Head.

I discovered for the first time that Holiday Plaza actually had three floors. I had already visited the shopping centre several times but had never gone beyond the first floor. But then, other than pirated software, cheap phone and car accessories, shoe shops and the odd bakery, there is not much else to buy here. Indeed, Holiday Plaza represents a real legal dichotomy for the authorities. Publicly, they are utterly determined to crack down on the rampant piracy and copyright infringement that bedevils the country and makes it the bane of companies like Microsoft. And there are occasional, token raids on warehouses that manufacture pirated discs to pacify Bill Gates and his corporate pals. But the reality is harder to swallow. Crack down too hard on the DVD and software piracy in Holiday Plaza and visitors from Johor and over the Causeway will go somewhere else and the place will die. Indeed, its precarious position was discernible on the almost deserted upper floors, where a number of units that once sold legitimate products had closed down. There were fewer illegal DVD shops on the upper floors, so there was not an incentive for most shoppers to take the escalators. As a result, a blind eye is frequently turned at Holiday Plaza to ensure the customers keep coming back. Indeed, when I walked past the Crocodile menswear shop, I saw two Malaysian policemen trying on shirts. Beneath their feet, *ah bengs* were encouraging browsers to visit their VIP rooms. The cops could have apprehended the lot without breaking into a sweat. Perhaps it was their lunch break.

My next destination was supposed to be Lido Beach. As it faces Kranji Dam across the Johor Straits, I had planned to make poignant comparisons between the two countries. But the taxi driver insisted that was not where I really wanted to go.

"You don't want to go to Lido Beach," he said, as if playing a Jedi mind trick. "There's nothing for you to see. You want to go to Danga Bay. I take you there instead."

In no position to argue, I allowed him to take me to a place I had never heard of. It proved to be a wise move. Danga Bay is a half-finished waterfront city that spreads out over 25 kilometres and will eventually be home to residential and commercial centres, an education hub and sports facilities. Building work started in 2001 and the RM15 billion project promises a cruise terminal, a marina and a spa village, among many other things. The location is not unattractive. Overlooking the sea, it boasted one of the most picturesque food courts I had ever seen and was complemented by a couple of beach bars, a street bazaar and a mini fairground, most of which were closed. But the taxi driver assured me that locals flocked to Danga Bay on weekends and I believed him.

When it is finished, Danga Bay will be a cross between East Coast and Sentosa Cove, with yachts and boats docked at its jetties, children playing beach sports and tourists having a drink by the sea. That is, if it ever meets its 10- to 20-year completion date. Pardon my pessimism, but I have visited several neglected Malaysian beach resorts in the last 10 years. Looking more like ghost towns than a seaside playground for holidaymakers, these sad, peeling relics are dotted all over Malaysia and Indonesia. For Danga Bay to survive, it clearly needs Singaporeans to pop over on the odd weekend with their families to patronise the eateries and play on the beach. There are certainly worse places to have a cold beer and a plate of tasty chicken rice.

When leaving, I noticed a surreal attempt to attract the attention of Singaporean visitors. It was one of those guys who sketched your portrait while you waited. For a few dollars, this artist painted in oils on a half-decent canvas. Normally, these painters display their talents with illustrations of international celebrities such as Brad Pitt or Julia Roberts. Not this guy. No, he had proudly pinned up portraits of Malaysian Prime Minister Abdullah Ahmad Badawi and Singaporean Prime Minister Lee Hsien Loong. Now, PM Badawi I could just about understand, but PM Lee? The painter clearly expects Singaporeans to admire the portrait and say, "Wow, I've never seen such a likeness. It could be my prime minister standing there right now. I'm so overwhelmed by the patriotism that I can almost feel a verse of 'Majulah Singapura' coming on. If the artistic genius can do that for my country's leader, just think what he could do for me. Show me where to sit!"

But most Western tourists, on the other hand, will spend several puzzled minutes staring at the portraits of the two prime ministers before one of them is brave enough to ask, "Excuse me, I don't mean to be rude and I certainly don't wish to denigrate your talents, but who are these two meant to be? I don't think I've seen any of their movies."

Two hours later, I was ready to kill the Marco Polo of Johor Bahru's taxi services. Danga Bay might have been a welcome diversion, but it was also miles from the town centre and the Causeway. I limped along Jalan Skudai beside the Johor Straits as the warm, sea air melted my skin. Buses sped past at regular intervals, but there appeared to be no bloody bus stops. The public transport accessories that I usually take for granted in Singapore are apparently unnecessary in the orderly, functional world of JB, along with public benches and shelters from the merciless sun.

My fractious mood took a turn for the worse when I struggled through the public toilet that was Lido Beach. Being so close to the town centre, this coastal spot has long been a popular picnic spot for locals, but it was difficult to see why now. Drains filled with the most repugnant and smelly sewage imaginable trickled down sandy trenches and into the open sea, much of which will wash up around Kranji's mangroves. The lack of subtlety was almost laughable. There were no discreet pipes or tunnels involved, just puddles of black, treacle-like sludge all over the beach. To complement the putrid smell, there was a dead cat on the pavement, across the road from the Straits View Hotel, which easily won the title for least original hotel name. The poor cat had obviously been knocked down several hours earlier and mini-beasts of all shapes and sizes were gleefully ripping its exposed organs to shreds. And this was on a main street, opposite a hotel, in the middle of a scorching day. In the same week, Malaysia had unveiled a typically ostentatious plan to build a new scenic Causeway bridge on its side of the Straits (the project was eventually halted, even though millions had been spent on the foundation work). But in generating headlines with such grandiose schemes, municipal planners still neglect the very basics of public services, like clean streets and decent sanitation.

Sidestepping the dead cat, I eventually found the spot I was looking for. I took out my binoculars, sat on the concrete wall above Lido Beach, surveyed the horizon line and there it was—Kranji Dam and the very bench I had earlier been sitting on to peer over at Johor Bahru. Staring across at my home for the past 10 years left me with a very sentimental, and very obvious, thought. In geographical terms, Singapore is nothing. It barely qualifies for that little red dot status. From certain angles within Danga Bay, most of the country was obscured and here the miniscule island looked so unremarkable. Singapore really is nothing more than a remote island of four million castaways. It is dislocated from the natural resources of the Malayan hinterland and, apart from its advantageous location for shipping fleets, it has very little else to offer. To call Singapore a mere success borders on an insult. It is a bloody economic miracle and the envy of most of its neighbours, including those who lived behind me. Singapore does not come up with daft, extravagant schemes to rebuild half a bridge, but it keeps its streets clean. For most people, that is more than enough.

But the Malay fisherman who sat beside me at Lido Beach was not impressed. He eyed my binoculars suspiciously, waiting for me to give an explanation.

"Singapore. I live there," I said to the fisherman. He could barely contain his indifference.

"I don't like it."

"Don't like what?"

"Singapore. I don't like it. Everything need a permit. I want to fish, need permit. Want to work, need permit. Drive a taxi, need permit. In Singapore, I need a permit for everything. In Malaysia, if I want to fish, I fish."

The tide was out by at least 100 metres and would not be in for another two hours. My fisherman friend clearly had too much time on his hands.

"Since I got retrenched, I come here to fish," he explained. "At my age, very tough to find work. So I sit here and fish, and I don't need a permit."

"No, that's true. You don't need a permit to do nothing. Well, I've got to get to the Causeway now. It's time to go home."

And I really meant it.

CHAPTER 18

Few people walk over the Causeway. There is a footpath on the left-hand side of the bridge, if you are entering from the Singapore side, but it is seldom used. That is because only an idiot would stroll across the 1,056-metre-long bridge. You will never hear a sensible Singaporean or Malaysian say, "It looks like it's going to be a lovely day. There's not a cloud in the sky. Let's take a gentle amble across the Causeway and marvel at the sights, sounds and distinct smells of the Johor Straits."

In the interests of authenticity, I thought it might be awfully windswept and debonair to return to my island home on foot. It was not. After spending several minutes explaining to the impatient immigration officer at Johor Bahru why I had entered the country illegally, I was allowed to leave once I had surrendered my train ticket as evidence. Malaysia is a country where dozens of *ah bengs* can illegally peddle pirated products while two coppers try on polo shirts in the same shopping centre, but an overzealous immigration official confiscates a used $2.90 train ticket.

I followed the railway line that brought me into Malaysia and realised I was on the wrong side of the Causeway. I dashed between crawling lorries, reversed around stationary cars and jogged alongside packed No. 170 buses. And those bloody motorbikes are relentless, aren't they? Standing at a small zebra crossing just a few yards from the footpath, I waited impatiently as the army of revving ants refused to stop. Getting across the Causeway is akin to playing a board game. You need to throw a six to start. In the end, I cheated death by marching across with my hands held aloft like a deranged messianic figure. They soon stopped then.

The walk across the Causeway was abominable. Opened officially in 1924, the bridge is drab and colourless and there was little to see other than the corrugated iron fences that some underlings had kindly put up to obscure any vista that might possibly be more arresting than that of a crawling traffic jam. And yes, it is not a myth—the Johor Straits really does stink. The odour from the sea, coupled with the carbon dioxide cocktails served up by the endless stream of zigzagging motorcyclists, created a combustible toxic stench that left me with a headache. The lengthy queues at the Woodlands Checkpoint followed by an even longer wait for the buses to clear customs left me to draw only one incontrovertible conclusion—if you are not driving, always take the train to and from Malaysia.

I found my way to Woodlands Town Park East. Naturally, I staggered around Woodlands Street 13 for a bit, looking in vain for the entrance, before I clambered up a grassy hillside and found a few canoodling couples and some people walking their dogs, who kindly pointed out that I had come up the wrong side of the park. There was a gentle path on the other side that I had missed completely. Annoyed by my myopia, I threw my bag down in a huff, removed my sweaty, sticky shirt with some difficulty, kicked off my shoes and socks and settled down on the grass for a nap. I lasted less than five minutes. Ants had apparently mistaken my hairy chest for a nest of twigs and were setting up base camp. And three foreign domestic workers were now sitting on a nearby bench, giggling at my perspiring, flabby stomach.

I left the park, which provided a wonderful view of the sunset, and cut through the tidy housing estates of Marsiling. The neighbourhood was so open and spacious. This tour was forcing me to stubbornly accept the fact that there were other roomier and more colourful estates than my beloved Toa Payoh. My suspicions were confirmed when I reached the junction of Marsiling Road and Woodlands Centre Road.

Woodlands Town Garden must be a contender for the country's finest town garden. Toa Payoh's pond and green penis tower look woefully inadequate in comparison. An impressive 11 hectares in size, Woodlands' green haven boasted two ponds and cleverly incorporated Sungei Mandai Kecil, a river that ran through the park. The ponds were separated by a tasteful stone bridge and the park also offered a couple of pagodas, good fishing, some great picnicking spots for the family and a middle-aged taxi driver groping a woman half his age on one of the benches. What more could you want? Standing on the stone bridge, I could still make out the Malaysian coastline, but this lovely garden, with its manicured lawns and tidy flowerbeds, seemed a million miles away from the putrid drains on Lido Beach. Not for the first time, I realised I was really going to miss this country.

The next morning I fulfilled a promise to Cliff. When the World War II veteran visited Singapore in 2005, I promised to visit Pulau Blakang Mati and the Sembawang Shipyard, which was once home to the British Royal Navy. Criminally overlooked in many history books and guidebooks here, the old Sembawang Naval Base played host to the British battleship HMS *Prince of Wales* and the battlecruiser HMS *Repulse* as preparations to confront the Japanese fleet off Kota Bahru, Kelantan, were finalised. With the men of Force Z, the vessels left Sembawang on 8 December 1941 and never came back. Like the American ships at Pearl Harbor, which had been pummelled a day earlier, they proved to be sitting ducks in the open sea. Military warfare was changing, with air power triumphing over heavily armoured warships, and over 760 British sailors and dozens of Japanese aircrew were sent to their watery graves off Kuantan.

It is one of many significant events in Singapore's modern history that is sadly neglected. Students can regurgitate facts regarding Stamford Raffles, the battle for independence, the rise of the PAP and the transformation from third world to first almost parrot fashion, but the sinking of the *Prince of Wales* and the *Repulse* gets scant coverage in comparison. It is deplorable. Apart from the loss of life, the decisive air attack had far-reaching consequences for mainland Singapore. With their enemies' major sea vessels destroyed, the Japanese were confident enough to launch a ground assault in the New Year and storm Singapore with a force roughly three times smaller than that of the British. Yet I have met many Singaporeans who have little knowledge of one of the most pivotal moments in the country's history. Fortunately in September 2005, the 60th anniversary of Japan's surrender, a memorial was finally dedicated to the men who lost their lives on both ships. It was unveiled on the very dock where the ships had set sail and I had promised Cliff that I would pay a visit one day.

The only problem was that I had absolutely no idea where the memorial was. I took the MRT to Sembawang and the No. 856 bus to Admiralty Road West. I headed past Sembawang Prison DRC, which is never going to be confused for NTUC holiday chalets. At the top of two watchtowers, soldiers brandishing machine guns observed me wandering down the street, flicking through my street directory. I gave them a cheery wave. Neither waved back. This part of Singapore has long housed the armed forces of Britain, the United States, Australia and New Zealand, among others, and the commodious black-and-white colonial houses and accompanying gardens certainly provide the officers with luxurious living quarters. There are Singaporean CEOs who do not live as well as this. The names of the streets were fascinating: Jamaica Road, Tasmania Road, Fiji Road, Falkland Road and Gibraltar Crescent. It is a dummy's guide to the rise and fall of the British Empire. I propose that if the Union Jack is ever lowered in both the Falklands and Gibraltar, then some street renaming might be in order in Sembawang.

I ambled along Admiralty Road East and passed the Terror Club. Now, isn't that a frightening name? It is a social club for the stationed or visiting naval servicemen of one particular country. There are no prizes for guessing which one. Only straight-faced Americans could come up with a name like the Terror Club and not laugh. At a push, the British might opt for the Slightly Scary

Club and the Canadians may plump for the genuinely applaudable We Never Go to War Club, but only the Americans could conjure something so terrifying and so pitiful at the same time. The young troops that passed me certainly looked scary. I had never seen so many crew cuts and pimples. Bouncing along wearing oversized shorts and baseball caps, some of these guys should not be trusted with a calculator, never mind a gun. A banner above the club's swimming pool read "The Terror Club Welcomes USS *Blue Ridge*". That only meant one thing for Singapore. The working women (and men) of Orchard Towers were in for a busy weekend.

After reading several news reports, I suspected that the memorial was behind the Port of Singapore Authority's (PSA) Sembawang Wharves in Deptford Road, which was a private building with security at the gate. I had neither my passport nor my employment pass with me. My chances of bluffing my way through were slim at best. I figured that I had more chance of eating a hotdog at the Terror Club with one of its dudes.

Well, I have to say, the security guards at PSA were wonderfully helpful and accommodating. They made a call and, within minutes, I was being driven around the extremely private shipyard by a petty officer in the British Royal Navy! A considerate chap by the name of Geoff Fawcett, he went way beyond the call of duty and gave me an informal tour of a place that is not open to Singaporeans, never mind a strange *ang moh* with no formal identification. It was an extraordinary, private world occupied by foreign military. The navies of the United States, Britain, Australia and New Zealand all continue to operate at Sembawang, which serves as a logistic base and an administration centre for visiting vessels. I passed a minimart, a money changer, a tailor's and a hairdresser's, all of which were managed by Singaporeans, yet relied exclusively on the foreign forces for custom. The tailor's shop was over 40 years old and the owner has measured up the same senior-ranking officers since they were teenagers. The local hairdresser is even allowed onto the gargantuan vessels to cut the hair of the rank and file on board. It was quite amazing.

Geoff dropped me off beside the memorial, which is along the west wall of the Sembawang Shipyard. It really was just a few yards from the store basin where the ships had left for the last time all those years ago. It was a simple sombre memorial, with a plaque detailing the events of 8 December 1941, enclosed by three pristine white walls. The plaque was made in Melbourne, significant because so many of the servicemen who died in Singapore or were imprisoned at Changi were Australian. According to Geoff, the British Royal Navy officers stationed in Singapore had long championed the importance of having a memorial to those in Force Z who had perished and that they should be credited for their perseverance. A considerate, respectful guide, Geoff told me he had taken several families to the memorial in the past year, including one who had flown all the way from Plymouth, an area in the southwest corner of England.

I stayed for about half an hour before the genial Geoff dropped me back on Admiralty Road East. I was glad I had visited, for Cliff and my late Uncle Johnny, both of whom had docked at Sembawang and Blakang Mati with the British Royal Navy sometime between 1939 and 1946. But I cannot help but feel that the memorial is a little wasted at the back of Sembawang Shipyard, tucked away beyond the private properties of the PSA. A little later, I visited the nearby Sembawang Park, which offered amazing views of the American vessels stationed at the shipyard next door. Perhaps the park might have been a more suitable location for the memorial. Although it is not the exact spot, the park's jetty does show visitors where the ships left and there is no reason why a simple plaque cannot still be added there by the National Heritage Board. Building such a tribute around Sembawang Park's jetty or beach might not be geographically precise, but it would be far more accessible. And a memorial is only a memorial if people can come to remember.

CHAPTER 19

Sembawang was really growing on me. The two-storey terraced houses around Jalan Basong that backed onto plant nurseries had a rustic feel about them and the northern town offered a gentler lifestyle more in tune with its Causeway neighbour than the buzzing multitudes around Orchard Road. More importantly, Sembawang is also home to Singapore's most eccentric ice cream vendor. I walked towards the entrance of Sembawang Park beside Kampong Wak Hassan when the ice cream vendor zoomed past and stopped at the lay-by. It was 2pm on Friday afternoon and the park was deserted. Queues of eager customers were out of the question. I took pity on the elderly uncle and treated myself to a raspberry ripple.

"You like a cone?" asked a pair of shoulders. His head was buried in the tubs of ice cream somewhere inside the trolley. He was down there for an inappropriate length of time.

"No thanks. I'll have a wafer," I replied, peering down into the trolley. If the guy resurfaced licking his lips with a face full of raspberry ripple, the dollar coin was going straight back in the pocket. But the robust chap suddenly reappeared holding a raspberry ripple wafer. Only then did I realise he was impressively tanned and had a shocking head of red hair. I had never encountered such an elderly *ah beng* before.

"Hey uncle," I asked, desperate to maintain eye contact and not focus on his red moptop. It was brighter than a baboon's backside. "Why did you stop here? How to get customers?"

"No lah, I come here to go swimming."

"Really? Is there a swimming pool here then?"

"There, lah," he replied, betraying a flash of irritation at the asinine nature of the question. "Can see the sea or not?"

I could indeed see the sea. But having examined the Straits at close quarters on both sides of the Causeway in recent days, I was aghast at the possibility that anyone might fancy a bit of breaststroke around floating turds. I thought only mad dogs and English tourists at Blackpool did that. But the ice cream vendor was obviously an exception. I found a bench that was a discreet distance away from his motorbike and tucked into my raspberry ripple while observing an old man with red hair prepare for a swim. He had a cursory look around and, satisfied that the coast was clear, stripped off in the middle of the street! His shoes, socks and T-shirt were insouciantly discarded and tucked away in the trolley with the tubs of chocolate chip. Then he dropped his shorts to reveal what can only be charitably described as a well-worn pair of Y-fronts. They were pinkish and baggy in all the least flattering places, not helped by the tanned potbelly that protruded over the waistband. Now appropriately attired, I assumed that he would trot down to the seashore. But no, the suave swimmer helped himself to a cornet first. He dove into his trolley holding his neatly folded shorts and re-emerged with a raspberry ripple. Casting aside the traditional notions of public decency, he stood at the end of Sembawang Road in his pink underpants, with one hand nonchalantly leaning on the seat of his motorbike and the other holding his ice cream cornet.

And he did not move. Even when a bus pulled into the Sembawang Road End Bus Terminal beside him, reversed and went back out again, he stayed by his bike in his underpants, licking his raspberry ripple. Only when he had finished the cornet did he finally decide to saunter down to the beach, where he swapped the pink undies for a pair of trunks under the cover of his towel. But he did not swim. Instead, he stretched out on his towel, lit a cigarette and let out a satisfied sigh. His ice cream cornets, it seemed, were better than sex.

I waited at a nearby picnic table for 15 minutes to catch a glimpse of him paddling in the Johor Straits, but he appeared to have dozed off. It then occurred to me that there was something deeply disturbing about loitering around a beach waiting for a near naked uncle to show off his doggy paddle so I wandered off into the park.

Sembawang Park is considered to be one of the country's most *ulu* spots because of its comparative isolation, and it was almost empty. But that suits some people. As I passed a shelter, a breathless Indian couple hurriedly stood up and the man adjusted his zip. There was something about Sembawang Park that made Singaporeans want to take their clothes off. The park also has several monkey puzzle trees, which are stunning Chilean pine trees, with symmetrical branches that make them look like Christmas trees. I only mention them because there is no other tree on the planet that has a better name than the monkey puzzle tree. According to legend, the name derives from some daft Englishman who, in the 1800s, remarked that its scale-like leaves and prickly branches made the tree a puzzle to climb for most monkeys. No one is quite sure what the Englishman had been smoking. The name does not particularly convey a romantic mood though. In *Dr No,* Sean Connery and Ursula Andress sang about being under a mango tree together, but I wonder if the Indian lovebirds were aware that they had shagged under a monkey puzzle tree.

Whistling the tune of "Underneath the Mango Tree", I set off to visit the jewel in Sembawang's comely crown. In 1909, a Chinese merchant by the name of Seah Eng Keong discovered something unique at the heart of the northern kampong—a hot spring. It did not take long for local residents to flock to the natural phenomenon, believing the water's purities tackled common ailments like arthritis and rheumatism. During the Occupation, the Japanese constructed several thermal baths to enjoy the warm water. And by the 1960s, there were plans to transform the area into a spa to rival the world's best resorts. Tourists were expected to come from far and wide to experience the curative benefits of the spring. But nothing happened and, by the 1990s, the spring had fallen into disrepair and most Singaporeans had forgotten about the place.

But a handful of older, wily Sembawang residents, who remembered the hot spring of their kampong childhood, began to quietly return when the opportunity presented itself. In early 2002, the landowners, the Ministry of Defence, cleared the surrounding land to build an extension to the Sembawang Air Base. The story reached the newspapers and suddenly hundreds of Singaporeans were springing up in Sembawang. And they were not amused that the Ministry of Defence intended to fence off the area. Before you could shout "Eureka", community leaders presented a petition to the government, demanding that the spring be preserved.

Singaporeans are certainly a funny lot when it comes to picking their protests. In previous general elections in my Bishan-Toa Payoh constituency, no opposition candidates have stood against the PAP incumbents, which meant a walkover, so voters were denied the chance to troop down to the ballot box. But there were no organised complaints or protests. Threaten to close the island's only hot spring, on the other hand, and the petitions come out. It is most strange. A few months after I visited the hot spring, the 2006 General Election was held and Bishan-Toa Payoh residents were, once again, denied the chance to vote. But in the build-up to the election, the populace was up in arms over a more pressing issue—the price of a cup of coffee had gone up 10 cents. To offset the rising price of coffee, stall owners had been forced to increase their prices. Letter writers to the media suffered an apoplectic fit at the injustice of it all. The message came through loud and clear. Singaporeans will accept a one-party state, but do not take away their hot spring and never mess with their coffee.

But credit must go to those at the Ministry of Defence. Not only did they accede to local residents' demands and keep the hot spring open, they also renovated the compound and replaced the dirt track with a cemented path and some bougainvillea bushes in mid-2002. Hoping to be cured of their various aches and pains, the crowds returned to the revamped spring while the Singapore

Tourism Board examined its potential to attract foreign visitors. And then, nothing happened. Interest from the media and the public waned and the attraction certainly did not end up in STB guidebooks. But it was still open and I was eager to see what had become of Singapore's legendary hot spring.

I bounded off the bus at the junction of Sembawang Road and Gambas Avenue. The spring was just a couple of minutes walk down Gambas Avenue, although it was easy to miss. There was no sign. No mention of the hot spring at all, in fact. Perhaps the Ministry of Defence hopes to downplay the fact that it sits within a restricted area. If that was the intention, it has worked. The Sembawang Hot Spring undoubtedly holds the distinction of having the ugliest entrance to an attraction that I have ever seen. Prisons boast more attractive façades. The fence around the compound stood at least 3 metres high and was topped off by the ubiquitous roll of barbed wire. Although there was no indication of what was actually inside, there was still a sign ordering visitors not to cycle, litter, skateboard, play sports, walk dogs and, best of all, sell ice creams. Guess my swimming friend is screwed then. In addition, the Ministry of Defence could not be held responsible for any injuries sustained and visitors entered at their own risk. I now understood why the coach parties were not queuing up.

The path was also bordered by green fencing and barbed wire. I ambled along for about 25 metres until the path abruptly turned right and there it was, the exotic Sembawang Hot Spring. Now I do not know about you, but when I think of a hot spring, I conjure images of the great Roman baths with their flawless, mosaic floors within magnificent temples that stood several metres high or the religious sanctuary at Lourdes in southern France, with its castles, apparitions and spas. What did the Sembawang Hot Spring offer? A concrete compound and half a dozen taps. I was devastated. I needed a pint of hot spring water just to overcome my sense of disappointment. The unprepossessing concrete square was about 30 metres across and surrounded by the omnipresent high, green fencing. In the middle were four taps, from which the hot spring flowed continuously from 7am to 7pm. There was no religious miracle before and after those hours—the Ministry of Defence turned off the taps. I noticed a few more taps in the corners of the compound, but they were slightly obscured by plastic buckets and chairs that kind souls had left for others to use.

But then, the kampong spirit still prevails here. The moment I entered, an elderly chap told me to help myself to one of the plastic chairs that hung over the fence. I realised later that he was the caretaker; his office nothing more than a tatty old shed. He directed me to an upturned bucket beside the four taps.

"Take, take. Spring, spring," he said, gesturing towards the bucket. But I hesitated. Being even more obtuse than usual, I had foolishly assumed that the hot spring was under the bucket. I was momentarily paralysed by the thought that I would lift up the bucket and unleash a roaring spurt of boiling water into the air, like a geyser at Yellowstone National Park.

"What's underneath?" I asked, taking a couple of tentative steps towards the bucket.

"It's okay. Take, take. Spring, spring."

That is it, I thought. There was a volatile geyser under the bucket just waiting to blow my head off. I flipped the bucket over and jumped back to avoid the thousands of litres of nothing. The bewildered caretaker was offering me an empty bucket to fill at the taps. Now he hesitated. He was clearly not sure whether to hand me a second bucket or call the staff at Woodbridge Hospital.

I filled my bucket, returned to my plastic chair and waited an hour for the boiling water to cool. Aside from the caretaker and myself, I counted four other people. A middle-aged Chinese couple massaged their feet in a bucket beside me while, in the far corner, another Chinese couple, possibly in their early sixties, treated the Hot Spring as a day out. Singing along to the tunes blaring out from a Chinese radio station, the guy relaxed in an old bathtub filled with spring water while the woman washed their clothes in a bucket before stepping into her bathtub—a blue plastic barrel cut in half. Oh, she did look a treat.

I dipped a big toe into my bucket, but the water had not cooled sufficiently. I am not a hypochondriac, just listen to this. In 2002, a 57-year-old carpenter lost six toes here. A desperate diabetes sufferer, he came here looking for a cure but ended up in hospital with gangrenous toes. Unfortunately, his medical condition contributed to his injury. His poor blood circulation meant that he did not feel the water scalding his feet and burning through his skin until it was too late. So I was more than happy to bide my time. Besides, the soothing atmosphere was addictive. There was a real sense of collectivism here. Everyone shared chairs and buckets and talked to each other. The caretaker knew every visitor and even tried to converse with me but my appalling Mandarin let me down. The couple beside me explained the procedure of cooling the water through hand gestures and some quite gifted miming. There might have been a hi-tech airbase next door and a swanky condo complex on the other side of Gambas Avenue, but the socialist kampong spirit had at least survived in here.

After the couple beside me cleaned up and cycled away, I was left with a singing Chinese bathtub and a woman lying in a plastic barrel. It was time to leave. I stood up to wave goodbye to the caretaker and almost knocked my chair over. He was nothing more than a floating head. No one had said that this place was haunted. On closer inspection, the caretaker had somehow contorted his body so it could descend into a barrel smaller than a beer keg. Only his head was visible. The barrel was filled to the brim with steaming spring water, which gave the surreal impression that a dislocated head floated over it. The caretaker's ghostly face appeared through the steam and smiled back at me, the woman in the blue barrel waved and her partner belted out another Chinese ballad from his bathtub.

It had been a fabulous day.

CHAPTER 20

Anyone who grew up in or around London in the early 1980s will be familiar with the concept of "red bus rovering". Before the uninspiring, all-inclusive travelcard was introduced, London Transport sold a one-day pass called a Red Rover, which essentially allowed you to travel on any red bus in London and its surrounding boroughs, including Barking and Dagenham, for the price of one ticket. It was marvellous. Children travelled out of their Essex housing estates around the city's fringes and into the exciting labyrinth of the nation's capital. Back then, the sun always shone, the buses and telephone boxes were always red and Ross and I could not get anyone to snog us in the school playground. And when you did not have a girlfriend to watch *Rocky III* with, you went "red bus rovering" with your best mate instead. The ticket was a gateway to a hedonistic metropolis that was a million miles away from the monotonous terraces of Dagenham. Any bus, any time, any place and as often as we wanted. Soho, Camden, Petticoat Lane, Tottenham Court Road, Notting Hill and Covent Garden—London called to us. The only problem was that our mums would not let us travel that far.

"Let's go red bus rovering," I would say excitedly as we watched Mickey's funeral in *Rocky III.*

"Yeah, all right, and this time let's go all over London. Even further than last time," Ross would reply as Rocky searched for his eye of the tiger.

"Where did we go last time?"

"Barking."

Barking is the town beside Dagenham. It was like buying a farecard in Toa Payoh and spending the day in Bishan. It was time to stretch our wings. We were almost 12 after all.

"We won't go to Barking again. Only spam heads go there. Let's go somewhere different up London."

So we went "up London". All the way to Upton Park, the home of West Ham United, and waited for Trevor Brooking to catch us kicking a tennis ball around the forecourt, whereupon he would immediately recommend us to the club's scouts. You see, we thought that the players lived in the stadium and we would join them once we had signed professional forms. But Upton Park is only 15 minutes away from Dagenham on the Tube. For all our bluff and bluster, Ross and I only ever went "red bus rovering" to the neighbouring Essex towns of Barking or Romford or to West Ham's Upton Park to demonstrate our ball control. We hardly needed a *London A-Z* as a guide.

And then it happened. We finally realised that we had exhausted every hang-out possibility in Barking and Romford, we were not going to dislodge Tony Cottee and Frank McAvennie from the West Ham first team and, more importantly, we had heard that you only needed to glance at a girl "up London" and her knickers would fall off. So Ross and I ventured into the city. We traipsed along to every major landmark we knew: the Tower of London, Madame Tussauds and the famous cinemas of Leicester Square. We only looked at them, mind you, as we lacked the funds to go inside any of them. Of all of London's landmarks, I loved Piccadilly Circus the most. With its gaudy advertising billboards, the statue of Eros and that roundabout leading to all the major shopping streets, the lively area seemed so glamorous to a 12-year-old. It was like standing on a real Monopoly board. Since then, I have taken every opportunity to visit Piccadilly Circus whenever I have returned to London.

And here I was once again, watching the cars, taxis and buses in Piccadilly Circus. Something was not quite right though. First, I did not have Ross beside me saying, "That girl across the street just winked at me. The one with the twitch. She definitely just winked at me. I reckon I could shag her." Second, I was not in London. I was in Seletar in northern Singapore. But it was Piccadilly Circus nonetheless, a mini-roundabout that was once the gateway to Britain's Royal Air Force and their largest airbase outside of the country in the 1930s. I had taken the MRT to Yio Chu Kang and then the No. 86 bus, which drove past the famous *prata* shops of Jalan Kayu and dropped me at the entrance of what is now the Seletar Camp of Singapore's Armed Forces. The former officers' village is also home to Singapore's oldest airport, 300 colonial properties and a cluster of bizarre street names that stand as a legacy to Britain's former military presence here. From where I stood at Piccadilly Circus, Edgware Road was the first exit, Maida Vale the second and Piccadilly the third. There was also Lancaster Gate, Knights Bridge, Battersea Road, Regent Street, Hyde Park Gate and The Oval, among many others; all in the quiet, remote Singaporean village of Seletar. Before you ask, there were no billboards, giant screens or statues at Piccadilly Circus. There was nothing except a sense of humour. It was just a mini-roundabout with a patch of grass in the middle and a miniscule road sign that cheekily said "Piccadilly Circus". I loved the irony. It was the only mini-roundabout I had ever come across that actually had a name, never mind one so historic and grandiose.

The black-and-white colonial bungalows and two-storey houses were lovely, with many complemented by large, well-tended gardens. Unlike the almost exclusively British community around Dover Road and "Little Kent", the Seletar village had a more cosmopolitan and homely feel. These houses looked like homes, rather than temporary stations for military personnel. The bungalows and gardens around Maida Vale were lived in, varied and inviting, probably due to the estate's eclectic mix of residents. Although there are a number of expatriates living here, there are also a number of Singaporeans, well-known names in some cases, from the arts and academic communities. And it all seemed more genuinely bohemian than the superficial Holland Village.

I strode down Park Lane, hoping to take a short cut to Seletar Airport, but a couple of soldiers at the School of Logistics halted my progress. That was a real Monopoly moment. I had gone round Oxford Street and passed Park Lane, only to be stopped and told to go back to the beginning and start again.

"You can't pass this way," the officer said. "Go back down Park Lane and head up West Camp Road to reach the airport."

"But if I don't pass 'Go', can I still collect $200?"

He had obviously not played Monopoly before. But I took the longer route to the airport, via Bays Water Road, where the houses and gardens were bigger, as were their snarling dogs. For heaven's sake guys, we all get the message. Your houses are palatial fortresses, the envy of Piccadilly and the rest of Singapore, but please, shut those bloody dogs up.

The breezy walk down West Camp Road was wonderful. The road was largely deserted and the welcome silence was only occasionally interrupted by a small private plane coming in to land on the runway to my right. Each flew so low overhead that I could make out the pilot's face. I waved at them as they approached but none of them turned and waved back, the miserable bastards.

Unlike the pilots, however, I almost missed Seletar Airport. Having been inculcated with the mantra "We've got the best airport in the world" so many times, I naively expected something of Changi Airport's proportions. After all, Seletar Airport had once been a magnet for the rich and famous, including actor Douglas Fairbanks and playwright Noel Coward. Today, however, it is almost hidden among old hangars, a roadside canteen and run-down buildings.

Opened in 1929, Seletar Airport consists of a small cluster of attractive single-storey buildings, reminiscent of other smaller airports in the region, such as Lahad Datu in Sabah, where they combine the services of baggage handling and customs. In other words, one man collects the cases from the plane, pushes them across the tarmac on a trolley, opens the doors to the terminal and throws them onto a table. Of course, nothing so slapdash would be tolerated at a Singaporean airport. I watched with not a little admiration as the staff effortlessly guided several shuffling passengers through the appropriate channels before they boarded a plane bound for Tioman Island. Then I went for a pee.

How many countries are there in the world where you can find yourself in a remote, tiny airport and yet the toilets are pristine, cleaned on an hourly basis and, best of all, free? Proudly take one step forward, Singapore. As I relieved myself, a bearded Scottish businessman joined me at the urinal. For reasons best known to themselves, middle-aged Scotsmen tend to favour beards. They also like to respond to every question and comment with the word "fine". This particular Scotsman did both, although he was reluctant to engage in any conversation initially, probably because I had a pen in one hand, my peeing equipment in the other and a notepad in my mouth. I have really got to stop taking notes in public toilets.

"So, er, what ye doin'?" he asked, not looking up.

"Oh, I'm researching a travel book on Singapore."

"Fine."

"So you're off on holiday then?"

"Aye. Well, been here on business. Now I'm off to Tioman for a few days."

"Oh, it's one of the best snorkelling places in the world."

"Fine."

I fancied asking him if, like most tourists, he thought Singapore was a "fine" city but he was bigger than me. I left the quaint Seletar Airport to find a bus stop in West Camp Road. There were a number of private planes parked on Seletar's tarmac. It can still be the airport of choice for those rich or famous enough to warrant a discreet arrival and departure. In 2002, Tom Cruise and his then girlfriend Penelope Cruz landed at Seletar to promote their film *Vanilla Sky* here. Tom and I have actually got quite a lot in common, you know. We have both been to Seletar Airport.

I took a bus back to Piccadilly Circus and meandered over to Baker Street. It was a sentimental journey. My mother was working at Marks & Spencer's old head office in London's Baker Street when she met my stepfather's backside. He was a porter; she was a secretary. He suggested he won her over with his sense of humour; she claimed he came in to empty her bin and provided her with a brief glimpse of his exposed crack. Either way, my youngest brother was the eventual result of that encounter. As one London street had inspired Sherlock Holmes, a fine song by Gerry Rafferty and my little brother, I felt the very least I could do was visit its Singaporean namesake.

Unfortunately, Baker Street could be a contender for the scruffiest street on the island. The untidy weeds gave it an unkempt look that was out of place among the tidy lawns of the neighbouring streets. There were skips full of car scrap and a shack with clothes hanging everywhere that resembled squatting quarters. Two empty boarded-up colonial houses only added to the eerie atmosphere. Even if a porter did come in and stick his backside in your face, you really would not want to live here.

I turned into the optimistically named Hampstead Gardens, which managed to be spookier than Baker Street (an impressive feat in itself) and was home to Singapore's creepiest house. Facing the Seletar Base Golf Course, a boarded-up, derelict property loomed large. The paint was peeling, weeds grew through rusted holes in the roof, the floorboards creaked and cracked and mould covered the walls. If Norman Bates ever bought a holiday home, this would be it.

I waded through the knee-deep undergrowth that bordered the front of the property, climbed over the barbed wire on the top of the fence and peered through a crack in one of the windows. The room was dank, dusty and full of cracked tiles. A filthy plastic chair was in the middle of the room. It looked like an interrogation room for the dead. Even in daylight, there was a sense of trepidation about the place. As I returned to the road to take in the dilapidated shack, I noticed a sizeable monitor lizard's head stick up above the grass beside the fence. It eyed me for a few seconds, then slunk off down the side of the house. In a country famous for its urban density and high-rise living, this crumbling hovel felt entirely incongruous.

I bid farewell to Seletar Village by dancing down a little street and singing a song my nan used to croon to me from her armchair:

"Any time you're Lambeth way
Any evening, any day
You'll find us all
Doin' the Lambeth Walk."

And I did the "Lambeth Walk" in Singapore's Lambeth Walk! London's original Lambeth Walk was known for its street market before World War II but became famous for the song of the same name in the 1937 musical *Me and My Girl*. It was a jaunty, Cockney ditty and its walking dance was nothing more than a cocky, playful strut down the street. My nan always sang it with such panache before finishing with her trademark—a quick flash of her knickers. We were used to her skirt-lifting, but it could get a bit embarrassing, especially when she did it in the supermarket. If my old nan sang "Silent Night" with a church choir on Christmas Eve, she would round it off by lifting her skirt and showing off her bloomers.

So I felt it only right to offer a poignant tribute to my beloved grandmother and one of her favourite songs by "Doin' the Lambeth Walk" in Singapore. So if anyone living there recalls an *ang moh* flashing each house by lifting an invisible skirt, do not worry. It was only me.

I ended up lost in Seletar West Farmway 4. Well, I did not think I was lost. On the contrary, I was enjoying a decent amble around the Jalan Kayu countryside. But when I reached the end of Seletar West Farmway 4, I found myself standing before an unnamed property and was about to turn back when a Malay chap on a bicycle appeared and informed me there was nothing to see here. So I strode irritably back down Farmway 4, blundered through a spider's web, removed the fractious spider from my forehead and ended up outside The Animal Resort in Seletar West Farmway 5. It was a real hidden gem and a fine place to take children. A 2.2-hectare animal farm, The Animal Resort serves as a care centre and a hotel for pets. As soon as I wandered in, some geese ran across my feet. Many of the animals roamed around freely. There were goats, horses, rabbits, dogs and an enormous wood stork that was standing guard over a turtle pond. Now there probably is an uglier bird than the wood stork somewhere on the planet but I have never seen it.

The high point of my brief visit was undoubtedly the School of Pet Grooming. As the title suggests, trainee pet groomers and stylists come here to learn how to give Lassie a ponytail or Rover a tight perm. There were three silver tables similar to a room service trolley, with a pampered dog on each one. Nervous stylists hovered over each dog, snipping, trimming, stroking and brushing. For some inexplicable reason, all the pets were those tiny, mini-me dogs like Chihuahuas and Shih Tzus with bows in their hair. One stylist was in the process of giving a toy poodle what I can only call furry pigtails. It looked preposterous. As she fussed over the yapping midget, I admired the stylist's restraint. She obviously wanted to push Toto off the table. The walls were covered with framed certificates of achievement for pet grooming. The awards included bizarre categories like Best Poodle Perm, Cutest Poofy Tail and Closest Scrotum Shave. I would gladly give out the certificates for that one.

"I've seen some dogs' bollocks in my time," I would say. "But I've never seen a pair shaved this well before. I'm not sure why Fido is whimpering; that's one flawless scrotum he's got there. They look like a couple of fine fish balls."

As I finished the day in Jalan Kayu, I feel it only appropriate to acknowledge the man who supposedly gave the street its name. As the principal building officer for the British Royal Air Force in the Far East in the 1920s, C. E. Woods designed the airbase at Seletar. In recognition of his sterling work, Jalan Kayu, the road that leads to the airbase, shares his name. In Malay, *kayu* means "wood". But in recent years, and particularly since the Malaysia Cup era, the word *kayu* has taken on negative connotations. "Referee *kayu*", for instance, means that the man in black is wooden or dim-witted. So if you translate it literally, Jalan Kayu will always be dedicated to the man who shaped Seletar's airbase and colonial village. A plank.

CHAPTER 21

I was on a mission. I planned to track down Singapore's last kampong. Somewhere out in Lorong Buangkok there was not just a traditional Malay village of wooden homes, there were the final remnants of a country's past. A world of collective spirit, shared hardships and togetherness. In its race to build a first-world economy in the 1960s and 1970s, Singapore swept away the kampongs of its founding generations without batting an eyelid. *Attap* huts, crumbling timber homes, inadequate sanitation and polluted streams were all systematically bulldozed, cleaned up and drained to make way for the city of concrete we all know and love today.

But one survived. Hidden from public view, the small kampong of fewer than 20 rustic homes escaped the blueprints of the Urban Redevelopment Authority to allow its mostly Malay residents to continue a rural way of life not dissimilar to their great-grandparents. Being an endangered species, the village enjoys an almost mythical status. Singaporeans are vaguely aware of the country's last kampong being somewhere in Lorong Buangkok, but few have actually seen it. I wanted to catch a glimpse of Singapore's past before the future took it away once and for all.

Following a short bus ride from Ang Mo Kio MRT Station, I sauntered past the brand new HDB blocks of Buangkok Link and ventured into the living time capsule in Lorong Buangkok. Little more than a country lane, it was not signposted and a wonky lamp post with a smashed light encapsulated the street's spookiness. I trotted up the slight incline as quickly as I could. With Woodbridge

Hospital to my right and whistling trees to my left, there really was not the inclination to loiter. I came to the end of Lorong Buangkok and discovered, to my consternation, not a kampong but a retirement community called Surya Home. It was a rather run-down establishment, and not the first time I had seen the poor elderly folk of Singapore get the short straw for living in a country that does not subscribe to welfarism. I called out to a couple of Filipino nurses to ask for directions, but an elderly Chinese woman appeared from nowhere and took charge of proceedings.

"You want kampong? I find you kampong," she cackled.

She was certainly a peculiar woman. She held a pink toothbrush aloft like an Oscar, but there was not a single tooth left in her mouth. That made it difficult to concentrate for two reasons. First, I could not work out what she actually used the toothbrush for. And second, it is difficult to understand someone whose organs of speech are limited to a pair of gums.

"Yeah, I'm looking for a kampong. In Lorong Buangkok."

"This is kampong. Kampong is home," she mumbled vaguely through her toothless mouth. "This is my home. This is kampong. Kampong here."

"No, no, I'm looking for the old Buangkok kampong, not too far from Jalan Kayu."

"Wah, Jalan Kayu had a lot of kampongs last time. Wah, so many. Now no more already."

"That's great, thanks. But what about the one in Lorong Buangkok?"

"That one here, look. Kampong here. Surya Home. My kampong, Buangkok kampong."

Clearly medication time, the nurses ushered the poor woman and her toothbrush away and left me none the wiser. I was plodding off back into Lorong Buangkok when a middle-aged Chinese chap chased after me. His unkempt hair had been cut several different lengths and he had only three or four tooth stumps left in his mouth. Were the nurses dipping their patients' toothbrushes in sulphuric acid? His fingers were yellow and he constantly sucked on a cigarette stub that was neither lit nor fresh. The reek of tobacco made me nauseous.

"You want kampong at Lorong Buangkok?" he asked, grinning a toothless smile.

"Yeah, that's right. You know where it is?"

"Yeah, yeah I do. You are very tall," he replied.

"That's true. But do you know where the Buangkok kampong is?"

"Yah, yah, I know where, I know where ... Wah, you very tall, ah." He was mad. Friendly and eager to help, but mad. "My father was tall, you know. You look like my father. Do you know my father? Do you know where my father lives? Where does my father live?"

I thanked him and wished him well but he continued to shout out to me as I marched back down Lorong Buangkok, asking me where his father lived. Poor sod.

I retraced my steps and found another single lane off Buangkok Link. Once again, the dirt track was not signposted and appeared to double up as a coach park and a dumping ground. When the road ended, I went behind it and into the forest. Stone pillars ensured the path was only accessible on foot and a statue of Buddha had been placed on one of the pillars. I squeezed between the pillars and stepped over a man-made barrier of sticks and twigs tied together. The dense foliage was not inviting. The wild elephant grass towered above me in some places while my clomping around triggered slithering noises through the undergrowth every few paces. I was certainly apprehensive. Pythons and cobras are extremely common here. In the distance, I heard chickens and made out the tops of zinc roofs. But they were too scruffy to be part of a kampong and it quickly became clear that I had inadvertently stumbled across a group of squatters. A stray dog picked me out through the grass and started howling. Now, if I have learnt one thing during my tour of Singapore, it is that feral dogs are not solitary creatures. Suddenly, half a dozen of them were running towards me. I did not wait for a formal introduction. I was eager to keep my testicles. I sprinted back through the elephant grass. My arms flapped around in front of me in a vain attempt to see where I was going. I crossed a stream, startled a few lizards, hurdled the man-made barrier and almost knocked over the sacred Buddha before ending up on a muddy path in front of a ramshackle workshop.

At a stroke, I had gone back 40 years. I had found the kampong. The workshop was made of timber, with a sloped zinc roof. There were a number of Chinese deities on shelves in one corner, next to countless tins of Milo. At least half a dozen bicycles were tied to a tree and there was a broken washing machine stuck in the mud. I nervously called out. Although the workshop's owner was not around, his possessions and tools were laid out in front of me. Remember when your parents said that in their day, they could leave their doors and windows open all day long and no one would steal anything? Well, this was their day.

Behind the workshop, I glimpsed a couple of wooden houses and stepped tentatively inside Singapore's last kampong. I realised that I had missed the village earlier because it was almost entirely camouflaged by the forest. Coconut and banana trees served as natural borders for the kampong, along with a few mango trees and the ever-present elephant grass. Some workmen were laying pipes at the entrance of the kampong, providing the only telltale sign of modernity. The first two houses I passed were dilapidated and on the verge of collapse. The roofs had caved in and coconuts from the trees above had performed the role of the Dambusters' bouncing bombs, smashing through the walls and floors. It was a terrible sight.

I crossed a stream via a tiny bridge constructed from two old wooden doors that creaked ominously and had a peek at two intact houses next door. They were enormous. Taking into account the gardens, each property was at least twice the size of my four-roomed flat. And according to one of the residents, they only pay $13 a month in rent. No wonder families are reluctant to move.

As I peered around one of the houses, the owner appeared. And at the risk of making a facile comparison, I have wandered around some of the more upmarket estates and postcodes of Singapore and been greeted with indifference, suspicion and the odd devilish dog specialising in human castration. The kampong owner, however, invited this nosy stranger into his home.

"You want to see how big it is? Come, I'll show you the back garden," the amiable Malay chap said.

Well, his garden was indeed bigger than any other that I have seen in Singapore. It was a veritable menagerie. The guy had a dozen caged birds, five dogs that I counted and other animals that I did not manage to identify. The garden also incorporated a veranda, a table and chairs, two old wells previously used for sanitation, an electricity generator and a stream, all for $13 a month. The guy had been born in the kampong and returned to take care of the property after his parents died. We walked over to the stream where there were hundreds of empty oyster shells on the bank.

"They're not all from this tiny stream, surely?" I asked incredulously. My host did not wait for an answer. Instead he jumped into the ankle-deep stream and fished around in the water for no more than five seconds before producing an oyster. I thought I was in the presence of a native from a forgotten rainforest tribe. He shrugged his shoulders.

"Once a village boy, always a village boy," he said. Two of his dogs then bounded off down the stream.

"They're looking for snakes," said my indifferent host. "That's why I keep them. They've caught two pythons for me in this stream. And I had to cut down all the trees behind the stream to keep out the cobras."

The rustic simplicity of this man's life was difficult to take in. Everything seemed so incongruous. I was only 15 minutes from the air-conditioned modernity of Hougang Green Shopping Mall and his kampong faced the expensive private properties of Gerald Drive on the other side of the canal. And here we were plucking out oysters with our bare hands and chasing snakes down the stream. My pessimism suggested it could not last, but my host was adamant that his way of life would be preserved for at least another eight or nine years.

"Those pipes they're putting in where you came in are to improve the sanitation of all the houses," he said. "They wouldn't bother if they were going to knock us down. We need them though. We've always had problems with flooding."

That is an understatement. During the monsoon season, flood waters reach knee-level here and the kampong is often washed out. In the 1970s, frustrated residents bestowed a new name upon the village, Kampong Selak Kain, which is Malay for "lift up your sarong". I just love that. But my new friend was not going anywhere just yet. As he walked me to the home-made bridge across the stream, he said, "I've got to paint the place and do a lot of work, but I hope to stay. It was my parent's house. I can't let it fall apart."

I admired his optimism and I sincerely hope Kampong Selak Kain is spared the HDB bulldozers. And I am not patronising the residents. Nor do I pity them. They neither need nor crave my pity; they just want to be left alone to live quietly in their family homes. But then, the kampong in Lorong Buangkok is not there for my benefit. Nor should it remain solely to enable tourists to turn up and marvel at the rural simplicity of life in equatorial Asia. The kampong must stay because it is the only one in the country. Through the commendable work of the National Heritage Board, the government is finally accepting that no amount invested in interactive museums and fancy 3-D exhibits can resurrect dead history. There is no substitute for living, breathing history. If those traditional wooden homes ever pay the price for urban redevelopment, then one of the most vibrant, colourful and proud chapters of the Singapore Story closes forever. And the elusive kampong spirit dies with it.

CHAPTER 22

I left the past and quickly returned to the present when I took the train to the most controversial station in Singapore. When the doors opened at Buangkok Station, I was astonished. The station is an architectural marvel. Flawlessly designed with dazzling local artwork around its fringes, Buangkok feels more like an art gallery than an MRT station. But then, more people probably visit an art gallery. Only nine other people alighted with me. As I passed through the turnstile at the cavernous but deserted station, I noticed one lonely guy manning the information counter. As he looked thoroughly bored, I took it upon myself to cheer him up a bit.

"Excuse me, sir," I asked, gently tapping on the window. "Can you tell me where the white elephants are?"

He was stunned. "You want to see the white elephants?"

"Yeah, of course. They're very famous, you know. They made news all over the world and, as you can see, I've come a long way to see them."

"No, no, they've been taken down already."

"Oh dear. That's tragic. Has the art exhibition finished? Are the white elephants now displayed somewhere else?"

"No. They were taken down almost immediately. They were just cartoon elephants. Nothing serious."

"Oh, I see. Why were they put up here? Outside Buangkok MRT?"

"It was nothing. Just someone playing a joke. It was nothing very serious."

I beg to differ. The white elephant debacle was a joke, but a serious one. In 2005, residents and grassroots leaders in Buangkok had just about had enough. A gleaming, brand new $80 million MRT station sat proudly on the edge of their town, with trains trundling through every few minutes on the North-East Line. But the trains did not stop at the station because it was not open. Train operators had originally suggested Buangkok Station would open in 2008 when there would be enough housing units in the area to justify the expenditure. This did not please residents, to say the very least, many of whom had moved to the new town on the proviso that they would be provided with adequate transportation services. So the empty, ghostly station sat there every day: a giant white elephant in the heart of an expanding community.

Then in late August 2005, eight cardboard white elephants mysteriously appeared around the station's grounds to coincide with a ministerial visit. I loved the impudence and applauded the residents' sense of humour. Others did not. The cardboard cut-outs led to a police probe to find the culprits, who had not obtained the necessary permit. Not for the first time, Singapore threatened to become a laughing stock on the international stage. But on this occasion, common sense prevailed. It was a great day for Singapore. Not because residents had actively engaged in a benign political protest, but because the white elephant furore showed that everyone from the top down was finally taking this business of a sense of humour seriously. A local politician once remarked that Singapore must take this business of a sense of humour seriously; arguably the daftest remark ever uttered by any parliamentarian anywhere in the world. But ironically, the government is trying really, really hard to do just that.

Just a few months later, it was decided that Buangkok Station should be opened after all. At the residents' party to mark the occasion in January 2006, some students sold "Save the white elephant" T-shirts to raise money for charity, which was marvellous. But at the risk of bursting Buangkok's radical bubble, the fact that only nine other people alighted with me at the station may suggest that the station was not ready to be opened. When I exited the station, I was met with a sweeping view of nothing. There was an open field on one side and a half-finished housing estate on the other. It did not look promising.

I had decided to go to Buangkok to sample the Singapore I was leaving behind. If the kampong in Lorong Buangkok represents the country's past, then the new towns of Sengkang, Punggol and Buangkok in the northeast are stepping stones to the future. All three offer modern, luxurious HDB blocks that can easily be passed off as condominiums and the estates have been touted as a 21st-century township. But a house alone is not a home. When residents began moving into Sengkang in the late 1990s, there was a flood of complaints. Aside from the initial teething problems of any housing estate, such as dimly lit lift lobbies, concealed block numbers and leaking roofs, there were more pressing concerns that astounded me. Inadequate public transportation and a lack of linking roads were so serious that the debate reached Parliament. Residents understandably rushed to move into their ultra-modern apartments only to find a lack of community centres, coffee shops, schools, medical facilities and banks. At one point, around 1,000 households moved into their new Sengkang blocks every month in a township that covers over 1,055 hectares. That is almost twice the size of Ang Mo Kio. Eager homeowners were moving in faster than the amenities were being built.

The perceived incompetence was extraordinary. How could the HDB get it so right with Toa Payoh in the 1970s and yet seemingly get it so wrong with the new estates around Sengkang? It intrigued me because my English hometown of Dagenham had suffered the same problems. When the London County Council built the estate in the 1920s to rescue working-class Londoners from the East End's slums, it was lambasted for providing nothing more than red bricks and cement. At the very heart of the so-called British Empire was the world's biggest housing estate, but it failed to provide decent shops, schools and medical facilities for its tenants. There were not even any pubs! How on earth can you transport an entire community of Cockneys and dump them in the Essex marshes without giving them a few pubs? Dagenham still suffers from the after-effects of the town planners' short-sightedness. When town councils break up extended families in their pursuit of urban redevelopment, there must be a trade-off. The public facilities and amenities of the new town should, at the very least, be the equal of the community that has been left behind. Otherwise, what is the point of uprooting a family?

I sauntered down Sengkang Central to see if the town had righted its wrongs and found myself in a huge housing estate off Compassvale Drive. Now the first thing you notice about Sengkang is its sea-shanty, seafaring, "ahoy there, shipmates" architecture. As it was once the town of the seafarer and a port, Sengkang's planners incorporated its past into their designs, hence street names like Compassvale and Rivervale. The marine theme can be seen everywhere, from the metallic sails that hang off most of the blocks at Compassvale to the lighthouses and timber ship that feature inside Compass Point Shopping Mall. It certainly was not subtle but it was quirky, with the highlight being the shark's fin. Have you seen it? There may be several poking out around the estate, but I only found the one and it was freakish. I walked past a badminton court and there it was; a life-sized silver shark's fin sticking out of the grass.

"Hey lads, what the hell is that?" I asked the two teenagers playing on the court. "It looks like a shark's fin."

"It is a shark's fin," one of them replied. "It's part of the fish theme here. Stupid, right?"

Well, I do not know about stupid, but it was certainly bizarre. If a drunk stumbled across it at night, he might think he was drowning. Every time I looked at it, I could hear the primeval sound of John Williams' cello. To me, the architectural feature said "*Jaws*". To many older Chinese, it must say "wedding dinner".

The badminton court was occupied and there were other teenagers waiting to play. I also noticed matches in full swing at the basketball court and the street soccer pitch. In fact, all of the public courts and playgrounds were filled with youngsters. I realised that the designers had pulled off a masterstroke here, not by emulating the superficial features of a condo complex, such as fancy lift lobbies and marble floors, but by fostering a sense of community. The enclosed nature of the estate provided security. Building the blocks around the recreational facilities gave the estate a focal point, in this case the various sports courts, to enable younger residents to come together and play. Because the apartments themselves bordered the facilities, they provided an element of safety, a literal physical barrier from the outside world. I was very impressed. Children cannot play like this in a sprawling estate like Toa Payoh. Aside from the lack of green spaces and sports courts, they would invariably need to cross streets, void decks and roads to find an appropriate venue. Toa Payoh's centrality makes it an ideal location for working parents, but I now wondered what the old town actually offered their children. Compassvale, on the other hand, was a great place for sporty, energetic children to grow up safely. The swanky estate had a real self-contained, communal feel about the place. I will not get carried away and say that the kampong spirit had returned to Sengkang—the days of borrowing a cup of sugar and dashing through muddy streams to catch fish are long gone. But the town's heart is in the right place.

As time was getting on, I found a willing tour guide to show me around the townships of Sengkang and Punggol—the LRT. For those of you who share my utter contempt for all short forms, abbreviations and acronyms, the LRT stands for Light Rapid Transit (LRT), a mini-transportation network set up to serve the far-flung estates of Sengkang and Punggol. The Sengkang LRT, a $302-million driverless system, opened in 2003. It followed the much maligned Bukit Panjang LRT, which opened in 1999 and has since spent much of the time breaking down. Now I like the LRT. It is cute and convenient. But it is not a train. I mean, it is a train in the technical sense, but it is not really a train. The LRT reminds me of little dogs like Chihuahuas, Shih Tzus or, my personal favourite,

Cockapoos (a cross between a Cocker Spaniel and a Poodle). They are dogs in the literal mammal classification sense but, let's face it, they have got far more in common with other four-legged animals. Like hamsters. You will never read the headline "Man mauled by Chihuahua". Or see armed police officers send for the Shih Tzus before a drug bust. They call themselves dogs but, really, they look more like cats with big ears and hormonal issues. Well, the LRT is the public transportation equivalent of a Chihuahua. Those driverless contraptions masquerade as a sleek, steel train but, if the operators painted a face on the front windows, the cuddly carriages could hang out with Thomas, Percy and the Fat Controller. As the automated, single carriage chugged along the track, I kept hearing the dulcet tones of Ringo Starr telling the mischievous Thomas to come back and pick up his driver.

Not that the LRT was not a comfortable ride. On the contrary, the carriage was spotless, as you would expect here, and television screens played movie trailers to while away the time. It just felt like I was being transported from Terminal One to Terminal Two. Furthermore, the skytrain at Changi Airport could stake a valid claim that it provides a more scenic ride than the Sengkang LRT. By the time I had reached Bakau LRT Station, it was difficult to distinguish one side of the track from the other. The blocks on the left were beige with an orange window sill and the blocks on the right beige with a blue window sill. That was the extent of the variation in design. When the sprawling estate in Dagenham opened in the 1920s, there were reports of new tenants going shopping and not being able to locate their home when they returned. How does that not happen here? I would not be surprised if Sengkang resembled the *Village of the Damned* on a full moon, with dozens of lost residents staggering aimlessly around the streets shouting, "Where the fuck's my apartment?"

Toa Payoh, like the neighbouring older towns of Ang Mo Kio and Serangoon, has its faults, but uniformity is not one of them. Tall, short, fat and thin—apartment blocks of all shapes and sizes are welcomed in the Big Swamp. From my window in Lorong 2

Toa Payoh, I could count six blocks that were different in shape and colour and all within walking distance. The view from a window in Rivervale must resemble Huxley's *Brave New World*. I switched over to the Punggol LRT and alighted at Riviera LRT Station because it sounded French and exotic and, according to my street directory, it overlooked the Sungei Serangoon River. I need not have bothered. The amenities at Riviera consisted of an HDB block, a car park and a bus stop. It must be like the Rio de Janeiro Carnival here at weekends.

I took a bus to the jetty at the end of Punggol Road, which once offered seafood restaurants by the sea. Pig farms also dominated the vicinity back then, so heaven knows what the area must have smelt like. Now there was a jetty for fishermen and a small plaque to remember the 300 to 400 Chinese civilians who were executed here on 28 February 1942 by the Japanese military police. They had not done anything of course. The executions were part of the nationwide Sook Ching operation to purge the country of suspected anti-Japanese civilians. The plaque was installed in 1995 by the National Heritage Board, which has redoubled its efforts in recent years to commemorate key incidents in Singapore's short history but rarely gets the credit it deserves.

Apart from some parents making sandcastles with their children, the seafront was deserted. Few people visit Punggol Beach now. It is a shame because the beach was surprisingly clean and the sunset was breathtaking. There were a few kissing couples waiting to get it on after dark, but I barely noticed them. With weary resignation, I accepted the fact that I am destined to stumble upon every shagging couple in Singapore.

I finished the day inside the lift of Block 187 in Punggol Central. I cannot explain it really. I caught a brief glimpse of the HDB apartment block and wandered over. With its underground car park, palm trees, marble floors and cream-coloured apartments with wide, blue-tinted windows, the block easily fitted the dream of a 21st-century township. I had never seen a more attractive HDB apartment block. But best of all, Block 187 had a sexy lift voice.

I travelled up to the top floor accompanied by a seductive, arousing female voice. I pressed the top-floor button and she groaned, "Going up". The woman's pouty voice was straight out of a pornographic movie. I had a quick peek around the top floor but there was not an unblocked view of Punggol. Besides, I was eager to get back to the female orgasm. She did not disappoint. In fact, she even lifted a line direct from a porno movie. "Going down," whispered the woman, clearly quivering with lust. At that moment, an unforgettable scene from the movie *Fatal Attraction,* involving a lift and Glenn Close, suddenly popped into my head. I was not displeased; I had been thinking about Punggol's old pig farms.

CHAPTER 23

It was not always easy growing up in England. My parents divorced when I was in kindergarten, my mother worked long hours and my younger sister had to eat my sausages and mash. Those burnt bangers just floated in the potato purée and it is no coincidence that she is now a vegetarian. But at the end of every school year, we packed our bags and headed off for our annual caravan holiday in Clacton on the Essex coast. Before outrageous property prices in Britain forced people to take out a second mortgage to buy a doll's house, caravans were the destination of choice for most working-class families. Cheap, homely and easy to maintain, caravans afforded us a little castle by the seaside. We would stay for the entire six weeks of the summer holiday and live on a shoestring. The journeys were always special. As we drove out of Dagenham, my sister and I would tuck into the chocolate goodies provided for the two-hour journey. Twenty minutes later, my sister would reproduce the chocolate goodies all over my A-Team T-shirt. My mother would tell her off and my sister would cry and blame me for complaining when I clearly should have sat in silence for the remainder of the trip covered in vomit. Meanwhile, I would sulk all the way to Clacton because I had to bare my bony, milky-white chest to giggling lorry drivers.

Nevertheless, those caravan holidays were glorious. At our caravan park, there was a swimming pool, a video arcade, a clubhouse and a playground, all ideal locations to target pretty girls. But as my mother gave me a wonky haircut and a red turtleneck to go with my perpetually runny nose, I looked like a heroin addict going cold turkey. So I spent most of my days on the swings listening to the *Rocky IV* soundtrack on my portable tape recorder, which, I seem to recall, was the size of my HDB apartment. We divided our time between the pool, the park and the beach. Evenings were always spent at the cosy clubhouse with the other caravanners, all of whom came together to watch me take part in the annual fancy dress contest. Each year, my giggling mother covered me in green food dye and threw me onto the stage as "the world's skinniest Incredible Hulk". Oh, how we all laughed.

Without a doubt, those caravan holidays were easily the highlight of my childhood, as they have been for countless working-class children growing up in Britain. Singaporean children really do not know what they are missing. I have always believed that the biggest drawback of growing up in a small country is that there are very few places for a child to escape to. There is no space for a caravan park here and even if there was, I suspect it would lose out to a more lucrative shopping centre, condo complex or integrated resort.

Of all the coastal towns in Singapore, only one comes close to simulating the communal, caravan culture of my British childhood: Pasir Ris. I love everything about Pasir Ris and it is easily my favourite town in Singapore. The fact that few tourists or expats visit the place is nothing short of criminal. Once the home of poultry farmers and fishermen, the northeastern coastal town has long been considered an idyllic destination for day trippers and picnicking families.

A holiday town, Pasir Ris is one of the country's newer HDB estates with younger, more active residents favouring a healthier, outdoor lifestyle by the sea. At one time, Pasir Ris MRT Station had more bicycle stands than any other station in Singapore, and the town boasts one of the most scenic cycling trails in the country. They are certainly not couch potatoes in Pasir Ris.

I asked a member of staff at Pasir Ris MRT Station how long it would take to walk to NTUC Lifestyle World-Downtown East.

He looked utterly horrified. "You sure you want to walk?" he asked. "There's a feeder bus, you know. No need to walk."

"It's okay, I want to walk. I know it's not that far."

"It's very far. At least a 15-minute walk."

It took five minutes. That is another drawback that comes with living in such a small country. Distance is relative. On several occasions during my trip around the country, I was advised to take public transportation only to discover that my destination was no more than a couple of streets away or on the other side of a shady park. By and large, Singaporeans do not walk anywhere unless it is on an air-conditioned treadmill. And while we are on the subject, the next time a teenager steps into your HDB lift and casually presses the button to the second floor, pick the lazy bastard up by the scruff of the neck and throw him back out into the lobby. Can't healthy youngsters walk up a couple of flights of stairs anymore? The social and economic ramifications for the country are terrifying. Seriously.

Downtown East is the main reason why most people visit Pasir Ris today. Built by the National Trades Union Congress, the entertainment complex was little more than a couple of public swimming pools beside some holiday chalets when I first arrived. Now the entire facility has been transformed beyond recognition; the swimming pools gave way to the marvellous Wild Wild Wet water theme park, with the usual tunnel slides and wave pools. I have been a couple of times at the weekend and the park is never less than packed. The Escape Theme Park is a poor man's Disneyland, but the few decent rides are reflected in the reasonable admission fee.

Still, there is a certain mocking cynicism when it comes to Downtown East. Like Sentosa, the resort draws unfavourable comparisons to the magical kingdoms of Florida, the Gold Coast and now Hong Kong. It is an unfortunate symptom of the "whacking" culture that permeates society here. As there is very little to complain about in the economic and political arenas, there is a tendency to "just whack" trivial stuff such as minor bus fare increases, taxi drivers and Downtown East. Town planners are damned if they do and damned if they do not. Addressing the age-old gripe that there is nothing to do on this tiny island, NTUC spent $30 million to redevelop Downtown East and then endured further complaints from those unfairly comparing apples with oranges. If those gambling behemoths pencilled in for Marina Bay and Sentosa fail to live up to international standards of an integrated resort, then public criticism will be more than justified. But Downtown East more than adequately meets the needs of its community, NTUC members and the accidental tourist.

I went into Downtown East through the back entrance via Aranda Country Club and encountered a world that bore close similarity to my caravan holidays. There were teenagers shooting and killing things in the video arcades, market stalls that sold sweets, crisps and the usual tat only sold at seaside resorts, a kiddies' play centre and ball pool, a theatre for movies, concerts and the odd circus and the usual fast food outlets. Every time I have visited Downtown East, changes have been implemented and they are always for the better. On this occasion, a stretch of shops leading to the chalets had been upgraded and now sold magazines, hawker food and, rather strangely, VCDs.

Outside the Wild Wild Wet water theme park, I glimpsed four teenage boys flirting with girls as they tottered past. That is what it is all about—getting away from the books and blogs for a little quality time with the opposite sex. With far too many teenagers going to single-sex schools here, they need to savour every opportunity they can get to mingle.

As it was Friday, the weekends-only Escape Theme Park was closed so I hired a bicycle and poked my nose around Pasir Ris Park. Built on reclaimed land, the massive 71-hectare park is a charming, well-maintained retreat for families, fitness fanatics and, well, just about everyone. The Fishermen's Village served up the kind of seafood on the water's edge that once packed them in at Punggol; children had a quaint cycling trail for beginners, a maze garden and an adventurous adventure playground; and the mangrove swamp boasted a new boardwalk for nature enthusiasts. There was even a birdwatching tower that provided some decent graffiti on its top level. Someone had written "You shit on me, I shit on you", which displayed a Corinthian spirit of fair play if nothing else. Another hand had scrawled "No Vandalism!". I loved that.

Convinced I could not embrace Pasir Ris any further, I whizzed past a couple of carpenters who were hammering in the final few nails of a brand new pony stable. The foreman told me that within a month, children would be able to come here for pony-riding lessons followed by dinner at the adjacent café, all within the secluded setting of a breezy park overlooking the sea. Until the glittering doors to those integrated resorts are opened, there is simply no better venue to take your children for a day out, and that includes the half-finished Sentosa. The fad culture makes the pony stable a bit of a risky business venture but I sincerely hope it survives. Singapore can always eke out a little space for an alternative leisure activity and I have long had a soft spot for horses.

When I first met my wife, she was 16 and an accomplished horse rider. She devoted every spare moment to her beloved pony Pepi, attending to his every grooming need. Anyone in the horsey fraternity will tell you that the magnificent sturdy studs are prone to uncomfortable penis scabs. Pepi was no exception, and my wife would clinically pick them off. Now, most teenagers usually spend their puberty years drowning in a maelstrom of hormonal insecurities and self-doubt. So have you any idea what it does to a teenager's self-confidence when he discovers that his girlfriend spends her weekends examining the sexual organ of one of the most prodigiously well-developed mammals on the planet? When she said her favourite companion was hung like a horse, she meant it.

Having returned my borrowed bicycle, I reluctantly left Pasir Ris. I planned to spend the rest of the day in the neighbouring town that still conjures evocative images and scarred memories for people across the Asia-Pacific region by the mere mention of its name: Changi.

Home to both the world's finest airport and the darkest chapter in Singapore's history, Changi generates pride, sadness, anger and bitterness, depending on your age, race and nationality. Younger Singaporeans are proud of their airport; older Singaporeans recall Sook Ching. Australians and Brits think of concentration camps, hardship and brutality. The Japanese do not really talk about the place. And Nick Leeson will always equate the town with a prison cell and colon cancer. It is many things to many people but, for me, it has always been about the history. So I took the No. 89 bus along Loyang Avenue to find Fairy Point Hill. I was going for three reasons. First, the name made me laugh. Second, I knew that there was something vaguely historical about the place. And third, no one I had spoken to had a clue where Fairy Point Hill was or what was actually there.

I alighted beside Hendon Camp, home to some of the finest commandos in Singapore, and almost bumped into a couple of Singapore's military elite. Surely, the buffed, bronzed pair would know where I was going.

"Hey guys, do you know where Fairy Point Hill is?" I asked.

They had no idea. "I've never heard of the place. Oh wait, do you mean the one over at Changi Village beside the hawker centre?" one of them ventured.

"No, that's the ferry point. I mean Fairy Point. It's supposed to be off Cranwell Road, which we're in now."

"Sorry, never heard of it. But I know for sure it's not anywhere around here."

Fairy Point Hill proved to be 200 metres away in the next street. Those commandos have got a wonderful sense of direction, haven't they? Not that I can blame them for being unaware of Fairy Point's whereabouts because, technically, I am not sure if it is even supposed to exist. Besides, they were not alone in their ignorance. After ambling past the government bungalows and reaching the end of Cranwell Road at Changi Beach Club, the security guard there also insisted that Fairy Point Hill did not exist. The road proved to be right behind him.

I turned back down Cranwell Road and noticed a side turning that obviously did not intend, or want, to receive any visitors. A striped barrier and concrete pillars ensured that vehicles could proceed no further. There were no street names, signposts, mailboxes, lamp posts, electricity cables or anything to suggest that the crumbling path was a street. But it clearly led to a grassy hillock and, according to my street directory, the location of Fairy Point Hill so I smothered myself in insect repellent and ducked under the barrier. I followed the cracked, uneven road up the hill, past the overgrown weeds. In the overhanging branches of a tree, a couple of green parrots screeched at me. The heat was insufferable so, after checking that there were no giggling lorry drivers around, I peeled off my drenched T-shirt and invited all the mosquitoes in Changi to attack my flabby nipples. They duly obliged.

I turned a corner at the top of the deserted hill and there it was—the most haunted of haunted houses. On the crest of Fairy Point Hill stood a stately two-storey colonial mansion. The majestic building was cream-coloured with bright, sturdy pillars that have long been popular in military architecture. There was a rusty flagpole on the roof. Several archways, flawlessly carved out of timber, adorned the façade and gave the doors and windows an undeniable elegance. You do not come across historic structures like this in Singapore very often.

Sadly, the house was falling apart. The interior had been gutted, the paint was peeling off every wall, chunks of plaster were strewn across the floors and electricity cables hung out of every crevice. With all the doors and windows either smashed or removed, I peeked into the rooms. They were all empty. I lacked the courage to step inside because signs all over the building warned that trespassers would be prosecuted and, if I am being honest here, the house was spooky, even in daylight. So I wandered around the back instead. Weeds covered the outside toilets and storeroom. I was desperate for a pee but the constant rustling in the undergrowth and the strange surroundings ensured I left Fairy Point Hill cross-legged. The place was just too damned eerie. At the bottom of the slope, I noticed a sign that I had missed earlier. It had been posted up by the Urban Redevelopment Authority to inform interested parties that Fairy Point Hill, now euphemistically named Changi Point Cove, was up for sale as a prime residential and entertainment site.

Now, at what point will all this stop? How many historic sites, sacred grounds or green spaces will be auctioned off, demolished or dug up before someone suggests calling it a day? With every parcel of historic land that is sold off, Singapore sells another piece of its soul to the highest bidder. It really is that simple.

I later discovered that the dilapidated building was originally a command house for British forces. Designed by colonial architects and completed in the 1930s, Fairy Point Hill's strategic location in the island's leafy northeastern corner ensured it played an integral role as a British air- and naval base. After Singapore's independence, the building was taken over by the Ministry of Defence and served as the SAF Command Headquarters. History oozes from every nook and cranny and the National Heritage Board could work wonders with the house. The dying site is crying out to be resuscitated and turned into a World War II museum or archive, a tribute to those imprisoned in Changi, a memorial to those who perished in the Sook Ching operation or even an administrative centre for the Heritage Board. Changi has more than enough hotels and chalets to take care of the future; what it does not have is enough buildings to take care of its past.

CHAPTER 24

I should point out that Changi is doing many things right. I left Fairy Point Hill and found myself on the exceptional Changi Point Boardwalk. Over 2 kilometres long, the boardwalk begins at the Changi Beach Club, follows the edge of the coastline and finishes at the ferry terminal in Changi Village. When I say the edge of the coastline, I mean just that. At one point, the platform took me above the rocks on the shore and within a couple of feet of the crashing waves. And its information panels are faultless. I learnt that a famously tall "Changi tree" (most likely *Sindora wallichii* and believed to have provided the town with its name) was removed by the British to stop the Japanese using the local landmark as a marker for their guns. I cannot help but feel that if the British had spent less time chopping down historic trees and more time worrying about the tens of thousands of Japanese troops who were making their way towards the Johor Straits, the events of 1942 might have been a little different. I also found out that Changi Village was a popular destination for tigers in the early 1900s. They swam over from Johor, stopped over in Pulau Ubin for a bit of wild boar and then made their way over to Changi. That route is now popular with illegal immigrants.

At the end of the boardwalk, I took a bus to Upper Changi Road North to have a quick peek at something that the National Heritage Board really has got just right. Opened in 2001, the Changi Chapel and Museum is housed inside a gentle, respectful white building and commemorates those who were imprisoned in the vicinity during the Japanese Occupation. Admission was free, as it should be for every museum, and there were excellent storyboards and poignant keepsakes, diaries and clothing that once belonged to the POWs. And the touching replicas of the Changi Murals, sketched by ailing bombardier Stanley Warren, have to be seen to be believed. Warren's story is truly one of the most uplifting accounts of World War II.

Increasingly sick from his incarceration, Warren kept his spirits up by drawing a number of religious murals, such as *The Last Supper* and *The Resurrection*, on the walls of Roberts Barracks, Changi Camp, which was used as a POW hospital, beginning in October 1942. Now, this was one brave man. He had eight kidney stones removed with no anaesthetic, and still worked on the murals. The Japanese were hardly going to provide paintbrushes and easels so Warren improvised. He used clumps of human hair for paintbrushes, brown camouflage paint and crushed-up billiard chalk for blue paint. When the war ended, Warren assumed the paintings had been destroyed by the Allied forces' bombing campaign, returned to England and thought no more about them.

Then the story took a remarkable turn. In 1958, the murals were uncovered, by accident, in Changi Camp Block 151. Stanley Warren was somehow tracked down in England, where he worked as an art teacher, and was invited back to Singapore to restore and finish the Changi Murals. He made several trips back and they were finally completed in 1988. He died in 1992. Due to their sensitive location, the originals are not open to the public, but the replicas at the Changi Museum are respectfully displayed. You must see them.

What I have always liked about the Changi Chapel and Museum is its sombre subtlety. I visited Pearl Harbor several years ago and it felt more like a Disneyland attraction. First, there was the film with the bombastic sound effects, accompanied by the ever-present chest-beating patriotism and bugle blowing. Then came the trip to the viewing platform from which you could peer into the sea and stare at the rusty USS *Arizona,* an experience that

I found rather uncomfortable. But that was only slightly less macabre than the sweaty tourists in floral shirts and knee-high white socks dashing around with their camcorders, ordering their children to pose beside the watery graves of dead servicemen. Americans just cannot do subtle, even when it comes to war memorials. But the quiet, reflective tone at Changi is perfect.

I continued down Upper Changi Road North and stopped outside the new, pristine Changi Prison. Part of the modern complex opened in 2004 to some controversy. Not for the first time, the authorities had not entirely considered the political and historical sensitivities when announcing that the old, decaying prison, built in 1936, would be torn down and replaced. For many war veterans around the world, as well as thousands of elderly Singaporeans who suffered Japanese persecution, the prison was a symbolic reminder of their horrific past. And we are not talking about a handful of aunties and uncles here. Between 1942 and 1945, around 76,000 POWs were interned in the area. Not surprisingly, letters to the press came from Australia and New Zealand, begging the authorities to respect their memories of the dead. But if cemeteries cannot be spared, then an archaic, crumbling prison has got no chance.

The original Changi was demolished, but a sensible compromise was made and I was here to see it. I strode quickly past the shiny Prison Link Centre, which bears more than a passing resemblance to a shopping centre with its gleaming glass frontage. I arrived at the main entrance to the prison and found what I was looking for. I could not miss it. An old, grey, 180-metre stretch of wall facing Upper Changi Road North, with a turret at each end, stood out among the new shiny structures. The stark, depressing façade now provides the only gateway to the site's past as it was rightfully gazetted by the Preservation of Monuments Board as a National Monument. Common sense prevailed as the authorities finally acknowledged the tremendous emotional value of the original Changi Prison. Even the present Australian foreign minister, Alexander Downer, whose father endured three years as a POW in Changi, applauded the decision.

I could not really see much of the old wall from the street so I approached a young Indian woman who was coming through the prison gates at that moment.

"Is there any chance I can go in and have a look around?" I asked.

"Can you go inside? This is Changi Prison." Her tone made it clear that she was dealing with a moron.

"No, sorry, what I meant was, is there a museum or an exhibition inside?"

"Of course not, it's a prison."

She hurried off to the nearest bus stop as a genial guard gently ushered me back towards the street. Security is certainly stringent at Changi Prison. And I do ask some bloody stupid questions at times.

The following morning I returned to the charming Changi Village in a very chirpy mood. The giddy prospect of a little sea travel always gets me excited and I planned to spend a rustic day on Pulau Ubin. I arrived at the new Changi Point Ferry Terminal to find it transformed into a modern, airy building with a bar on its roof overlooking Serangoon Harbour. The only downside was the bumboat drivers are more finicky now. They will not start their engines until there are 12 passengers waiting to travel (or you are willing to charter the entire boat for $24 to match the $2-per-person fee). But I was suitably entertained while I waited. A couple of perspiring, overweight Chinese gentlemen sat on the bench beside me. If you needed a stereotypical profile of two loan sharks, these greasy guys fitted the bill. Three students joined us, one of whom was a tall, attractive Chinese girl. Well, that was it, wasn't it? In a mixture of English, Singlish and Hokkien, the guys remarked how sexy the girl was, what they would like to do to her and in what positions. I have always found these conversations utterly engrossing. Do such guys really believe that all that lustful snorting, guffawing and hand signalling will lead the beautiful young woman to say, "Do you know what? I've succumbed to your irrepressible charm. Come, let's find an empty bumboat. I want to have sex with you both right now."

The nifty journey took 10 minutes and I stepped onto Pulau Ubin's jetty and back to the 1960s. Whatever route you take, whether you walk, cycle or drive, Pulau Ubin is a peaceful, beautiful getaway. Its very charm lies in its simplicity. The island offers a rustic retreat of kampongs, wooden jetties, undisturbed wildlife, old plantations and a traditional agrarian lifestyle, in which residents rely on prawn farms, fishing, provision stores and renting bicycles to survive. Being an island of undulating, granite hills, granite mining once provided work for thousands of settlers in the 19th century. This occupation also gave the island its name; Pulau Ubin means "Granite Island" in Malay. But the quarries are no longer in operation. They are now filled with water and vegetation is recolonising the areas. In fact, I noticed reforestation taking place all over the island, which was most pleasing. Across most parts of the island, the sound of silence is still deafening. Of course, you will still occasionally encounter wearisome types who carp on about there being nothing to do on Pulau Ubin. Shoot them.

I rented a mountain bike from an ebullient woman who had lived on the island for over 40 years, whizzed past the shops, eateries and stray dogs (those buggers could not catch me on a bike) and headed into the countryside. It was delightful. I cycled through old coconut and rubber plantations and around the picturesque Pekan Quarry, stopping twice to allow monitor lizards to swagger across the road, and then headed west along Jalan Endut Senin.

One of the joys of cycling is being part of the secret society of fellow cyclists. It is like the masons. There are secret signals, expressions and comments shared only among cyclists and only when passing each other. A brief downward glance denotes a serious cyclist not to be trifled with. Raising your eyes to the sky followed by a brief sigh and a smile indicates a social cyclist who is not as fit as he should be. Looking down at your pedals suggests a red-faced, panting cyclist who is in no mood to talk to anyone. While open-mouthed, wide-eyed horror insinuates that you are about to collide with your fellow secret society member and you might wish to get out of the way.

There are also the snatches of conversation. The quick "Hello, lovely day" is always practical when cycling downhill. But in Pulau Ubin's unhurried, tranquil setting, there was time for slightly longer exchanges. There were comments like "The countryside here is beautiful", "We must be mad to cycle in this weather", "Hang in there, the jetty's just up ahead", "Gee, that's a nice bike" and "You don't get many of them to the pound, do you?".

I stopped at a kampong where a homeowner sold cold drinks to day trippers. I already had a bottle of water in my bag, but I loved his hand-painted sign which read "Oh yeh, oh yeh, y u so like that? Buy a drink lah!", so I did. Remembering my manners, I stood at the door and called out to the guy. He appeared, but was clearly none too pleased that I had called him out to the front door. He ushered me into his kitchen and left me to pick out a drink from a cool box while he turned his back on me and returned to his washing up. He was not being rude. He trusted me. They still do not feel the need to lock their doors on Pulau Ubin.

I pedalled past the new Marina Country Club, which I must say has been blended in with its rural environment rather well. Partially covered by trees, the simple wooden chalets with their mock thatched roofs were not ostentatious. No one hankers for another concrete jungle on Pulau Ubin, but the sports and adventure retreat actually matches its habitat. If the Urban Redevelopment Authority insists that further construction is required on the island, let's have more of this please.

I was heading towards Jalan Wat Siam and Kekek Quarry when a small sign caught my attention. The sign caught my eye because it was written in English, German and Chinese; a linguistic combination you do not expect to find on Pulau Ubin. The sign said "German Girl Shrine" and an arrow pointed towards a narrow gravel path. Now I do not know about you but I will always make time to visit the shrine of a dead German girl at the end of a country lane in a remote corner of a tiny Asian island. I raced off down the track and soon found myself bouncing over ragged rocks, chipped stones and fallen branches. I puffed my way up a steady incline and found myself in an open field surrounded by *lalang* grass. The gravel track was uneven and slippery. It was like taking part in a motocross race. I swerved down a sharp left slope and stumbled upon a striking yellow hut. It was shaded beneath two trees; other than that, the area was deserted. I peered through the window of the hut and jumped back. There was a lavishly decorated altar at the far end of the room with a large white urn in the centre. This was the dead German girl's shrine. I turned the handle of the bright yellow door and, to my utter disbelief, it opened. The smell of joss sticks was overwhelming and there were half a dozen lit candles scattered around the room. Someone had been here before me. On the altar were a number of pitiful offerings to a teenage girl, including cheap perfumes, soaps and make-up mirrors. There was also a newspaper clipping about the German girl that some kind soul had nailed to the timber.

Her tale was undeniably fascinating. According to local folklore, the dead girl was the daughter of a coffee plantation owner on the island. After World War I, British soldiers did not take too kindly to having Germans making a good living on one of their crown colonies so they marched in to intern the parents. The young girl apparently escaped through the back door, lost her footing at the edge of the quarry and plummeted to her death. Chinese workers carried her remains to the crest of a quarry hill and gave her a proper burial. Then, of course, devotees began turning up to pay their respects and pray for good fortune. One or two must have hit the jackpot because devotees are known to come from as far as Myanmar and Thailand to pray for wealth and happiness. According to folklore, quarry excavation meant that the grave was exhumed in 1974 and the girl's remains were rehoused here. At weekends, devotees still light a candle for the girl, leave a small present and pray for a little something in return.

It is a great story. But there must be an easier way to strike 4D and get rich.

I spent no more than five minutes at the northern beaches of Noordin and Maman. Unlike the packed beaches around Sentosa and the East Coast, the sand was untouched, the sea was reasonably clean and there was not a single tanker on the uncluttered horizon. But all of that was academic, thanks to the bloody awful fences that have been erected just past the water's edge to keep out illegal immigrants. I cannot begin to express how depressing and unsightly it all looked. The immigrants may not be able to get in but snorkelling Singaporeans cannot get out either and heaven knows what detrimental effect the bamboo barricades have had on Ubin's indigenous wildlife.

At the point where Jalan Maman and Jalan Sam Heng meet, I had stopped for a drink when I heard an intense, high-pitched squeal echo through the trees. I nearly fell off my bike. Being the shameless coward that I am, I waddled from side to side and pulled back from the edge of the forest. Although the foliage was thick, I spotted a short, stubby hairy tail wagging through a narrow clearing. It was a wild boar. Satisfied that it was a safe distance away and the road was downhill if I needed a quick getaway, I crept towards the animal. Wild boars are generally harmless, but they will attack with their tusks if they feel cornered. A deep snort followed by a quick rustling through the undergrowth stopped me dead in my tracks. I crouched and peered through the trees again. There were two of them. Grey, heavy and over a metre in length, the boars snorted in my general direction and continued to sniff the ground. As it was getting dark, the nocturnal creatures were foraging for food. It was a priceless moment. But I was not going to test my good fortune by venturing any closer, even if I had paid my respects to the dead German girl. The burly boars continued on their merry way through the forest, grunting at each other in a dismissive fashion that was uncannily reminiscent of my grandparents.

I love Pulau Ubin and I know I will dearly miss its traditional, rustic simplicity when I leave Singapore. Around 300,000 people visit the 1,020-hectare island every year. Of that figure, a substantial number are tourists and there are over four million people living in Singapore. The figure could be much higher and the residents would almost certainly welcome the additional revenue. So go to Pulau Ubin. Find $2 for the bumboat and go this weekend. I cannot promise you anything but peace and quiet, the shrine of a dead German girl and, if you are lucky, the odd glimpse of a wild boar. But the island does provide a temporary escape from that jungle on the other side of Serangoon Harbour.

CHAPTER 25

And so to Singapore's biggest and most popular park. East Coast Park stretches across some 20 kilometres of reclaimed land in the southeast of the country. Boasting just about every outdoor and indoor pursuit imaginable, the park's theme is one of "Recreation For All" and I do not disagree. At weekends, families enjoy barbecues on the beach under breezy coconut trees while fitness enthusiasts cycle, skate, bowl, swim or smack a few golf balls around a driving range. The only slight problem I have with the East Coast is that it has a higher proportion of wankers than elsewhere.

On any given Sunday, the cycling and skating paths are undeniably swamped with idiots. After gathering at the nearby Idiot Club, these skaters don their wraparound sunglasses and knee and elbow pads and spend the afternoon irritating as many people as possible. The Idiot Club generally accepts two classes of skater: Beginner and Expert.

The beginner's task is simple: totter along the skating path for three steps, then fall over in front of half a dozen cyclists and pedestrians. Repeat. All bloody day long. The expert skater's job, on the other hand, is to define coolness with every effortless stride. With their aviator shades, Lycra shorts, bare chests and hands behind their stooped backs, these guys are so cool it hurts. To everyone else, they look like silly sods with lumbago. But when the two groups come together, as they frequently do at East Coast Park, they form a congested traffic jam of Rollerblades, such that the casual walker cannot cross the path without being poleaxed by a giggling beginner or knocked into a bird sanctuary by a speeding extra from *Starlight Express*.

Taking refuge from a heavy downpour, I stood under a shelter beside the old Big Splash water slide park and waited for my clothes to dry. When the rain stopped, members of the Idiot Club quickly resumed their weekend's activities. A French couple pulled up at a barbecue pit beside me to allow the woman to adjust her skates while her partner perfected his spins. With his slicked back hair and enormous aviator glasses, he had clearly gone for the Alain Delon look. But his appearance suggested that he had just escaped from the early 1980s. Do you remember the TV series *Magnum, P.I.*? Well, this guy looked like the butler. With legs apart and hands on his hips, he performed numerous spins, much to the admiration of his sophisticated companion. Now I know the French believe their European neighbours across the English Channel are an uncouth lot. The Brits might lack fashion sense and stubbornly insist that leggings go with anything. We might drink more beer, swear at football referees and eat chips with everything. But I am proud to say that if an Englishman wore anything Lycra and pirouetted on a pair of roller skates in a public park, his embarrassed partner would say he looked a prat.

I arrived at the Big Splash end of the East Coast because that is where Scott and I first went 10 years ago. Singaporeans had told us that the Big Splash swimming pool was a popular hang-out (times change so quickly, don't they?) and we decided to pay it a visit for no other reason than the name of the water slide park sounded like "dick splash", which is a childish vulgarity in Britain. I wandered along the path near Big Splash for a bit. There was a persistent drizzle in the air but that did not stop a middle-aged Malay couple from insisting that they could defy science and get a barbecue going in the rain. The husband fussed over the satay sticks while his wife held an umbrella over both their heads. Every few seconds, the husband made a futile attempt to light the wet charcoal and the wife shouted at him when the charcoal predictably failed to ignite. This went on for several minutes. It was better than Punch and Judy.

Then I made an impetuous decision. I noticed a sign that offered kayaks for rental and impulsively decided that what I craved in my life at that moment was to sit in a plastic hammock, in damp clothes, in the drizzle, on the sea. I collected my bright yellow kayak from the shop inside Big Splash and felt entirely satisfied with the $6 rental fee. I had to pick up the kayak and, through a combination of lifting and dragging, carry the thing out of Big Splash, across the skating and cycling paths, around the excitable members of the Idiot Club, down the beach and drop it into the sea. By the time I had finished, I was ready to take the kayak back. But I must say it was worth it. The rain took a breather, the heavy clouds parted and the sun peeked through for the first time that day. I felt quite the mariner, rowing along the shoreline, waving at fishermen and disturbing their fish, narrowly missing children's heads with my paddle and generally making a decent stab at joining the Idiot Club. Exhausted after 10 minutes of, quite frankly, ineffective rowing, I decided to lie back for a bit and go wherever the sea took me. Five minutes later, I looked around to find a thick film of oil floating on the surface of the sea around the kayak. It was black, gritty and extremely unpleasant. Just 20 metres away, children splashed around in the sea. The East Coast is a fine place to go kayaking but I am not sure that I would want to swim in it.

After I had dragged the kayak back to the shop, I jumped straight onto a hired bicycle. Big Splash is at the far western end of East Coast Park. Knowing that it is 20 kilometres long, I had plenty of ground to cover and set off for the National Sailing Centre at the opposite end. The number of extended Malay families I passed was remarkable. Children, parents, grandparents, aunts and uncles were gathered around various barbecue pits, cooking, eating, drinking, pitching a tent, listening to music, reading newspapers, kicking a ball or playing board games. I hold the deepest respect and admiration for the Malay community's ability to still appreciate and enjoy the simpler things in life despite living in a frenetic, urban metropolis. Watching the happy children mess around on the beach while their parents prepared their picnic lunch brought back memories of my family's unostentatious beach holidays when I was growing up in Essex. It made me smile.

East Coast Park has always been a curious place because it has not always been there. It is an underwater world brought to the surface. Built on reclaimed land after 1966, East Coast and the Marine Parade estate behind it arose from the seabed. In just over 20 years, over 1,000 hectares of land was reclaimed for recreational and residential development. But there is always a cost. Just past the underpass at Amber Road, I noticed the by-product of rapid land reclamation—erosion. A sizeable area along the coastline had been roped off because it appeared on the verge of collapsing. Huge chunks of the shoreline, riddled with plant and tree roots, lay on the empty beach and, if the unstable ground I stepped on was any indication, more will follow. The very land that was extended, over a period of many years, is receding quite quickly. Apparently, the stone and concrete structures built to protect the new coastline from excessive erosion, known as breakwaters, might not be up to the task. Originally, the sea went between them, which lessened the impact of the waves and explains why you see C-shaped beaches along the East Coast. But stronger, more aggressive waves are now going over the breakwaters and smacking into the reclaimed land. Coastline erosion is a natural phenomenon, of course, but not a popular one here I would have thought. East Coast Park is barely 40 years old, but the number of areas cordoned off is clearly increasing. The next time you visit the East Coast, count the number of benches inside those roped-off zones. There are a lot. And yet Singapore marches towards higher population targets (eight million has been mentioned more than once) by investing billions in land reclamation to eventually house everyone. But the sea is gradually taking the land back, free of charge.

I cycled past the bustling Marina Cove; a football clinic, where two mini-Hitlers barked orders at terrified seven-year-olds; a sandcastle corner; and four teenage boys performing handstands and cartwheels on the beach together. It was certainly an eclectic mix. At the bird sanctuary, I spotted my favourite sign to date. In a swampy area covered with long grass was a sign that read "Long Grass Area". Whatever next? Signs that say "A Really Big Tree" or "An Empty Muddy Field"? I assumed the sign served as a public safety notice. If it were not there, perhaps the sanctuary would be littered with fallen cyclists shouting, "Who forgot to put a bloody sign here? Why didn't someone tell me there was long grass in here? I cycled right into it, couldn't see anything and tumbled over a bird's nest."

The extensive makeover at East Coast Lagoon was amazing. The venue had recently been converted into Singapore's first cable ski park in which wakeboarders are pulled along by cables suspended overhead from pylons in one loop around the lagoon. I watched several skiers somersault and backflip off ramps with begrudging admiration. I cannot even skateboard. A young couple joined me at the lagoon to marvel at the East Coast's latest and, I have to say, most impressive attraction.

"It's great, isn't it?" I said cheerily. "But it looks like they've lost their speedboat, eh?"

The guy stared at me with the utmost seriousness. "No, no, they don't use a speedboat here. No need."

"I know that. It's just as well because that guy's obviously lost his."

"No, he hasn't. He doesn't need one. Look. The cables pull him around."

The couple gave me a blank look. I suspect they give many people blank looks. I reminded them to look both ways when they crossed the road and pedalled off.

It was getting late and I still planned to get over to Katong Park so I upped the pace a bit. As I passed yet another bird sanctuary, one of our feathered friends, and I swear this is true, defecated on my exposed shoulder. That had never happened to me before and I fancy myself as a bit of an amateur ornithologist. But here I was in a public park, travelling downhill on a mountain bike and yet somehow a bird managed to smother my shoulder with something that bore a remarkable similarity to pork rib soup. Optimistic types will intercede at this moment and insist it is lucky to be covered in the excrement of another animal. And do you know something? They are completely wrong.

No more than two minutes later, I cycled purposefully towards Bedok Jetty. Cycling towards me was a chubby Chinese girl who decided at that very millisecond that she fancied a breezy ride down the jetty. Being a junior member of the Idiot Club, she waited until she was certain it was a kinetic impossibility for me to avoid a collision before turning right. As the oblivious girl manoeuvred her bike to ensure maximum impact, I hit the brakes and they squealed like a traumatised pig. Performing a melodramatic emergency stop, my bike skidded in a straight line for an impressive 10 metres. I almost retained my balance but my momentum forced the back wheel to swerve 180 degrees to my right and I landed on that side of my body. For several, not uninteresting, seconds, I continued to slide along the ground, removing much of my skin's outer layer in the process, while still sitting on the bike. It was quite a feat. I eventually came to a halt in front of Bedok Jetty. Eager to milk the sympathy from bystanders, I remained prostrate for a bit with the bike on top of me, nursing my cuts and complaining loudly about "these bloody kids today". The back wheel was still turning slowly, adding a theatrical touch to the scene. One cyclist offered to help me to my feet and another shouted at the girl to stay in her lane. The girl was fine, of course. My sensational emergency stop had permitted her just enough time to move out of the way before I tumbled over. She peered down at me, muttered a brief "sorry" and pedalled off into the sunset.

"Well, at least you're all right," I shouted after her. But the moment had passed. Public sympathy was no longer forthcoming and devoted members of the Idiot Club were hurtling towards me. So I returned the bike to the rental shop, washed my cuts, took the underpass beneath the ECP and found myself at Singapore's original park by the sea.

Before the East Coast, there was Katong Park. In the 1950s, when land reclamation was still a pipe dream, Singaporeans flocked to the park that boasted a coastal swimming bay. Built in the 1930s, Katong Park is one of the oldest parks in the country. Famous for its coconut plantations, the place began life as a fort, protecting what is now Keppel Harbour, then became a Japanese war factory during the Occupation before ending up being the place to be seen by the sea. At weekends, Malays held popular dances and the Peranakans, Eurasians, Jews, Arabs, Ceylonese, Punjabis and the seriously wealthy flocked to Katong Park (the condos and swanky houses around Meyer Road are their legacy). They came for the swimming bay. It is interesting to note that the bay was enclosed by a fence to protect paddlers from the strong currents and the odd stray shark. Similar fences are used around Pulau Ubin's beaches today to keep out illegal immigrants.

Katong Park is also a historic site. On 24 September 1963, the park was bombed as a result of Indonesia's Konfrontasi (Confrontation) campaign against the formation of Malaysia. Two more bombs exploded there in the following two weeks, triggering two years of violence across the country. Then in 1966, land reclamation started on the East Coast and England won the World Cup (the latter has no relevance whatsoever but I thought I would mention it). The construction of East Coast Parkway left Katong Park overshadowed, in every sense. I stood at the edge of the park now and all I could see was a dog-run area and the concrete leviathan of the ECP. Fifty years ago, I could have jumped into the sea from here. It is extraordinary really.

I glanced through the long list of rules and regulations for the dog run, one of which stipulated that "bitches on heat are not allowed in this facility". I have been to Essex nightclubs that had a similar ruling. I wandered past the dog run and noticed a fenced-off area. It was the fort! Partially excavated, it was clearly part of Fort Tanjong Katong, the 19th-century British fort. I was excited. Built in 1879 to protect Singapore from a possible Russian invasion, the fort is one of the oldest in Singapore and is commemorated by the adjacent Fort Road. The military structure appeared to be in the process of being excavated as it was only partially exposed.

The section was made of brick, spoon-shaped and about 10 metres long and 3 metres across at its widest point. Little slats provided spyholes and what must have been a good vantage point to spot incoming vessels off the eastern coast of the island. But the site was extremely odd. I could not find any information panels or plaques; nothing to indicate what the structure was. Dog walkers, joggers and foreign domestic workers all drifted past the archaeological dig without giving the historic gem a second glance. Why should they? It was fenced off, unnamed and offered the curious visitor no information. Without that, it was nothing more than a lifeless lump of dusty rock.

I found out later that the fort had been reburied during the 1960s (the British made a real hash of their original attempt to bury it in the early 20th century) and rediscovered by a Katong resident who spotted some incongruous rocks sticking out of the ground in 2001. Three years later, a community project kicked off a dig to determine the size of the fort. Diggers chipped away at the soil for 10 months and much of the perimeter wall of the 6,000-square metre fort was revealed. But no one was quite sure what to do next. So, and you really could not make this up, a decision was taken to rebury the fort—again—to protect it from the weather. By early 2006, there was just one section left uncovered. The one I stood above now. It was crazy. Having been buried, reburied, dug up and reburied again, the fort's future remains uncertain. It could be declared a national monument but there has been no firm decision because historic sensitivities must, as always, be balanced with economic sensitivities. Katong Park occupies prime real estate and is surrounded by condos, with more to come judging by the noisy construction sites that I saw. Perhaps the government could turn Fort Tanjong Katong into a casino.

I hope something is done to preserve the fort because Katong Park was certainly a comely little spot and deserves more visitors. Not that the park was empty. On the contrary, I was impressed by the number of residents using it. A Caucasian father was organising a game of cricket with his son and some Eurasian lads while Indian

Sikhs, Malays, Chinese and Eurasians played football on the opposite field. It was only a five-a-side game, but just about every race was represented. It is a real melting pot in Katong. I know the areas around Mountbatten Road and Tanjong Rhu Road are more affluent and perhaps more English-educated, but you would not see this in Toa Payoh. It is just not cricket.

I left Katong Park and drifted down Mountbatten Road in the hope that I might discover a minimart hidden among the condominiums. Instead I stumbled upon a street that made me do a cartoon-like double take. Barely discernible in the darkness, I made out the words on the sign from the other side of the street—Ramsgate Road! I had visited "Little Kent" off Dover Road and had hoped to find a Ramsgate Road there, but it had been here in Katong all along. Ramsgate Road, a street named after the English town where my family now lives and the town where I spent several happy holidays as a child. I checked the street directory and discovered that there was also a Margate Road, a Clacton Road and a Walton Road further down the street. Those four roads pretty much incorporated every caravan or chalet holiday I ever had growing up in England. Being a sucker for nostalgia, I called my mother in Ramsgate, England, from Ramsgate Road, Singapore. She informed me she was busy cleaning out the dog's ears and had no time to talk, which took a bit of shine off the serendipity.

But the coincidence crowned an entertaining day by the sea. I had already said goodbye to one country with a place called Ramsgate. And here I was, over 10,000 kilometres away, doing it all over again.

CHAPTER 26

I had never been to Joo Chiat, a little enclave of Peranakan shophouses and seafood restaurants that separates Geylang and the East Coast and provides some colourful pre-war architecture. However, in recent years, Joo Chiat has taken in the overspill of prostitutes and pimps from Geylang, much to the chagrin of its residents. Always keen to explore a little local nightlife, I took a bus to East Coast Road and ventured down Joo Chiat Road.

The street's tone was set immediately by a poster pinned to a KTV lounge window. It promised "Free Pool, 4.30pm to 7.30pm". The poster was surrounded by photographs of half-naked women crouched on all fours to ensure ample views of their ample charms. How the hell did they play pool in this joint? Not one of the women held a pool cue. I did not want to contemplate where they might have put it. I passed several KTV lounges, bars with blacked-out windows and massage parlours. Then I spotted a shop that had a sign that read "Crabs And More". I thought that was a bit forward. Everyone knows the Joo Chiat stretch offers more than just a massage, but few patrons wish to consider the medical implications. On closer inspection, the shop was a seafood restaurant and appeared to be doing a roaring trade. But if I were a lady of the night, I would avoid standing under a sign that promised "Crabs And More".

Joo Chiat certainly provides an eclectic mix of goods and services. Shops sell Tibetan artefacts, fish tanks and marine supplies, DIY products and spare parts for cars, all of which are sandwiched between family eateries, the omnipresent karaoke bars and short-stay hotels. This diverse range of retailers complicates the efforts of Joo Chiat's working women. Standing outside a bar with the word "angel" in its name may attract the punters, but pouting outside a paint shop offering discounted tins of vinyl is far less appealing.

Just after 8pm, the prostitutes appeared. When they stepped under the street lights, their appearance alarmed, rather than aroused. They wore so much make-up that they looked embalmed. If one or two of them died on the job, as it were, it might be difficult to notice. Within moments of the women tottering along the cracked pavements, the foreign workers were suddenly two strides behind them. It was uncanny. Just half an hour earlier, Joo Chiat had been nigh on deserted. Now, I found myself surrounded by Indian and Bangladeshi workers strolling together arm in arm. That close physical bonding among Asians, particularly Indians, still surprises me. If I returned to England after being marooned on an uninhabited island for 25 years, I would receive nothing more than a hearty handshake from my closest friends. But foreign workers will cuddle each other when they come back from a coffee shop. It is most impressive.

But it is not all hookers and crabs in Joo Chiat. Visitors are drawn to the area, which was once a massive coconut plantation, because of its colonial architecture. The Hotel 81 Joo Chiat might earn much of its living from the women outside but its colourful façade was stunning. It picked up the Singapore Architectural Heritage Award in 1996 and it was not difficult to see why. On the corner of Koon Seng Road and Joo Chiat Road, another two-storey masterpiece, built in 1928 with beautifully carved archways, stood out from the seedier shenanigans on the street. Although the building now houses a KTV lounge, the owners must be credited for respecting the Peranakan architecture.

On the subject of KTV lounges, why are all their doormen ugly? Is it a job requirement? Outside almost every establishment in Joo Chiat stood an individual who appeared to be auditioning for *Richard III*. At most nightclubs, the bouncers are invariably young, buffed-up beefcakes in ill-fitting tuxedos. KTV lounges, however, clearly favour fat, middle-aged, chain-smoking types, whose job description involves leering at the hostesses and greeting them with the occasional grope. That was not a pleasant sight.

Understandably, Joo Chiat residents are tired of the KTV lounges, the massage parlours and the budget hotels offering hourly rates. I wandered behind the main stretch along Tembeling Road and passed many decent, comfortable family homes. These people do not want hookers on their doorsteps, quite literally in one or two cases. In 2004, an expatriate engineer complained to the media that he had heard strange thumping noises outside his Joo Chiat home one night and found a randy pair going at it like rabbits on his car bonnet.

As the hookers were increasingly overshadowing Joo Chiat's proud Peranakan and Eurasian heritage, the locals bravely stepped in and took matters into their own hands. Eleven residents formed the Save Joo Chiat Working Group in 2004 to register complaints about disreputable businesses with the authorities. Their efforts were rewarded quickly. According to media reports, there were 400 arrests for vice-related activities in the neighbourhood in 2004, a marked increase over the 50 arrests made the year before. The Joo Chiat residents' proactive stance can only be applauded. With illegal Chinese immigrants still working the streets here, the residents need all the help they can get.

At the northern end of Joo Chiat, I had originally planned to turn left into Geylang Road and venture into Singapore's infamous red-light district but I took a brief diversion. Geylang has been the heart of the island's ethnic Malay community ever since the British impolitely removed their floating village at the mouth of the Singapore River in the mid-19th century. By the 1930s, distinct Malay districts had formed and evolved into Geylang Serai, where I was now standing. In a bid to replicate the community's proud heritage, the Geylang Serai Malay Village opened here in 1989. The attraction promised authentic cuisine and costumes, traditional dances, museums and galleries.

There is only one problem with the Malay Village—it is monumentally crap. I have visited some lame Singaporean attractions in the last 10 years (Sentosa's Lost Civilisation and the now defunct Clarke Quay Adventure Ride spring to mind) but nothing comes close to the Malay Village. And that is a real tragedy.

Although it was almost 10pm when I popped in, the Malay Village was still open, not that it made any difference. I was the only visitor. Built in the traditional kampong style with sloped roofs and timber frames, its entrance had the misfortune of resembling a ferry terminal at one of the many seaside resorts dotted around the region. Most of the retail units had clearly been closed for some time, the food stalls were out of action and the Kampong Days exhibit was a joke. Apart from a few interesting panels on prominent Singaporean Malays in the art gallery, the ghost town was a faded, peeling mess, a truly shameful tribute to the vibrant heritage of Singapore's indigenous community. I later discovered that a new management team had recently taken over control of the Malay Village, the fifth in 17 years. Although the bosses have promised a new restaurant, a resource centre and shops selling art and traditional clothing, the Malay community is not holding its breath. The Malay Village has been down this road four times before. If this makeover does not work, then the artificial attraction should close its doors for good. It is an embarrassment to the community it claims to represent and offers nothing to tourists. Chinese visitors have Chinatown, Indians gravitate towards Serangoon Road and Westerners head for Orchard Road and the colonial district. But Malaysian and Indonesian coach parties have no compelling reason to leave countries steeped in indigenous tradition to sample this replicated rubbish. The Malays deserve something better.

In some respects, Geylang has not really changed. Historians believe its name is a corruption of *kilang,* the Malay word for "factory". Coconuts and lemon grass were once processed in factories around the area, hence the name. In the alleyways behind Geylang Road today, the factories remain productive after dark although there are marginally fewer coconuts now. Everyone knows the place. Sex websites provide top 10 lists, tourists occasionally visit for a cheap thrill and Singaporean teenagers are guaranteed an easy classroom laugh with the mere mention of its name. In a country famous for its transparency and strait-laced conservatism, Geylang is synonymous with seedy sex. Everyone knows that. But appearances can be deceptive. I sauntered down Geylang Road from the east and the street initially promised nothing more sordid than a new chandelier. Like Balestier, much of Geylang Road is dominated by lighting shops, offering the latest fittings and designs. I know most men harbour ambitions of leaving Geylang glowing in the dark, but not like this.

In fact, Geylang Road provides a subtle route to its red-light district. It sneaks up on you. The odd pub and KTV lounge gradually overtake shops selling fluorescent tubes and household appliances; it is a surprisingly discreet process. By the time I had reached Lorongs 22 and 20, the transition was complete. Neon lights dazzled from overhanging signs, special offers on jugs of beer were scribbled outside every bar, skinny Chinese girls with bad teeth grabbed at my arm to coax me into their drinking dens and sex shops sold terrifying plastic cylinders with pumps that promised to inflate my penis.

I stopped for a drink at a coffee shop and immediately aggravated the beer promoter by occupying an entire table with one can of Coke, thereby depriving her of four potential beer guzzlers. As she treated me with such cold contempt usually reserved for the parasitic pimps operating in the alleys behind, I reciprocated by staying put for an hour, pretending to be completely engrossed in the Chinese drama on TV that had something to do with martial arts and a eunuch.

After dark, Geylang gives you the opportunity to briefly see how the island's invisible people live. Singapore's much maligned foreign workers dominated the vicinity at every turn. On the ground behind me, four Bangladeshis were huddled together in the darkness, passing around a bottle of beer. The ground was filthy. Half-finished containers of take-away food, bags of rubbish and cat excrement cluttered the damp ground around them as they sat, cross-legged, beside an open drain. As it was Friday night, they were obviously wearing their best clothes. It was a pitiful image I will never forget. A little later, another foreign worker, possibly Thai, sneaked between coffee shop tables. Crouching the entire time, the young man hid among the patrons' legs while hawking contraband cigarettes from a plastic bag. I watched him for five minutes and he did not stand up once. His business was illegal but it appeared to be thriving.

I finished my drink, gave the beer promoter a tip (wear less make-up) and followed the throngs of foreign workers and *ah peks* into Geylang's underbelly. The real red-light district runs parallel with Geylang Road in the scruffy alleys that stretch from around Lorong 22 to Talma Road and Lorong 8. Visibility was almost negligible and I could barely make out the women sitting on plastic seats. It was so dark that I am surprised punters do not inadvertently end up having sex with each other in those gloomy alleyways. Being the only white face in the crowd, I stood out like the Raffles Lighthouse and found myself an easy target for the pimps, who had clearly attended the same school of charm and deportment as the Joo Chiat doormen. Standing about 3 metres away from "their" girls, they blocked my path as I passed and occasionally grabbed my arm, all the while gesturing towards the women sitting in front of the drains and some garishly lit shophouses. The pimps' sales patter was usually the same. They emerged from the shadows, appeared at my shoulder and whispered, "Massage, special service, blow job for you?" No matter how many pimps stopped me, their spiel rarely changed. At one point, I contemplated turning back and asking, "Excuse me, can I change the order? What will happen if I have the special service first and the massage last? Will it fall off? Will I get 'crabs and more'?" But squeezed in among the gangs of foreign workers, *ah peks* and pimps, I was a conspicuous figure in the darkness and thought better of it.

Then I was accosted. A slim Indian girl, still in her teens, threw her arms around my waist and held on tightly. She would not let go. Instead, she smiled and shrieked, "Come with me! Come with me!" I was not aroused; I was petrified. Half a dozen Indian men, who had just been talking to the girl, eyed my every move. Rather melodramatically, I threw my arms into the air and kept them there. I marched along in the shadows, arms still aloft, as the girl clung to my waist and her teenage friend followed in hot pursuit. I was desperate for the girl to release me but lacked the inclination and the courage to physically remove her. I was left with no option but to pray she released her grip somewhere after Geylang's Lorong 12 so I could escape the prying eyes of her admirers, but preferably before Toa Payoh. I did not fancy greeting my wife with my hands in the air and a teenage hooker attached to my hips crying, "Come with me! Come with me!" The young girl released me, finally, when she bumped into some washing poles hanging in the alley. They clattered to the floor which ensured we briefly captured the attention of every punter in Geylang. Fortunately, the incident embarrassed my young friend enough to admit defeat and she slunk away into the darkness.

I reached the budget hotels around Talma Road, the heart of the red-light district, and witnessed the very entrepreneurial zeal that Singapore's government now demands of its people. Behind the prostitutes standing outside the hotels, I noticed an ice cream vendor who was doing more business than all of the hookers put together! Whenever the ice cream van stopped near our house in Dagenham, only teenagers and young parents queued up for a cornet. But the ice cream queue at Talma Road comprised four hookers, two of their customers and a pimp. It was marvellous. In Britain, adults light up cigarettes after sex. In Singapore, they lick a chocolate chip cone.

Time was getting on so I took a bus to Jalan Besar, marched purposefully through its empty street and turned into Desker Road. I had been to Desker Road only once before when David played tour guide around Singapore's saucier streets. We stumbled across the finest pair of breasts ever created that night. The only drawback was that they were the work of a gifted plastic surgeon and attached to a man. Older Singaporeans often refer to Desker Road as *Kin Jio*

Ka, or "banana foot" in Hokkien. This has no relevance whatsoever, I just think that "banana foot" is a superb name for a street. I am also particularly fond of Kay Poh Road off River Valley Road. It is childish, I know, but before I leave Singapore for good I am determined to tell a taxi driver that I live in a condo there. What a spectacularly brief conversation that would be.

"Where you go?"

"Kay Poh."

"Yeah? Well, balls to you, *ang moh.*"

Like Geylang, Desker Road is internationally recognised for its nocturnal services. Instead of hookers, however, it specialises in transvestites. I wandered down the street just before midnight and the only nightlife I came across was a bustling fruit and vegetable market that reminded me of my short career at Spitalfields Market. I lasted two weeks working with my uncle at East London's famous fruit and vegetable market before someone offered me cannabis behind a lorry and my mother promptly ordered her brother to sack me. No such social concerns in Desker Road though. The most serious threat to public order came from a group of mercurial Indians shouting at a TV in a coffee shop. I thought they were watching a political protest or hearing about news of a natural disaster back in their homeland, but they were watching WWE Wrestling. As they waited for The Undertaker to make his grand entrance, I enquired if Big Daddy or Giant Haystacks was on the bill. I was quickly shooed away.

I ambled over to Syed Alwi Road and found myself in the middle of a shopping maelstrom; Mustafa Centre was packing them in. Desker Road might have been largely deserted, but this 24-hour shopping district had families, couples, singles and tourists queuing up to get in. Midnight had come and gone but a security guard directed traffic into a burgeoning car park while another pedantically checked the bags of every shopper entering the store. Singapore harbours pretensions of becoming a round-the-clock global city. Although it is not there yet, Mustafa's and the coffee shops around Little India are on the right track.

I was ready to call it a night when I reached Serangoon Road but I saw a small crowd of foreign workers gathered around in Rowell Road. I took a peek and realised that the famous transvestites of Desker Road had apparently moved to the next street. As it was still only 1am, they had not yet ventured onto the streets. Instead they sat on the stairwell of the two-storey shophouses behind a locked gate as prospective punters peered through the cracks. This peculiar setting may have been for the prostitutes' own protection, but the scene seemed so desperately sad.

I walked a little further down Rowell Road when a voice beckoned me over. I peered through the gate and thought I had confronted the American rock group Kiss. Five male faces, practically obscured by long, straight hair and startling amounts of make-up, were crouching on the staircase and smiling back at me. As they sat beside, above or below each other on the stairs, they formed a neat circle of talking heads in the shadows. For one fleeting moment, they reminded me of Queen in their "Bohemian Rhapsody" video. One of the transvestites, who bore an uncanny resemblance to the singer Robert Plant, blew me a kiss, licked his lips and asked if I fancied having a good time. I politely declined his offer, wished him well and headed back to Serangoon Road for supper.

I have absolutely no problem with transvestites; I am just not a big fan of Led Zeppelin.

CHAPTER 27

On a damp November morning in 1996, Scott and I set foot in Singapore's most famous street for the first time. Being enthusiastic tourists, we arrived an hour before the shops opened and shuffled along an empty Orchard Road desperately trying to fathom what all the fuss was about. We reached Ngee Ann City, spotted a monstrous billboard advertising an ongoing *Star Wars* exhibition and immediately concurred that this was the very country for us. Scott was also pleased that Singapore had been courteous enough to name the adjacent shopping street after him, reinforcing the belief that kismet was firmly in our corner. From a historical perspective, it now seems particularly apt. I explored Orchard Road for the first time with Scott, a street that took its name from Captain William Scott's orchards. In the 1830s, Scott was both harbour and post master of Singapore and his plentiful orchards, pepper farms and nutmeg plantations were dotted all along the street, partially concealed by colourful shrubbery and shaded by thousands of breezy trees. Now, Orchard Road boasts several Coffee Beans, a handful of McDonald's and a number of 7-Elevens. Singapore's premier shopping district has come such a long way.

Fortunately, Orchard Road boasts two of the finest city parks in the world at either end: Singapore Botanic Gardens in the north and Fort Canning Park in the south. Being in absolutely no hurry to drift along in a sea of a thousand shoppers on a Saturday afternoon, I happily strayed over to the Botanic Gardens. Originally established by dear old Tommy Raffles in 1822 at Fort Canning to satisfy his naturalistic tendencies and provide his house with a decent view, the first garden closed just seven years later. An agri-horticultural society set up the present one 30 years later and, today, the Botanic Gardens is maintained by the assiduous National Parks Board. It is over 52 hectares of lakes, gardens, heritage trees, rainforest trails, sculptures, fountains and cafés, with a children's garden on the way. Unfortunately, it pissed down when I visited.

As I admired one particular tree, the extraordinary 47-metre-tall *jelawai*, one of the tallest indigenous trees in Southeast Asia, it started to drizzle. I am no botanist but I was desperate for a pee and examined the tree's girth to determine whether it was broad enough for me to nip behind. To my consternation, the low, menacing clouds decided to release their water before I could so I dashed to the bandstand and narrowly escaped the deluge. I have always relished the unexpected equatorial downpours here. In Britain, the incessant drizzle that passes for rain is uncomfortable and irritating, rather like a baby dribbling down your face. It is neither here nor there, just gloomy. But there is nothing remotely babyish about Singapore's rain. Oh no. This is primeval Neanderthal stuff. It roars down from the heavens, thunders along the streets like a Hobbesian brute, beats you around the head for an hour and then swiftly disappears to terrorise another neighbourhood. I will miss it a lot.

I sheltered in the bandstand with four couples. It was like hanging around for the next meeting of the Social Development Unit. To compound matters, a young couple occupied their time by fondling each other. He was discernibly French and she might have been Japanese and they spent the first 15 minutes of the thunderstorm declaring their unfettered love for each other and groping various erogenous zones. When I was young, and this is true, I thought an erogenous zone was part of the London Underground. I knew the Tube network was broken up into zones and just assumed that the erogenous zone was off the map somewhere past Upminster. I have been to Upminster and have since concluded that this might well be the case.

After about an hour of chest rubbing and doe-eyed staring at the relentless rain, however, the Frenchman's patience was clearly wearing thin. His exotic girlfriend continued to expound upon the romantic virtues of a tropical storm and he responded with a forced smile and a nod. But his stiff, fidgety body language really said, "It's just rain, darling. I can no longer feel my legs and I'm desperate for a curry."

I shared his impatience so I took my chances in the blustery conditions, splashed blindly through the puddles and headed for the toilets beside the National Orchid Garden. They were the best that I have ever had the privilege of relieving myself in. Whoever designed the public facilities at the Botanic Gardens must be recognised at the next National Day Awards. The toilets boasted freshly laid tiled floors and ceilings that were cleaner than most hawker centre tables. Tropical plants adorned the three individual basins and every immaculate toilet and urinal had an automatic flush. Not only did the toilet provide a welcome respite from the rain, its open concept, a familiar feature at Singapore's parks, made it breezy and cool. I would live in here. Do not come to the Botanic Gardens for its rainforest trees and free Symphony Stage shows, come for its toilets. The National Parks Board even provided a helpline above the urinals for visitor feedback. I was so impressed that I called and notified the bemused operator that I had never peed in a more welcoming toilet.

I toyed with visiting the National Orchid Garden next door but thought better of it. I know the importance orchid breeding plays in Singapore and, as flowers go, the orchid is one of the most attractive. I even had them at my wedding to give the ceremony a Singaporean flavour. However, the idea of paying $5 to see bunches of flowers in the middle of a free garden covered with all kinds of tropical flora and fauna strikes me as a trifle odd. I would not visit the Sahara Desert and hand over $5 to peer into display cases of sand. Instead I sauntered past the majestic Symphony Lake and watched children feed bread to the ducks. There are far worse ways to spend a Saturday afternoon.

It was here that I encountered one of those anal pet owners who believe that their pets are human beings. When these poor souls are not barking at the moonlight, they are dressing their pets up in human clothes and putting pigtails in Rover's hair. The storm had stopped by now, but this particular woman thundered towards me dragging a yapping sausage dog in a blue rain mac. Only the helpless canine's stumpy legs and perspiring, panting face protruded through its ill-fitting coat. Why do owners bestow such a cruel punishment upon their pets in the tropics? It is a dog. It is already wearing a bloody coat. As the woman marched past me, I registered my displeasure by releasing a distinct odour that the poor dog would have been proud of and headed for the exit.

Orchard Road has never really appealed to me. It has no identity other than being a street full of shops, a characteristic that barely distinguishes the place from Toa Payoh Central. Orchard Road is revered by most tourists, even though it has no central feature to attract those with interests other than credit card abuse. The pagoda-shaped Singapore Marriott Hotel at the junction of Scotts Road and Orchard Road comes close to being a national landmark, but it is hardly the Sydney Opera House. For a road that is namechecked in every guidebook and tourist guide written about the country, Orchard Road offers no iconic building or structure, no vivid history and little in the way of heritage. London's Regent Street and Oxford Street boast glorious histories. New York has Times Square and the Champs Elysées relies on the Arc de Triomphe to fill its Parisian postcards. Singapore has its fair share of famous buildings and tourist attractions: the overrated Merlion, Raffles Hotel, the Padang, the Singapore River, Boat Quay, Clarke Quay, Chinatown and Little India are just a few. But none of them are in Orchard Road.

To borrow the vague language of Scott's favourite shopping centre sign, Orchard Road offers shops, more shops and even more shops. What is more, most of them are the same. It is like a day trip to Toon Town. Do you remember watching older cartoons such as *Scooby Doo* in which the hooded villain always raced past that same nondescript backdrop every few seconds? Well, that is Orchard Road. In *Scooby Doo*, it is tree, grassy knoll, house; tree, grassy knoll, house. In Orchard Road, it is McDonald's, 7-Eleven, Coffee Bean; McDonald's, 7-Eleven, Coffee Bean. Originality is not high on the street's list of priorities. That is why it has plenty of familiar retail outlets behind polished glass frontages, but no identity. It undoubtedly does the all-under-one-roof concept very well. But then, so does Lakeside Shopping Centre, a characterless suburban behemoth on the borders of Kent and Essex that serves the populations of both English counties. And tourists are not clocking up air miles to visit that place.

Orchard Road's only real function is to satisfy one's materialism and the annual Great Singapore Sale is proof of its success. Every year, the Singapore Tourism Board sets higher targets of visitors and the media gleefully reports the record-breaking retail revenues as those tills just keep on ringing. The desire to create a nation of soulless shoppers who flood Orchard Road to upgrade their phones, buy electronic gizmos they do not need and toast their efforts with a well-earned latte is relentless. To help achieve the dream, one of the street's last green lungs, Orchard Turn, was recently sold off for redevelopment with the caveat that the site must house premier residential and retail outlets. The small grassy hillock beside Orchard MRT Station is just 1.8 hectares in size and has long been a popular spot for maids to meet for picnics as well as providing space for the occasional funfair. But the sale of Orchard Turn for over $1 billion dispelled any confusion or ambiguity regarding Orchard Road. The message was unequivocal: fuck 'em. The bulging Boss wallets and Prada purses from China and India are coming and more shops are needed to satisfy demand. So the maids can scurry away to the Botanic Gardens and the funfairs can stay in Chinatown.

I sat on a wall in my least favourite place in Singapore and watched the multitudes shuffle out of the underground exit of Orchard MRT Station. Humming The Kinks' "Waterloo Sunset", I watched as hundreds of youngsters scurried off in every direction to spend a few hours staring into shop windows at branded goods that they either could not afford or planned to throw onto a credit card that they probably should not have. I know they are all doing their national service by boosting their country's GDP, but there must be more fulfilling ways for young Singaporeans to spend their weekends than this.

I have always been fascinated by the design of Orchard MRT Station. I still struggle to comprehend how someone sat down and said, "Let's take a hot country with stifling humidity on the equator and build the exit to its most popular station underground. Then attach the station to a labyrinth of shopping lanes with a myriad of retail outlets selling essentially the same thing and link it all up with slow escalators and an inadequate air-conditioning supply. Now, watch the people come."

And the sad thing is, they do. They come 18 hours a day, 7 days a week. I gloomily observed the shoppers shuffle through the crowds, carrying too many bags, the sharp edges of which banged against people's knees and babies' buggies. No one seemed to smile and no one looked particularly happy.

I fled the retail prison and took a welcome stroll down Orchard Road above ground, which was practically deserted thanks to the grey weather and damp pavements. I may have escaped the shopping hordes but fell into the clutches of the roadshow MCs instead. You cannot walk 10 metres down Orchard Road without being blown under a bus by a booming speaker promising credit cards with lower interest rates, a free car, a condo and sex with the TV artiste of your choice. And those faux-American accents are exasperating, aren't they? It is bad enough that you cannot switch on a radio station here without suffering a 21-year-old giving you tips on how to lead your life in a voice that suggests she was schooled with Forrest Gump; now we also have to endure roadshow MCs convinced that they were raised in Boston rather than Buangkok. A guy selling a ladies' credit card considered approaching me, but checked himself when he noticed the steam coming out of my ears.

Orchard Road does have its plus points though. I ambled up Emerald Hill to admire the beautifully restored Peranakan shophouses. A certain William Cuppage had a nutmeg plantation around here in the 1840s before the Peranakans moved in and built many of the stunning pre-war houses that I now wandered around. Some have been converted to bars, restaurants and office units, but they have been stylishly done and most of the original façades remain intact. Emerald Hill provided a timely breather from the credit card salesmen. It is also home to Chatsworth International School, which I indulgently mention because my wife taught there for five extremely happy years.

At the junction of Orchard Road and Bras Basah Road stands the historic Cathay Building, which, I was delighted to see, had been renovated and reopened. It is the high point at the end of an otherwise drab street. One of Singapore's oldest cinemas, the Cathay Cinema, originally opened here in 1939 and was the focal point for the entire Orchard area. Even my dear war veteran friend Cliff fondly remembers enjoying an ice cream outside the building and watching the girls go by in 1945. After being closed for a few years, the building (now known as The Cathay) has opened its doors again with a new multiplex and renovated art house with, of course, the predictable shopping outlets to follow. More impressively, its original art deco façade was recently declared a national monument and restored. As dusk approached, I stood in front of the building's grand entrance, which once led to Singapore's first skyscraper, and was reminded of the cavernous odeons of my Dagenham childhood. Those eccentric, pre-war gems were eventually converted into bowling alleys or demolished and replaced by generic multiplexes. But The Cathay is still here. Critics have complained that only the original façade remains, but with the construction workers whistling their way over to Orchard Turn, I would be grateful for small mercies.

Just after midnight, I returned to Orchard Road and walked the same route again. There has been plenty of talk in recent years to turn the shopping precinct into a 24-hour playground with a vibrant street life to rival Nanjing Lu in Shanghai. London and New York supposedly never sleep and Orchard Road is eager to join the exclusive club of city insomniacs. It is already a bit of a chameleon. Once the final train has trundled out of Orchard MRT Station just after midnight, the day tripping shoppers go away and the prostitutes, transvestites and rent boys come out to play. Before dark, Orchard Road harbours ambitions of becoming the region's answer to Regent Street. After dark, it bears closer similarity to King's Cross. I stood outside Tanglin Mall and watched several foreign workers scavenge through the dustbins, looking for any gems that might have been thrown away at the flea market earlier in the afternoon. Not a great start. Between Tanglin Mall and Tanglin Shopping Centre, I encountered three people and they were all security guards. Were they bravely protecting their properties from each other? There was more life in Toa Payoh on a Saturday night.

Fortunately, Orchard Towers can always be relied upon to provide the area with a splash of colour and a sense of humour. Often referred to by locals as the "four floors of whores", Orchard Towers supplies alcohol, women and song in ample quantities at the right price. I made my way past the fidgety taxi drivers who were doubling up as pimps, ambled up the steps and brushed past the biggest pair of breasts in Singapore. I felt a right tit, and so did she. The lady of the night momentarily blocked my path until she accepted that I was not going to be her next client and all three of her left.

I climbed the three escalators that had been cheekily turned off by the building's operators. By the time that I had reached the top floor, I needed to lean on a handrail. A plump lady tottered over and enquired if I needed a special service. I asked if she had a defibrillator. As I battled in vain to get my breath back, I watched with nothing but admiration as these working women traipsed up and down the stairs hunting down customers. Occasionally, they got lucky and strode off with their client, arm in arm, to the nearest hotel. I will never know how they manage to have sex after all those stairs. I observed men twice my age climb all three escalators, agree a price with a woman and leave. I have no idea how they got it up in the bedroom. I struggled to get it up the stairs.

If I were going to invest in a Singaporean business, I would open a tattoo parlour on the top floor of Orchard Towers without any hesitation whatsoever. Drunk Americans with close-cropped hair were queuing up to go under the needle in these places. It had never occurred to me before, but setting up a tattoo parlour beside a bar is sound marketing savvy because, as we all know, when you have had a few, those babies sell themselves. When you are sober, a tattoo is for people who believe that collecting semi-automatic weapons is no different to collecting stamps. But when you are drunk, that spider's web on your left buttock is the very thing that has been missing from your life all these years. I walked quickly past one young American who could not decide whether to get an eagle tattooed onto his back or punch his reflection in the shop window. I peered inside another tattoo parlour and saw an *ang moh* who had fallen into the deepest of sleeps while sitting in the waiting room. His video camera was still switched on and recording his crotch while a steady stream of saliva dribbled down his chin.

Unlike Geylang or Joo Chiat, however, I have never regarded Orchard Towers as seedy. Tacky, certainly; unsubtle, definitely; but there is an overriding sense of the tongue being placed firmly in the cheek here. From the taxi drivers and the club doormen to the working women and the guy in the wheelchair selling red roses to drunks at exorbitant prices, everyone knows the score. Orchard Towers offers sex quite openly, but if you do not want it, no one is going to think any less of you. They will still usher you inside to buy a few beers, enjoy the house band and have a good night. Unlike in Geylang, you will seldom find hundreds of greasy men sniffing around filthy back alleys here. Instead, I discerned families, couples and friends of all races and ages eating and drinking at the various restaurants and pubs in the building. Orchard Towers provides the street with a convivial ambience that, with the exception of Emerald Hill, is lacking elsewhere.

I crossed the road and sat outside Forum—The Shopping Mall, near to a Malay motorcycle gang. Clearly going through their James Dean phase, the bikers were stretched out along the steps, sipping spirits from plastic cups and admiring each other's tattooed forearms. To be honest, it was difficult to spot an arm that did not have any ink on it. I had never noticed biker gangs in Orchard Road before. The black-clad group, some of whom had a fawning girlfriend attached to their waist, numbered at least 30. Now and again, they disappeared to race down Orchard Road on their mopeds and scooters. They were neither rowdy nor threatening and I found their homage to The Who's iconic movie *Quadrophenia* fascinating. But one or two of them reminded me of some of my Dagenham peers growing up. That was not necessarily a good thing.

Just after 2am, I took a rest on a bench near Le Meridien Hotel and was quickly joined by an attractive, middle-aged woman. "I've been watching you walk up and down," she said. "Where are you from?"

"Toa Payoh," I replied chirpily. She was the first person that I had spoken to in hours.

"Ah, not too far from me. You want a good time tonight?" She put her hand on my shoulder. The woman was old enough to be my mother. It then occurred to me that I had not been propositioned by a single prostitute under the age of 35. How bloody old did they think I was?

"No, no, it's okay, really. I just came out for the exercise."

"I understand," she said. Her warm, maternal smile betrayed a hint of rejection. I wanted to hug her. It was after 2am, most of Singapore was asleep and here she was talking to a sweaty stranger on a near-deserted, damp street. This was no way to earn a living. "Well, it was nice talking to you," she continued. "But it's getting late, you know. Maybe it's time for you to go home."

She gave me that kind, maternal smile again. So I did as I was told.

CHAPTER 28

I will never forget the day I discovered what an archaeologist did for a living. I thought it was the most glamorous, and easiest, job in the world. Take a shovel, dig up your front garden and discover the complete skeleton of a *Diplodocus* before lunch. Thus, the following weekend, my best friend Ross and I set to work in my Dagenham side garden with a pitchfork. We had certain advantages. Undisturbed land is an obvious boon for any budding archaeologist and no one in our family had touched the side garden since 1822. We made light work of the sodden soil and recovered a historic gem in less than two hours. The moment the pitchfork hit something metallic, we dove into the dug-up earth and pulled out a round, off-green object caked in mud. Once we cleaned it up, we deduced that it was a military helmet left over from World War II! As Dagenham had suffered some bomb damage during the Blitz, it must have belonged to a soldier in the Home Guard.

I waited impatiently for my mother to return home from work to inform her that she could quit her job immediately as my archaeological discovery guaranteed untold millions from a forthcoming Sotheby's auction. When she walked into the house, I handed her the treasure and told her, with some authority because we had recently covered World War II at school, what it was. She laughed and told me that it was not a military helmet but an old bedpan. I had not dug up part of a valiant serviceman's uniform; I had retrieved a potty from some old dear with incontinence. Despite that minor setback, I have been intrigued by archaeology ever since and decided to spend a morning at the site of Singapore's most productive dig.

I really like Fort Canning Park. Hidden away from the hubbub of Orchard Road, the historic site sits quietly, and most majestically, on a hill away from the maddening crowds. Old Raffles took one look at Bukit Larangan (Malay for "Forbidden Hill", as it was then known), and said, "That'll make a nice back garden." Before you could say "Mind that heritage", the jungle was cleared and animals were shot to facilitate the building of Raffles' bungalow here in 1822. He died four years later, which was a bit of a bummer. After his death, Raffles found it quite difficult to return to the bungalow so Singapore's governors lived there until 1860, when some bright spark realised that the hill's incomparable vistas made it an obvious choice for a military fort.

I mention old Raffles because it is hard not to conclude that Singapore's history was wilfully determined by just two men. I have read several local history books, particularly school texts, and the same two dates take centre stage: 1819, when Raffles first landed in Singapore, and 1959, when the People's Action Party was first voted into power. No one seriously disputes the impact these two events had on Singapore but the country existed, and thrived, before both Raffles and Lee Kuan Yew entered the picture. Fort Canning Park, the history of which can be traced back to Singapore's golden age of the 1300s, is living proof of that.

I planned to have my lunch of sweaty cheese sandwiches at the site of Singapore's oldest known house. In the 1300s, the Mongol rulers of China referred to the island as "Dragon's Tooth Strait", probably due to a large pillar of rock off Labrador Point. How I wish the island still went by that name. Just consider the marketing potential for T-shirts for tourists. In the 1300s, Dragon's Tooth Strait was ruled by a number of Malay kings, the fifth and last of whom, Sultan Iskandar Syah, was driven out of the country but went on to found Malacca before dying around 1413. The royal palace of Iskandar Syah and his predecessors probably stood at Bukit Larangan's summit. There is also the belief that his final resting place is also here as the hill was once a *keramat,* a traditional burial ground for revered Malay leaders. Muslims have prayed here since the 1820s. They are convinced that the area is a 600-year-old tomb and, considering the island is largely starved of juicy history, I am content to agree with them.

The *keramat* that now stands on the site is built in the traditional Malay style. Twenty wooden pillars support a replica of a 14th-century roof. At the centre is a tomb with Iskandar Syah's name inscribed on the side. When I visited, an Indian Muslim was leaning on the tomb and praying so I took my shoes off and sat a respectful distance away. I was starving but refrained from eating my sweaty sandwiches. First, I was not sure if it was disrespectful to eat in a *keramat.* Second, I found myself donating blood by the litre to the local mosquito population. When I was not swiping them away, I tried to make a grab for a sandwich but intimidating pigeons kept hovering fearlessly in my face. And it is not right to punch a pigeon in a *keramat,* is it?

So I had lunch at the wonderfully informative Archaeological Dig & Exhibition. I spent a happy hour there examining the artefacts and playing with the automated fan and lights system. But the exhibition also underlined the lack of understanding about Singapore's history. There just is not enough evidence. When I was growing up in Dagenham, farmers and fishermen frequently stumbled upon ancient Roman relics in the bogs of the Essex marshes beside the River Thames. Coins, pottery and jewellery were often unearthed, to the indifference of the blasé local populace. But at Fort Canning, archaeologists are ecstatic if they find tiny fragments of 13th-century pottery or a piece of an indecipherable coin because it is all that they have got. It is so sad. The information panels even referred to the period of Singapore's golden age as ancient history when, of course, it only took place 700 years ago and falls under the medieval period in the West.

That is not to say that human indifference or neglect is not occasionally at fault. As almost every centimetre of land on this minuscule island has been bulldozed, reclaimed or tunnelled through since the 1960s, archaeologists believe that the only undisturbed sites left that might throw up some historical clues are the Padang, the Armenian Church and St. Andrew's Cathedral. And economic and religious sensitivities are likely to keep the shovels away from all three.

There are also unforgivable stories that highlight the contempt people can have for a country's heritage. Consider the discovery of the Singapore Stone. Now the Singapore Stone should have been a key to the locked door marked the Dark Ages. Discovered at the mouth of the Singapore River in the 19th century by British engineers, the ancient boulder was around 3 metres high and 3 metres wide and contained approximately 50 lines of engraved text. Believed to be a variant of old Sumatran script, the stone has been dated from the 10th to the 14th century. Its scholastic importance to Asean history should have been obvious to all and sundry. The Singapore Stone could have been its country's "Rosetta Stone". (The Rosetta Stone was unearthed in an Egyptian port by invading French forces in 1799 and, because it was written in Hieroglyphic, Demotic Egyptian and Greek, allowed historians to finally decipher hieroglyphs and unlock the language of the pharaohs.) Comparing the Singapore Stone with the Rosetta Stone may smack of hyperbole, but we will never know now. Because in their eternal wisdom, British engineers blew up the Singapore Stone to prepare the ground for Fort Fullerton. Only a few fragments remain today in the National Museum of Singapore and they are either too small or too badly damaged to determine the date of or the language used on the stone. It was a gross error of judgement that can never be rectified. Singapore wields the financial clout to purchase water from Malaysia, rice from Indonesia, fresh milk from Australia and cheap labour from the subcontinent but it cannot buy back its own history.

Fort Canning Park has two trails: the 14th Century Walk of History, which includes the *keramat* and the archaeological dig, and the 19th Century Walk, which focuses on the impact Raffles had on the hill. Strangely, the former felt more authentic than the latter. In

2003, Fort Canning Park opened Raffles Terrace, which showcases reminders of the British Empire's contributions to the vicinity. There was a replica of the flagstaff originally erected by Singapore's first British Resident William Farquhar, a largely pointless time ball and a replica of the old Fort Canning Lighthouse. There was even Raffles House, a replica of the old man's bungalow, which, I believe, is available for private functions and conferences. That is always good to know, I suppose. I found the information panels enlightening, but Raffles Terrace seemed so artificial after spending time at the very real archaeological dig.

But Fort Canning is a remarkable park. I have not even mentioned the Battle Box, where the British made the decision to surrender to the Japanese on the morning of 15 February 1942; or the Sally Port; or the historic cemetery; or the simple fact that the city's green refuge is an ideal spot for a family picnic. More pertinently, Fort Canning provides a little insight into the increasingly forgotten island of Dragon's Tooth Strait, ancient royal palaces and fleeing kings. The sacred hill is a constant, physical reminder that the country was not born in 1819 or reborn in 1959. For that reason alone, the park should be revered as a national treasure.

I left Fort Canning, walked along Hill Street and entered the historical site that gave me the initial idea of writing this book. Sitting at my desk in the *TODAY* office in late 2005, I received an email request to cover the anniversary of a small church that served a tiny community within Singapore. I was not interested. Its name—the Armenian Church of St Gregory the Illuminator —was not familiar so I stopped reading the press release after the first few lines. A couple of days later, my boss asked me when "that Armenian Church story" was coming out so I sighed, reluctantly retrieved the email and read it properly. I was stunned. The church claimed to be the oldest in Singapore and was finalising its 170th anniversary celebrations. Surely that was a typing error? A 70th birthday seemed acceptable, but a building that was 170 years old in Singapore was absurd. This is a country, remember, where a good deal of the history syllabus in schools focuses on events after the

Japanese Occupation of 1942. And here were church volunteers claiming that their particular house of worship was constructed just 12 years after Raffles sailed away from Singapore for the last time and when most of the country was still a swampy jungle. I was not having it.

Of course, it all turned out to be true and it really is a wonderful story of dedication, application and perseverance from a community that has punched above its weight in Singapore for over 180 years. In the 1800s, 12 Armenian families came together to commission the Armenian Orthodox Church. Never a community to take half measures, they employed the services of George Coleman, one of the country's most respected architects and responsible for the Old Parliament House (now The Arts House). Construction began on the Hill Street site on 1 January 1835.

Just to reiterate, that is 1835. There were more Malayan tigers roaming freely around the jungles of Singapore than there were Armenian families. I am not joking. According to the helpful staff at the superb Raffles Museum of Biodiversity Research, one person was killed every day by a tiger in 1835. That is seven deaths a week. That is a lot of tigers.

But nothing stopped those resolute Armenians. The church opened its doors in late 1835 (in those days, they could commission, plan and build a stately neoclassical structure in less than a year. At the time of writing, Wembley Stadium was still not finished.). And those doors have stayed open to the public ever since. In the meantime, the surrounding jungles were cleared, the last of the tigers was shot in Choa Chu Kang in the 1930s, the British were attacked, the Japanese wreaked havoc, the British returned, communism loomed large, race riots threatened social order, HDB flats went up all over the island, reclaimed land was redeveloped just south of Hill Street and the banks at Raffles Place were built to clutter the skyline. Yet a small, unremarkable church still quietly goes about its business, serving the same community after 170 years.

But then the Armenians are a resilient bunch. Ignoring the adage that size matters, the tiny group has certainly left its imprint on the country. The Sarkies brothers conceived Raffles Hotel, which opened in 1887, and the botanist Agnes Joachim cultivated the *Vanda* Miss Joachim, the hybrid orchid that later became Singapore's national flower. When you consider that there are now around 40 Armenians still living in Singapore, their impact is nothing short of extraordinary. There are more people at my local coffee shop on most week nights.

The Armenian Church was everything I expected it to be. An elegant, white-washed building with flawless marble floors under grand porticos, it was neither garish nor ostentatious. It was a charming church with a graceful spire on top. I had walked down Hill Street a dozen times before but had not noticed the historic gem. Perhaps that helps to explain its longevity. Out of sight, out of mind, the Armenian Church has been pretty much left to its own devices by the British, Japanese and now Singaporean governments. A little too much perhaps. A collection box proudly stated that the building sustained itself without government subsidies. Now, if central funds can be allocated to build artificial tourist fluff like Raffles Terrace, then surely a few dollars could be handed out to help preserve one of the island's oldest structures?

I ambled around its manicured garden and discovered the grave of Agnes Joachim. She died in 1899 and the headstone, rather like the church, paid an unpretentious tribute, with a small plaque acknowledging her role in discovering Singapore's national flower. Some kind soul had left a pot of orchids by her grave.

It suddenly started to rain so I took shelter under one of the church's splendid porticos and watched soaked Singaporeans splash their way through Hill Street. The church did not seem to mind. It has been providing shelter for over 170 years.

CHAPTER 29

This island tour is fast reaching its conclusion so I thought I would recognise the people who made this glorious country what it is today. Revered for their honesty, transparency and lifelong commitment to a common goal, their contribution to society is acknowledged across the world. They helped bring a fledgling nation together to celebrate its independence every year. Indeed, the debt Singapore owes these fine, upstanding citizens can never be repaid.

I am referring, of course, to the Dagenham Girl Pipers. Or more specifically, Peggy Iris, Sheila Nobes and Carole Granfield of the Dagenham Girl Pipers. Those three women helped make Singapore's National Day Parade (NDP) what it is today.

As we all know, Singapore celebrates its independence on 9 August with an extravaganza at either the Padang or the National Stadium. (If you are thinking of attending the next one, the colour scheme tends to be red and white.) These glittering occasions give the country a chance to show off their Chinook helicopters and disturbingly energetic hosts who get paid a dollar every time they screech, "Singapore, make some noise!" They earn an additional 50 cents if they cry "woo", "awesome" or "Are you ready to par-ty?". These well-drilled affairs display a military precision that betrays a year of stringent planning, choreography and rehearsal. I have heard that even the "woos" are rehearsed.

But in 1967, it was a different story. In the first quarter of that year, preparations for the next NDP began in earnest. Having declared its independence in 1965, Singapore staged its first parade in 1966 and the show was an unqualified success. So the word from the top was "The NDP is to become an annual event so make sure that the second one is a marked improvement upon the first." But how do you top an exhilarating first act? How do you make the sequel more entertaining than the original? Simple. You get on the government hotline and call Dagenham.

That NDP organising committee meeting, comprising military bigwigs, political figures and members of the People's Association, must have been mind-blowing:

"We need to top last year's smash at the Padang. Don't think Malaysian standard, Indonesian standard or even Asian standard. The world will be watching so think world standard, people. I'm thinking foreign talent for this one. So where do we go to get world-class foreign talent?"

"Dagenham."

"Dagenham? No way! Out of the question! I don't want anything to do with Australians."

"No, it's in England, sir. In Essex. You know, the world's biggest council housing estate?"

"What? Bigger than our plans for Toa Payoh? Impossible."

"No, it is, really. It's also got the Ford car plant, Dudley Moore, Sir Alf Ramsey, Jimmy Greaves and that singer Sandie Shaw. She's in the charts right now, actually. You know, 'A Puppet on a String'?"

"Oh, that is a catchy song. Is Dagenham anywhere near Cambridge? We like Cambridge."

"Er, yeah, it's close enough."

"Right then. Let's call Dagenham and get them to send over some world-class talent. Who knows? Dagenham could become a veritable factory of foreign talent for this country."

I am milking this, I know, but my hometown and the adjectival "world-class" are seldom found in the same sentence. But in 1967, the Dagenham Girl Pipers was an internationally renowned marching bagpipe band that toured the world. So when *The Straits Times* reported in February 1967 that Singapore must have a 36-member all-girl bagpipe band, Dagenham's Iris, Nobes and Granfield were flown over, on business class I hope, to form the Singapore Girl Pipers and prepare them for the NDP. According to the report, the girls had to play the pipes and the drums and learn to dance the Scottish reel. I have no idea what encompassed the Scottish reel, but I suspect it involved drinking a copious amount of whisky and falling over.

Dagenham's coaches had to work with pipers who had good physiques and shapely legs, according to the government, which took time out from its busy schedule of building a country from scratch to discuss young girls' legs. Dr Goh Keng Swee, the Minister for Defence back then, pointed out that girl pipers are usually attired in tartan skirts so the need for well-formed legs should be obvious to all. In other words, fatties need not apply.

Dagenham's finest delivered the goods. The all-new Singapore Girl Pipers made a spectacular debut at the second NDP in 1967 and, by all accounts, stole the show. The girls went on to become a regular, and popular, feature at subsequent Padang parades. Under the tutelage of the People's Association, the Singapore Girl Pipers evolved into the Singapore Pipe Band, which is still going strong today. And, if I might be permitted to jut out my chest for just a moment, it is all thanks to my tiny hometown.

I sat on the steps of City Hall and looked across at the Padang. It was Sunday morning and there were a handful of tourists snapping pictures with Singapore's skyline as their backdrop. City Hall, a glorious building with its imposing colonnade, is steeped in history. On 12 September 1945, the Japanese climbed these very steps before formally surrendering to the dwindling British Empire. Twenty years later, Lee Kuan Yew announced the country's independence. Again, after climbing these steps. Now, I could pretend that I was pondering the magnitude of these events and their indelible imprint upon Singapore's history, but I was really picturing several pairs of "well-formed legs" marching up and down the Padang. I once watched the players of Liverpool Football Club jog around this hallowed turf and tried to recall which Reds were there that day. But it was no good. I got as far as Robbie Fowler and

Michael Owen before they were swiftly elbowed aside by startling images of the Fat Girl Pipers stomping across the Padang. I had to leave.

After a quick look at the old Supreme Court, a classically designed masterpiece that will soon be wisely converted into a national art gallery, I drifted down the small side street that separates City Hall and the old Supreme Court and was confronted by the new Supreme Court. Now, I have encountered some pitiful erections on this tour; the green penis in Toa Payoh's Town Garden will stay with me forever. But the new Supreme Court is spectacularly awful. Not untypical of modern monstrosities, it is covered in gloomy glass and pales in comparison to the old Supreme Court. That stately structure, with its respectful nod to St Paul's Cathedral via its majestic dome, was preoccupied with a much sillier concern: its appearance. However, its frighteningly functional successor is topped off with a disc-shaped structure that suggests it has just fallen out of a Steven Spielberg film. Irritated that such an incongruous design had ever been commissioned to stand behind two classical buildings, I marched across Anderson Bridge and took a bus down Beach Road to a place where heritage has been treated with a little more respect.

Kampong Glam (or Gelam) existed before Stamford Raffles. Named after the *gelam* tree that grew in the area, the kampong was located at the mouth of the Rochor River and populated by the Malay and Orang Laut, or sea people, communities. In 1822, Raffles beat the People's Action Party to its racial quota policy by carving up the areas around the Singapore River into racial districts. Kampong Glam, rather sensibly, was kept for the Malays and Bugis traders. Arab, Javanese, Boyanese and other Muslim merchants soon joined them. Ironically, the population surge put pressure on the land and Kampong Glam's original occupants moved away to places like Geylang Serai. Today, their descendants are stuck with a crappy Malay Village, so you could argue that they got a raw deal.

But Kampong Glam's new settlers gave the area an exotic feel still discernible today. With road names like Baghdad Street and Muscat

Street, the Arab Quarter is certainly one of Singapore's most unique places. As you leave Beach Road and wander down Arab Street, you enter a Middle Eastern world of two-storey shophouses selling the finest silk, fabrics, handicrafts, rattan, willow and bamboo. Arabs invite you to peruse their Persian rugs, tourists snap up batik shirts, sarongs and saris and locals come to be fitted out in traditional ethnic costumes. I even noticed elderly Malay fishermen haggling with a shop owner over some archaic-looking fishing tackle. But this is nothing new. In the 1950s and 1960s, Kampong Glam was the place to be on balmy nights when shoppers from across the region hunted down the cheapest textiles and hawkers pushed food carts selling *rojak, popiah* and, of course, satay. In 1989, the Urban Redevelopment Authority wisely declared Kampong Glam a preservation area and many of the pre-war shophouses around Arab Street, Baghdad Street and Bussorah Street were renovated.

The only problem was that the place was more or less empty when I visited. The pedestrianised Bussorah Mall had a slightly manufactured touristy feel, sprinkled with the usual backpackers' essentials: Internet cafés, cheap egg and bacon breakfasts, postcards and, most important of all, soap. The restored street looked great but, apart from a handful of backpackers, an expat family and some locals eating lunch at a halal coffee shop, I had the street to myself.

I also had the Malay Heritage Centre largely to myself, too. I originally had no intention of visiting the museum. I drifted over only because the building was the former Istana Kampong Glam, built in 1840 by Sultan Ali, the son of Sultan Hussein Shah (Singapore's first sultan). But the girl at the counter stared at me with such imploring eyes that I went in. I had reservations. I suspected that the museum would be nothing more than old kettles, some artificial timber boats and golden artefacts from royal ceremonies. That pretty much summed up the contents of the first floor, but the second floor was superb. The Malay community's cultural contribution to Singapore was its central theme and the gallery displayed Zubir Said's handwritten music and lyrics for "Majulah Singapura", the country's national anthem no less. There they were, right in front of me. I was impressed. One of the other galleries focused on the prodigious work of actor/writer/director/composer P Ramlee, an extraordinarily talented man who dominated Asean cinema in the 1950s and 1960s. Singapore's most recent artistic offering to the region has been Phua Chu Kang. I suppose that is progress.

My favourite exhibition centred upon Malay home life and the evolution from kampong to HDB flat. Although it banged the government drum a bit, the museum had recreated a generic Toa Payoh flat from the 1970s, complete with cheesy furniture, a television the size of a car and a wireless that must have required the services of a crane to get into the flat. I know it is kitschy but I am a sucker for this sort of stuff. With no one around, I sat in one of the dusty armchairs and imagined that I was wearing bell-bottoms and a polyester shirt, drinking warm Anchor beer and watching West Ham's Trevor Brooking knock one in on the *Star Soccer* black-and-white highlights show. It was fabulous.

I returned to Arab Street and had another look around the shops. They were all very exotic, but I did not urgently need a silk scarf, a tablecloth or a wicker basket so I shuffled back to Beach Road. On the way, I spotted a shop sign that read "Oriental Biggest Belly Dancer Boutique". I was intrigued. I had never seen a belly dancer's shop before and was not aware that Singapore had one. But the shop's name was ambiguous. Did the retail outlet promise an extensive range of costumes or did it just cater to fat dancers? Besieged by images of obese belly dancers, I went to Raffles Hotel for a quick pee.

Raffles Hotel is a charming hotel, a national landmark and the birthplace of the Singapore Sling. It is also a great place to have a pee. So let me give you an invaluable tip here. If you are caught short anywhere in the City Hall or Beach Road area, pop over to Raffles Hotel to relieve yourself. If you are going to go, you might as well go in style. A few years ago, I discovered that the toilets that serve the famous Long Bar (where the Singapore Sling was originally concocted) are outside the bar and just down the corridor. They are even air-conditioned, which is rather ironic as some of the bars and restaurants in the courtyard are not. So I sauntered casually along the red carpet at the hotel's grand entrance, took a sharp left past some fountains, perused the meagre selection of books in the hotel's gift shop, climbed the stairs, nipped past the Long Bar and whipped the old willy out in the most luxurious of surroundings. I will only pee in the best. And Raffles Hotel is my kind of toilet.

I stumbled upon the agreeable public facilities beside the Long Bar quite by accident. In 2001, the former Manchester United and England midfielder Bryan Robson was in town for a charity football tournament. His job as Middlesbrough manager was under threat at the time and I, the intrepid sports reporter, was tasked with tracking him down to find out if he intended to resign. A phone call informed me he was enjoying dinner at the Long Bar Steakhouse so off I went in hot pursuit. When I arrived, the head waiter said that I had no right to interrupt Mr Robson while he was eating and ordered me to wait outside. Unperturbed by this setback, I improvised. Captain Marvel had to empty his bladder at some point so I staked out the toilets. I stood at the door and smiled at each patron who entered. My appearance suggested a high-class rent boy. One or two visitors even went to give me money, which I quickly refused. What kind of service did they think they were paying me for?

The more I perspired in the sweltering heat, the more suspicious I must have looked. Ninety minutes passed and we were well into extra time, but old Robbo failed to make a late appearance. His assistant manager Viv Anderson, however, did. When he saw my reporter's notepad, he tried to bloody autograph it. But Captain Marvel steered clear of the Long Bar toilets. He was a combative midfielder in his day, one of the all-time greats, but Bryan Robson's physical attributes extend beyond the football pitch. He can hold his bladder for England.

It was a relatively cool evening so I took a slow walk across Esplanade Drive and watched the festivities below. There was a decent country band giving a free concert outside the Esplanade

Mall. The band played to a full house. The Esplanade's design may leave a lot to be desired but there is no doubt that the Theatres on the Bay concept has brought a much-needed vibrancy back to the Marina area.

The casino should do the rest. After visiting one of Singapore's oldest urban centres at Kampong Glam, I wanted to see the location of a glittering metropolis yet to be constructed. I hurried through the ghostly Clifford Pier, which had recently been closed down and moved to Marina South, and sat at the end of a jetty. Although it was now dark, I could make out the twinkling lights on the cranes across Marina Bay. On the left of the Bay, work has already begun on the Marina Barrage, which will eventually create a 48-hectare reservoir to host water sports events and perhaps even National Day celebrations. On the right, another construction site marked the colossal condo project The Sail @ Marina Bay. Sandwiched between the two, of course, will be the roulette wheels and the blackjack tables.

After years of debate, Singapore's government finally allowed the building of two casinos: a smaller one at Sentosa and a major integrated resort here at Marina Bay. The Bay's complex should be ready by 2010. Apparently, an integrated resort houses conference centres, artistic venues, hotels, galleries, restaurants and high-end retail outlets. That is all window dressing, of course, because if there was not a casino at the heart of the project, bidders from Las Vegas to Genting would not be queuing up to get a piece of the action. Not that the government really had a choice. Singaporean gamblers flood the casino in Malaysia's Genting Highlands and they are not spending their weekends on Star Cruises to spot marine life either.

And, dare I say it, the integrated resort is probably what Singapore needs. If it attracts the right nightlife, Marina Bay promises to be everything that Orchard Road is not. Urban planners are finally recognising that glass and concrete will build towns and shopping centres indefinitely, but they can destroy a country's soul. To avoid this, the National Parks Board recently launched an international competition for planners to come forward with their designs for three waterfront gardens. There will be a 54-hectare garden behind the integrated resort, a 30-hectare water-themed park in Marina East and a 10-hectare park that will neatly line the waterfront of Marina Centre. Now, that is more like it. The gardens should be ready by 2010 to accompany a twisting, 280-metre-long pedestrian bridge that will stretch across Marina Bay. It will be the longest bridge in Singapore. By that stage, the Singapore Flyer, an observation wheel modelled on the popular, if rather overrated, London Eye, should be packing them in. At 170 metres, it is projected to be the world's tallest revolving structure. This is Singapore. I would expect nothing less.

Honestly, it all sounds rather exciting. Singapore has to get the Marina Bay project right and it will. It has no choice. The government now accepts that a five-roomed flat, decent education and pristine trains that always run on time no longer impress younger, restless Singaporeans. They need to have some bloody fun in their own country and should not be forced to travel to California, Queensland or Genting to find it. Singapore may be a tiny country, but it can still accommodate both the history of Kampong Glam and the hedonism of Marina Bay. And as I stood on the edge of an empty, gloomy Clifford Pier, I promised to return to sample a bit of both.

CHAPTER 30

My Singaporean journey was almost over. In every sense. There was just one gigantic, gaping, green hole in the middle of the country left for me to cover. And I foolishly intended to cover it in a single day. On foot.

I got up at 6am, dressed quickly, kissed my wife goodbye and assured her that I would not die. I strode briskly through the quiet Toa Payoh streets, crossed over the already busy Thomson Road and headed into MacRitchie Reservoir Park. Knowing that a day-long trek was ahead of me, I performed my usual warm-up routine. I stretched my legs half a dozen times, bent over twice, ate half a cheese sandwich and waited for Benjamin Lee to join me. A lovely, accommodating man, the Senior Conservation Officer at the National Parks Board had offered to meet me at MacRitchie to point out the safest route on a map and underscore the importance of sticking to the trails. When he arrived, Benjamin insisted that I would enjoy the walk, but his uncertain body language betrayed his real opinion: the *ang moh's* gonna die.

I had wanted to tackle this walk for a long time. Eager to dispel the stubbornly persistent myth that Singapore is nothing more than an island of concrete, I planned to circumnavigate the Central Catchment Nature Reserve and Bukit Timah Nature Reserve in the middle of the country on foot. Now, that is a pretty daft plan. Comprising the reservoirs of MacRitchie, Peirce and Seletar, the Central Catchment area covers around 3,043 hectares. Bukit Timah is another 163 hectares. So I foolishly intended to trek through rainforest that covered 3,206 hectares. As one hectare (100 metres x 100 metres) is slightly shorter and fatter than the football pitch inside Cardiff's Millennium Stadium (120 metres x 79 metres), you will realise that Singapore's major green lung is a respectable size. It could be bigger of course. Those 3,206 hectares constitute 4.6 per cent of Singapore's total land area, but I have noticed reforestation taking place across the country and those three splendid gardens planned for Marina Bay should ensure that you bequeath a green island to your children, rather than a charred country. That said, 4.6 per cent of Singapore's land area is still a bugger to walk.

I planned to hike around 4.5 kilometres to the TreeTop Walk in MacRitchie, then cover another 6 kilometres or so to reach Bukit Timah Nature Reserve and eat my remaining cheese sandwiches. After lunch, I would follow a biking trail out of Bukit Timah, skirting the fringes of Upper Peirce Reservoir Park and Seletar Reservoir Park, turn right at Mandai Road, my northernmost point, then venture south along Upper Thomson Road, pop into Lower Peirce Reservoir Park, sneak around the Singapore Island Country Club, return to MacRitchie and be back home in time for tea. For some strange reason, Benjamin was not convinced.

"You shouldn't really go on your own, you know," he said, making a mental note to keep a search party on standby. "Have you got enough food and drink, plenty of insect repellent and your mobile phone? Oh, and don't forget to take down our helpline."

I laughed. He did not. So I took out my notepad like a penitent schoolboy and reluctantly jotted down the National Parks Board's helpline. I noticed Benjamin watch me write down every digit. There was no doubt in his mind. He clearly thought that the next time we met, I would be strapped to a stretcher and dangling from a helicopter.

I ventured onto the MacRitchie Nature Trail and was impressed by the number of eager middle-aged trekkers I passed. They powered along, always taking the time to smile, say "hello" or wish me a pleasant morning. I encountered one particular middle-aged group engaged in a bizarre conversation. Peering nervously into the undergrowth, one chap said, "Got a lot you know. I see them all the time. Must be careful."

"Yah, it's true," said a plump woman in a tracksuit with a beach towel round her neck. "The park ranger never talks about it, might scare off visitors."

"Yeah, loh. But the park ranger must take responsibility, right or not?"

"But he bites, right?"

"Of course he bites. Cannot keep secret. Park ranger must tell the public. He's damn fierce. If he bites you, must get antidote or sure die one."

I was not sure if they were discussing a snake or a psychotic park ranger.

I reached the TreeTop Walk remarkably quickly. Not through choice, though. I was pursued mercilessly by a group of expatriate housewives. There were six of them, all armed with walking sticks and one-piece Lycra suits, stomping through the forest at breakneck speed and knocking casual walkers into the reservoir. Then they closed in on me. Now, I should have been a mature grown-up and kindly stepped aside and allowed the Lycra ladies to pass. Instead I decided to race them to the TreeTop Walk. It was not their gender, you understand, it was their inane chattering. They never stopped talking. How did they do it? I panted, wheezed and swore at every chipped rock that stubbed my toes. Yet the far from desperate housewives breezed along and still found the energy to swap jokes and waffle on about the aesthetic value of black Lycra. I was insanely jealous of their fitness and vowed to spread my legs and jump on the nearest tree stump if so much as one of them surged past me.

I paid the price for my puerile behaviour. By the time I had dragged my shaking legs to the entrance of the TreeTop Walk, my vision was blurred and I thought I was hallucinating. Everywhere I turned, the forest was filled with those singing and dancing Ribena berries from the TV commercials. They were everywhere. I sat down, downed an entire bottle of Coke and belched so loudly that several startled birds flew out of the trees. It was just what I needed. The Ribena berries disappeared and I was ready for Singapore's greatest bridge.

On a trip to Western Australia a few years ago, my wife and I took four hours to drive south of Perth to reach the Tree Top Walk in the Valley of the Giants near the town of Walpole. Singapore's TreeTop Walk, on the other hand, was just a brisk 90-minute stroll from my apartment in Toa Payoh. And it was spectacular. In a country that is so small, there is a tendency to overlook things that are on your doorstep. I have met Singaporeans who have been to Australia's Valley of the Giants but would not consider visiting MacRitchie's TreeTop Walk. That is such a shame. Opened in 2004, the free-standing suspension bridge is 250 metres long and stands majestically over the forest canopy, which is about 25 metres below. As the bridge connects MacRitchie's two highest points, its panoramic vistas of the forest are breathtaking.

As I shared the bridge with only a handful of other visitors, I took my time. The bridge reaches 27 metres at its highest point but it was still dwarfed by many of the surrounding trees. It is awe-inspiring stuff and feels more like Sabah than Singapore. Of course, the adorably *kiasu* signs are always on hand to remind you where you are. On a list of dos and don'ts, it was suggested that, in the event of a thunderstorm, visitors must see the ranger on duty to avoid being struck by lightning. Why? Is he on a higher spiritual plane than the rest of us? Does the National Parks Board employ shamans? No disrespect to the young ranger who was sitting in his booth at the edge of the bridge but, if lightning had struck at that particular moment, I would have followed traditional protocol and screamed like a little girl and dashed for the exit.

Halfway across the bridge, I spotted a long-tailed macaque sitting pretty at the top of a tree some 30 metres above ground. I was delighted. It was the first monkey I had seen on the tour, which was rather surprising considering they are one of the more common wild mammals in Singapore. The macaque was certainly the first exotic animal I saw when I arrived in the country. Some colleagues took me to Bukit Timah Nature Reserve and the playful primates were everywhere: on dustbins, car bonnets, house roofs, rest shelters, benches and any other location where they could be guaranteed human interaction, some potato chips and the odd Mars bar. The idea of glimpsing monkeys in their natural habitat was exciting, but it was quite an anticlimax watching a fat kid feed them some Pringles in the car park.

But that is all changing. The monkeys are being forced back into the forest whether they like it not. There has been a discernible shift in attitude towards feral creatures in recent years, both in the media and in public forums. Heavier punishments are being handed down to animal abusers and the National Parks Board is doing a tremendous job in raising public awareness. I noticed massive billboards placed strategically in areas that were once popular with scavenging monkeys that reminded visitors to let the wild animals feed themselves. According to the billboards, offenders can even be fined now for feeding monkeys. NParks is determined to get the message across and the positive results were self-evident. From the bridge, I glimpsed at least a dozen monkeys foraging for fruits and seeds under leaves and branches. A decade ago at Bukit Timah Nature Reserve, a fearless macaque climbed nonchalantly onto a bench and stole a bag of potato chips from my lap. The cheeky bugger then sauntered over to the other end of the bench and ate them in front of me. But that is less likely to happen now. The monkeys are trooping back to the trees. Keep them there.

I embarked upon the long walk along Rifle Range Link and Rifle Range Road. Perhaps understandably, I met a lot of young men carrying weapons. National Servicemen were dotted all over the place: under tents, at checkpoint barriers or marching in single file through the forest in their camouflaged uniforms. To make a rather obvious point, the soldiers were so young. They were just kids. I know it is not politically correct, but I will never be comfortable with teenagers brandishing guns. They should be out chasing young women at Zouk, not chasing inanimate objects in the jungle. When I was their age, I felt uneasy with a pint of cider and blackcurrant in my hand, let alone an assault rifle. They looked bored, too. I knew the way to Bukit Timah Nature Reserve but, to make conversation, I asked one lonely serviceman for directions. He sat alone in the middle of the Central Catchment Nature Reserve and fiddled with his cable. He probably was not the first soldier to do so, of course.

"Hey man, how's it going?" I asked enthusiastically. "Am I going the right way for Bukit Timah?"

"No, you want to go back that way," he replied, gesturing in the opposite direction.

"Are you sure? That's MacRitchie. I've just been there. Bukit Timah should be this way."

"Ah, okay, if you're sure. But I really think Bukit Timah is the other way."

"Well, I'll soon find out. What kind of exercise are you doing out here anyway?"

"Navigation."

I had to look away and cover my mouth. With navigational experts like that in the Singapore Armed Forces, who needs an enemy?

I followed the trail into Rifle Range Road and was overcome by the putrid stench of rotting flesh. It was inescapable. With my T-shirt pulled up over my nose, I saw two scavenging crows pick away at a dead snake in the middle of the road. The snake had not been dead for long and could consider itself unlucky. In the hour that I had plodded along the road, only four military vehicles had passed, one of which had presumably squashed the snake's head into the tarmac. It was a mashed-up, bloody mess. Ignoring my close presence, the birds' beaks poked at the snake's organs like a surgeon's probing scalpel. It was a fascinating scene I had seen many times before, but it was usually through a small screen and accompanied by David Attenborough's narration. Now I understand why smell-o-vision never took off.

I reached Bukit Timah before noon, ate my sandwiches, replenished my water supplies, informed Benjamin that I was still alive, rinsed out my sweaty T-shirt and had a surreal conversation about local politics with a half-naked man in the toilets. Eager to get away, I plunged back into the forest at Senapang Link and trekked north along the biking trail that runs alongside Bukit Timah Expressway.

Now there is one obvious problem with biking trails; they are designed for rugged, all-terrain mountain bikes and not tiring hikers. The path was extremely narrow, with sharp, jagged rocks sticking out of the ground, mischievously camouflaged by thick vegetation to ensure that the soothing songs of the cicadas and the cheerful chirping of the birds was occasionally interrupted by cries of "Argh! Where the fuck did that rock come from?".

Somewhere in the Taban Valley, short bursts of rapid gunfire sent the entire forest running for cover. I am not joking. I was admiring the number of macaques playing in the trees when a series of gunshots exploded into the air like a dozen thunderclaps. I foolishly dove into some grass and grazed my arms and knees on some rocks. But I was not the only petrified primate. Troops of screeching monkeys scattered in every direction and I noticed a few squirrels jump from trunk to trunk in utter panic. The periodic gunshots were deafening. Through a clearing in the forest, I made out a number of targets and realised I was peering down at the Bukit Timah Rifle Range. Every time, the sharp shooters fired, there was pandemonium. The monkeys hopped up and down in the trees and bared their teeth, the birds flew away and the undergrowth moved as various reptiles slunk away. The forest obviously did not like having a rifle range next door. Neither did I.

Coincidentally, Benjamin sent a text message a little later to check that I was still conscious. I was in the process of replying when a helicopter circled overhead and appeared to follow me. It would disappear above trees only to reappear the moment I stepped back into an open clearing. It tracked me for several minutes as I trudged through the Dairy Farm area. You may call me paranoid, but the moment I replied to Benjamin and confirmed that I had not yet passed out, the helicopter disappeared.

Then the rainforest decided to live up to its name and ruin any chance of completing the tour on foot. I was deep inside the forest, on the Chestnut Track just before Bukit Panjang Road, when the heavens opened. I was pleased at first as the blustery conditions blew away the humidity. But it rained. And rained. And rained. Climbing a gentle incline at the time, I struggled to make headway as the soggy path quickly turned into a mudslide and I found myself ankle-deep in water. I found it all rather exciting initially, but the rain refused to relent and my map, street directory and mobile phone were soaked. I left the path and took refuge under some trees, but it made little difference. The contents of my bag were saturated by intermittent big blobs of water rather than a constant shower. There was no shelter anywhere and standing under a tree during an intense electric storm did not really appeal. I had little choice but to return to the flooded track. I ran blindly through the rain, cutting my ankles on jagged lumps of rock and stumbling through trenches of water that occasionally came up to my shin. At least 18 kilometres into my journey by now, my heart pounded and my tired legs were threatening to go on strike.

Fortunately, salvation came in the form of the Zhenghua Flyover of the Bukit Timah Expressway. I took refuge beneath the flyover, along with several motorcyclists, in Bukit Panjang Road. Some renovation work had recently been abandoned and there were tins of paint and bags of cement lying around under the flyover. I found an old pair of paint-spattered trousers and gladly used them to dry myself. I hope the owner did not mind.

The ferocious storm continued for another hour and I could not risk ruining my map, notepad and the rest of the contents of my rucksack by plodding on to Mandai Road. Nor would I entertain the prospect of rambling around Nee Soon Swamp after dark. Hikers do get lost out there and I did not fancy becoming another statistic for the National Parks Board's rescue team. So I dried my clothes and relied on public transport to get to Lower Peirce Reservoir Park. The flesh was just about willing, but the logistics were weak.

I like Lower Peirce Reservoir Park. The reservoir provides a charming backdrop for a picnic and a great place to go skinny-dipping with your mates when you are drunk at 3am. For legal reasons, I cannot say anymore on that particular subject. The park also has a gentle, amiable boardwalk through mature secondary rainforest and, most important of all, provided the location for my daft Stamford Raffles scenes in *Talking Cock, The Movie.*

When I arrived, I had the entire park to myself, but that was probably because it was pissing down on a Wednesday afternoon. I climbed over a gate to take a short cut through the Singapore Island Country Club (SICC) to get back to MacRitchie when Mr Kiasu appeared. That guy is like a bus or a policeman, isn't he? He is always there when you do not bloody need him. My feet had barely touched SICC ground when he descended down an immaculate grassy slope, waving at me frantically. Remembering my manners, I smiled and waved back. My flippancy irritated him.

"Cannot, cannot, cannot," he shouted as he thundered across one of the greens. "Cannot come in here. No, no, no." Mr Kiasu liked to repeat himself.

"It's okay. I'm just going to take a short cut through the golf club to MacRitchie. I've done it before." That was true, albeit with a nature group that had first obtained written permission from SICC.

"Cannot, cannot, cannot," he reiterated, waving a finger near my face. "Must go back to Upper Thomson Road." His authoritarian demeanour and aggressive tone annoyed me.

"Okay mate, calm down. I was just trying to take a short cut."

"Cannot, cannot. This is a private golf course. Cannot. No, no, no."

"All right, don't wet yourself. I'm not going to steal the grass off your bloody greens, am I? "

I will not miss Mr Kiasu when I leave Singapore. I will not miss private golf clubs either.

But there are so many glorious things about this country that I will miss. As I trudged wearily down Upper Thomson Road in the rain, a kindly taxi driver tooted his horn and enquired if I needed a ride. I declined, but his unexpected, benevolent gesture made me smile. I will miss Singaporean taxi drivers and their insistence that I tell them which way to go. Theirs is the only profession where the customer must provide directions to get the job done. I had a tonsillectomy at Singapore General Hospital and the surgeon did not seek my opinion on which way to go in.

I will miss a country where you can call a referee "a plank", "talk cock" and "fuck spider", often at the same time. A country where cheeky children step into a lift and shout "Wah, *ang moh!* So tall, ah" and inquisitive aunties insist on knowing your life story before you reach the ground floor. This is the country that gave the world the chicken chop, the contents of which remain a mystery to me, and Romancing Singapore, a festival of love that offers conclusive proof that the government has finally taken the business of a sense of humour seriously.

In Singapore, I can walk along any street, *lorong*, country lane or forest trail at any time, day or night, without fearing for my personal security. Having been mugged twice in England, I have never taken my safety for granted here. Nor should you. Cherish it. In Singapore, it is possible to have a politician's son, a lawyer's son, a doctor's son, a hawker seller's son, a bus driver's son and a cleaner's son sitting together in the same classroom. I know. I have taught them. In Singapore, aunties and uncles are still revered and treated with respect, quite rightfully, even when they jab a bony elbow in your kidneys to get on a bus. And they still look over their shoulder and speak in hushed tones when discussing the PAP at coffee shops, convinced that Lee Hsien Loong is sitting at the next table.

I know that I will never again live in a country where I can get a decent meal 24 hours a day. Or in a country where food courts, shopping centres, cinemas, hotels, massage parlours, surgeries, schools, train stations, bus stops, taxi stands, libraries, community centres, public swimming pools, parks, reservoirs, primary rainforest, a treetop trail, monitor lizards and wild monkeys are all within walking distance of my apartment. There is even a gynaecologist at the end of my street. I have never needed one, but it was always reassuring to know that there was one on my doorstep.

And to thoroughly dispel that persistent myth, Singapore is a charming, beautiful, green country where I can walk continuously for over eight hours and never leave a forest or park trail. I started my trek at 8am and by the time I had reached the end of the MacRitchie Nature Trail, it was almost 6pm. In total, I had covered approximately 27 kilometres on foot. My hike had included MacRitchie, Rifle Range Road, Bukit Timah, Upper Peirce and the fringes of Upper Seletar, Lower Peirce and Upper Thomson Road before returning to MacRitchie and Toa Payoh. And exotic flora and fauna surrounded me the entire day. The Central Catchment Nature Reserve boasts 1,190 recorded species of plants, 207 birds, 44 mammals and 72 reptiles. I saw a monitor lizard, two squirrels, some monkeys and a dead snake. It was a great day.

I reached home just before dark. I was exhausted. My wife opened the door, curtly informed me that I stank and ordered me to remove my shoes and most of my clothes outside. So I stood in the public corridor in my sweaty boxer shorts and looked out at Toa Payoh. As I craned my neck, I could just about make out my first apartment in Lorong 8, where Scott and I had mistaken a void-deck funeral for a coffee shop the night we arrived in Singapore. It was not that far really. If I walked briskly, I could probably cover the distance in just over 10 minutes. But the journey had taken me almost a decade to complete and I was extremely sad that it was coming to an end. I knew I was not just leaving a great island. It was much more than that. I was saying goodbye to the best 10 years of my life.

ABOUT THE AUTHOR

In 1996, Neil Humphreys turned down a lucrative offer to train as a London stockbroker and travelled to Singapore instead. Armed with an arts degree, he initially felt about as useful as air-conditioning on a motorbike. By 2001, he was one of the country's best-selling authors. His first book, *Notes from an even Smaller Island,* became an immediate best-seller and travelled across Southeast Asia, Australia and Britain. The book appeared on the Singapore best-seller list for over three years. In 2003, his second book, *Scribbles from the Same Island,* a compilation of his popular humour columns in *WEEKEND TODAY,* was launched in Singapore and Malaysia and also became an immediate best-seller. Humphreys believes more young Singaporeans should be brave enough to take arts degrees.